BACKPACKING

ESSENTIAL SKILLS TO

ADVANCED TECHNIQUES

BACKPACKING

ESSENTIAL SKILLS TO

ADVANCED TECHNIQUES

by Victoria Steele Logue

MENASHA RIDGE PRESS
Birmingham, Alabama

© 2000 by Victoria Steele Logue
All rights reserved
Printed in the United States of America
Published by Menasha Ridge Press
Distributed by the Globe Pequot Press
First edition, second printing, 2002

Library of Congress Cataloging-in-Publication Data:
Logue, Victoria, 1961–
    Backpacking: Essential Skills to Advanced Techniques
by Victoria Logue
        p.cm.
Includes bibliographical references (p.) and index.
ISBN 0-89732-323-8
1. Backpacking. I. Title.
GV199.6.L62 2000
796.51—dc21   00-039446

Photos of equipment by Bud Zehmer. Other photos by Frank
Logue or the author. Special thanks to Alabama Outdoors for making
equipment available for the production of this book.
Illustrations by Tami Knight
Cover photo by Dennis Coello
Cover and text design by Grant Tatum

Menasha Ridge Press
P. O. Box 43673
Birmingham, Alabama 35243
www.menasharidge.com

CAUTION

Outdoor recreational activities are by their very nature potentially hazardous. All participants in such activities must assume the
responsibility for their own actions and safety. The information con-
tained in this guidebook cannot replace sound judgment and good
decision-making skills, which help reduce risk exposure, nor does the
scope of this book allow for disclosure of all potential hazards and
risks involved in such activities.

Learn as much as possible about the outdoor recreational activities in which you participate, prepare for the unexpected, and be
cautious. The reward will be a safer and more enjoyable experience.

Table of Contents

PART TWO: On the Trail

Author's Notes

"Make voyages. Attempt them. That's all there is. "
-Tennessee Williams

While introducing my daughter to the pleasures of
backpacking in the Southwest recently, I was astonished
to discover what appeared to be the entire population
of the United States and Europe there as well.
Everywhere we went, German and French were heard
alongside accents as diverse as those from lower
Alabama, northern Maine, and eastern North Dakota.
We had gone out West to seek the wide open spaces

and instead we found ourselves elbow to elbow with all humanity. But once we wandered away from the well-worn tourist paths and headed into the backcountry, it was a different picture entirely. As soon as we stepped off the approach trail into Arches National Monument's Courthouse Wash, the bumper-to-bumper traffic and its noise and exhaust disappeared behind us. As we headed toward the towering sandstone walls of Petrified Dunes, the only sounds were the trickle of water, the drone of insects and the whisper of a breeze in the cottonwoods.

By the time we had backpacked a mile down the wash, we could have easily believed we were the only humans in the entire park. That night, as we camped high above the wash, well away from the danger of a flash flood, it was easy to remember why we so often put thirty pounds or more on our backs and head away from civilization. With a million stars glittering above us, bats flitting over the dunes, and the distant murmur of the wash, we could have stepped back in time.

Although some people enjoy backpacking for the physical challenge, more and more people are turning to nature to escape the stress of city life and jobs. They seek solace from the earth to help them with changes in their lives, whether it be as dramatic as death or divorce, or as simple as seeking an added dimension to life. Once on the trail, they start to experience nature on many different levels. Before long they realize that they've learned things without being told—the habits of wildlife, where water can be found, the patterns of weather. If they don't incorporate this increased sense of observation into their daily lives, they at least return to their lives refreshed. They soon find as much pleasure in a walk on a misty morning as on a clear, bright day. And if they hike the same trail time and again, that trail offers something different each time they hike it—the season, the weather, and their mood can all contribute to different perceptions and experiences. I've hiked on Georgia's Cumberland Island many times and each time has been different; I've spent sweltering days beneath the live oaks; I've taken cold and windy rambles along the beach; I've chanced upon a wild pig and her piglets rooting in the undergrowth; and I've watched feral horses prancing in the surf.

Fortunately, as people search for ways to communicate with the earth, public and private groups are developing programs that will open up greater possibilities for discovering the planet. Within the United States alone, the number of greenways and the extent of the National Trails System grow each year as federal, state, and local governments, volunteers, and corporations work together to provide everyone with a chance to put on a pack and "get back to nature." In Canada, Europe, and throughout the world, numerous organizations have been founded to increase the number of trails and greenways worldwide.

Though backpacking as recreation is a relatively new idea, people have been carrying loads on their backs for thousands of years. For hunters, soldiers, and members of a multitude of expeditions, backpacking has provided a means for getting one's gear and one's self to a required destination. It wasn't until the end of the nineteenth century that backpacking began gaining popularity as a recreational sport. At this time, clubs like the Appalachian Mountain Club and the Sierra Club were formed in order to protect land from development, build footpaths, and foster interest in the outdoors. The popularity of outdoor recreation continued to increase in the early part of the twentieth century. Though it slowed during World War I and again during World War II, interest in the outdoors boomed after each of these wars, especially as surplus materials became available to the public. As gear continued to improve throughout the fifties and sixties, the number of backpackers also grew.

The hippie movement in the late sixties and early seventies saw another increase in backpacking as people sought to commune with nature. The next ten years saw a decrease in the number of backpackers, but backpacking regained momentum in the mid-eighties as people become more aware of the environmental movement.

Now as we venture into a new millennium, backpacking is experiencing a heretofore unseen burst of growth. There is an overwhelming amount of new equipment geared toward making backpacking easier. Yet, in spite of all the advances in technology, backpacking is fundamentally the same sport it was one hundred years ago—there's no way around putting one foot in front of the other as you carry your home away from home on your back. I wrote *Backpacking* to help you do exactly that. You won't find incessant lists of equipment characteristics, or endless treatises on whether fastpacking is the only way to go. Instead, I focus on the basics of backpacking: I tell you what you really need to know to head off into the woods safely and confidently.

Unfortunately, I cannot guarantee an entirely comfortable backpacking trip. If you backpack often enough, eventually you will have a less than ideal experience—with vicious bugs, endless rain, steep inclines, icy streams, excessive heat, or physical pain. But I can almost guarantee these troubles will be quickly forgotten as you reach the summit of a particularly steep mountain and a neverending vista takes your breath away. Besides, getting through those adversities will make you feel good about yourself.

Fundamentally, this book takes you from the germ of an idea to its fruition—in this case, your desire to complete a backpacking trip. This book will help you plan and prepare for a trip; it will guide you in taking your first steps on the trail; and it will help you find and set up your backcountry camp.

Backpacking: Essential Skills to Advanced Techniques presents you with everything you need to know to successfully and safely complete a basic backpacking trip, and it includes numerous tips to make your trip as pleasurable as possible.

The three sections of *Backpacking* reflect the process of planning and executing your backpacking

trip. The first section focuses on plans and preparations. Initially, I talk about different types of hikes and
the numerous destinations you might choose. Then I
discuss how to prepare for a trip, readying yourself
physically and gathering the equipment you need.
Choosing the right equipment is as much a matter of
preference as pragmatism, and you'll find information
describing all your options so that you can make the
choice that's best for you.

In the second section of the book, On the Trail, I
talk about actual hiking techniques, including suggestions for cold-weather and desert hiking. Following this,
I discuss finding your way, maintaining your health,
handling medical emergencies, and dealing with problem animals.

In the final section of the book, I walk you through
what to do when you've finally made it to the point
where you can set up camp. From organizing your
camp to fixing broken gear, you will learn how to take
care of yourself once you remove your pack. I also discuss your backcountry kitchen and the types of meals
you can prepare while enjoying the great outdoors.

These hikers are ready
for a weekend trip on
the coast of Georgia.

One chapter of this book specifically discusses first hikes, offering special tips to make your first outing a little bit easier. Another chapter is devoted to long-distance hiking; it will help you decide, beforehand, whether or not you are suited to that kind of backpacking trip. If you decide long-distance is for you, suggestions are offered on how to make that trip flow a bit more smoothly. There are tips on hiking with children and with dogs—for those who wish to share this sport with the ones they love. And, because we've entered a new millennium, I also offer tips on how to make your hike more ecologically friendly.

I am not what you'd call a heavy-duty backpacker. I have had the opportunity to hike several thousand miles, but I racked up most of those miles during the trip of a lifetime—when my husband and I hiked the Appalachian Trail. Since that trip, I have continued to backpack but on a much smaller scale. I have also introduced the sport to my daughter, who now has dreams herself of completing the Appalachian Trail. Although backpacking is a big part of my life, it is not all-important. Basically, I am just someone who likes to head out into the woods every once in a while. Once there, my everyday problems and worries just seem to slip away. I enjoy the crunch of leaves under my feet, the weight of the pack on my back, and the whisper of the wind through the trees. I treasure the freedom that comes from having everything I need to survive resting on my back. I hope you will too.

Getting Ready

PART ONE

Planning Your Hike

Many people perceive of trails as isolated destinations, but in reality, most trails interconnect with others to form a fine spider web. For example, a short hike on a sidewalk will take me from my father's apartment in Alexandria, Virginia, to a hiking-biking path that runs from Mount Vernon to Washington, D.C. From there, the Chesapeake and Ohio Canal Towpath leads west toward Harpers Ferry, West Virginia, and the Appalachian Mountains. Having hiked to Harpers Ferry, I could turn north on the Appalachian Trail and follow it to Vermont, and from there I could hike all the way to the Canadian border via the Long Trail. Or, I could decide

3

to head south on the Appalachian Trail to Georgia, and then I could continue along the Pinhoti Trail through Alabama to Florida, eventually joining the Florida Trail. But even more astounding is that from the same juncture of the Appalachian and C & O Canal Trails in Harpers Ferry, I could turn west on the American Discovery Trail and hike all the way to California, and no doubt, at its juncture with the Continental Divide Trail, I could turn and hike south to Mexico or north to Canada, and at the Pacific Crest Trail, I could do the same thing again!

Thousands of miles of trail are already accessible to me less than a mile away from my father's urban home. From the long trails system to the natural corridors called greenways that are appearing across the United States, Americans are seeking the outdoors. And in many cases, the outdoors is right at their doorstep.

This chapter will help you decide on and then plan out a hike. The chapter begins by telling you about the numerous destinations available for backpacking trips, and it discusses how to find and use a guidebook. It then describes the different types of hikes you might like to attempt from a short, overnight or weekend backpack to a long-distance trip. There is also information on desert and cold-weather hiking and on backpacking with children and pets. The chapter ends with technical information such as how much to carry in your pack and how to arrange transportation.

As you read this chapter, you need to ask yourself several questions: Where do I want to hike? Do I prefer to stick close to home or would I rather try something farther abroad? How far do I want to hike? And how long do I want to be away from home? When do I want to hike—which season do I find the most pleasing? And finally, do I want a wilderness experience or would I prefer a more established trail?

TRAIL DESTINATIONS

Greenways

Linking the urban world to the outdoors, greenways can be as complex as a paved, multiuse path in an urban downtown or as simple as an abandoned road. Technically, a greenway is a corridor of protected open space managed for conservation or recreation purposes. Greenways often follow natural land or water features and link nature reserves, parks, cultural features, and historic sites with each other and populated areas. Trails, on the other hand, are paths used for walking, cycling, horseback riding or other forms of recreation and transportation. Some greenways are also trails, but because some greenways are made to attract nothing but wildlife, not all greenways are trails.

More than five hundred greenway projects are underway in the United States in an effort to provide Americans (of whom more than 80 percent live in cities) with the opportunity to take advantage of the outdoors. Thousands of volunteers are working to establish greenways that criss-cross the country and link long trails such as the Pacific Crest, Continental Divide, and Appalachian Trails to the country's major cities—Brooklyn/Queens, Washington, D.C., San Francisco, and Minneapolis.

Citizens are being joined in their effort by private corporations and companies. Some gas companies have established greenways over pipeline rights-of-way, and other companies are doing their part to fix up areas in cities, particularly in decaying neighborhoods.

Greenways are "the paths to the future," linking people to the outdoors. They meet an ever-growing need, the need to leave the hectic city (if only for a moment) and to experience earth beneath your feet and to breathe fresh air in your lungs—the need to feel life and to feel alive.

But greenways are not meant for humans alone. The protection of these scenic regions is beneficial to the migration and needs of many animals. The rapidly disappearing Florida panther could be rescued from the brink of extinction by the addition of only 15,000 acres of greenway to a 58,000-acre wildlife management area near Loxahatchee, Florida. This is true for many of the indigenous species whose survival is based on the need for large, undisturbed territories or ranges.

Rails-to-Trails

Each year, more than three-thousand miles of railroad tracks go out of service as trucking becomes the most popular way to haul freight around the country. Transforming these abandoned tracks into trails has become especially popular in urban areas where large tracts of land are expensive or unavailable. The level grade and narrow corridor of railroad beds are often perfect for hiking-biking paths, and rail-to-trail conversions are springing up everywhere. The Rails-to-Trails Conservancy was formed in 1986 to promote the transformation of these tracks to trails. Of the approximately 150,000 miles of abandoned lines in the United States, more than 10,000 miles have become rail-trails.

While rail-trails still seems to be predominantly a midwestern phenomenon, this new trail system is quickly spreading all over the country. Canada and Europe have also joined in the phenomenon, although because Europe uses its rail system so extensively, there are fewer abandoned railroad grades to develop. Among the more well-known rail-trails in the United States are the 75-mile Greenbrier River Trail in West Virginia, the 200-mile Katy Trail in Missouri, the 165-mile Taconite State Trail in Minnesota, and the 114-mile George S. Mickelson Trail in South Dakota.

National Trails System

Each year millions of people take advantage of this country's National Trails System. From the thousands who hike a short section of the Pacific Crest Trail in California's Yosemite Valley to the intrepid few who attempt to hike the Continental Divide Trail's 2,600 miles, the system offers a wide variety of experiences. On the East Coast alone, approximately four million people each year spend a day or more along the Appalachian Trail, only a fraction of the number of people the whole system sees each year.

The Appalachian Trail was designated the country's first National Scenic Trail in 1968, and it has served as a model for all trails in the National Trail System. Later that same year, the Pacific Crest Trail was added to the system. Ten years later, five more trails were added, including the first National Historic Trail—the Oregon Trail. Historic trails follow roads and rivers as well as footpaths.

Once a trail is designated by Congress as a national trail, the law directs the Department of the Interior to fix the route of the trail and publish it with maps and descriptions. This process can take several years. States along the trail then have two years to acquire any portions of the trail corridor that are privately owned. Once the two-year period ends, the National Park Service takes whatever action is necessary to preserve and protect the trail. If all else fails, the park service is allowed to use the law of eminent domain (whereby the government has the right to take over private land for public use) to purchase the trail corridor. Of course, acquiring land for a national trail corridor is dependent on annual funding by Congress, and that funding does not always come through. The entire process from designation to trail completion can take decades. The California and the Pony Express Trails were both designated as National Historic Trails back in 1992, but their formal routes are not yet fixed.

Here is a sampling of some of the more established national trails:

Appalachian National Scenic Trail

The Appalachian Trail is the only member of the National Trails System that has been completed. Its 2,167 miles wind northward from Georgia through North Carolina, Tennessee, Virginia, West Virginia, Maryland, Pennsylvania, New Jersey, New York, Connecticut, Massachusetts, Vermont, New Hampshire, and Maine.

Less than seventy-eight miles of the trail's corridor remain on unprotected land. The most popular sections of the trail pass through Great Smoky Mountains National Park, Shenandoah National Park, and the White Mountains of New Hampshire.

Continental Divide National Scenic Trail

Established in 1978, the Continental Divide Trail begins

Typical sign on the
Appalachian Trail.

Typical sign on the Appalachian Trail.

at a white obelisk marking the U.S./Mexican border. Traversing New Mexico, Colorado, Wyoming, Idaho, and Montana, the trail ends at the Canadian border. According to the Continental Divide Trail Society, more than 2,100 miles of this 2,600-mile trail have been completed. The Continental Divide Trail passes through the Rocky Mountains and both Glacier and Yellowstone National Parks.

Florida National Scenic Trail

Established in 1983, more than one thousand miles of this 1,300-mile trail have been completed. Traversing the length of Florida and passing through the Everglades and Canaveral National Seashore, the trail links the western end of the Florida panhandle to Lake Okeechobee and continues on to Big Cypress National Preserve. Because some segments of the trail are on private land, only members of the Florida Trail Association can hike the entire length of the trail.

Ice Age National Scenic Trail

More than 450 miles of this 1,000-mile trail have been completed in Wisconsin. The Ice Age Trail was established in 1980 and follows the ridge of hills defining the southern advance of glaciers that occurred thousands of years ago. This chain of moraines criss-crosses Wisconsin from Door County to the Saint Croix River.

North Country National Scenic Trail

Established in 1980, 1,200 miles of this 3,200-mile trail have been completed. The trail will pass through New York, Pennsylvania, Ohio, Michigan, Wisconsin, Minnesota, and North Dakota—from the Adirondacks of New York to the Missouri River in North Dakota.

Natchez Trace National Scenic Trail

This southern trail, established in 1983, travels from Natchez, Mississippi, through Alabama and on to Nashville, Tennessee. It parallels the Natchez Trace Parkway, a 450-mile roadway that commemorates the historic Natchez Trace, an ancient road that began as a series of animal paths and Native American trails and was later traveled by settlers. Because of the historic significance of this trail, it may soon be changed to a National Historic Trail.

Pacific Crest National Scenic Trail

To date, all but eight miles of the Pacific Crest Trail's 2,638 miles have been permanently located. Beginning at the border of Mexico in Southern California, the trail traverses the length of the state before crossing into Oregon and Washington, and ending at the Canadian border. The trail passes through many national parks and national forests including Yosemite, Lassen, Shasta, the Cascades, Mount Ranier, and Crater Lake.

Potomac Heritage National Scenic Trail

Passing through Virginia, the District of Columbia, Maryland and Pennsylvania, approximately half of this 704-mile trail has been completed. Official segments of this trail, which was established in 1983, include the C & O Canal Towpath, the Mount Vernon Trail managed by the George Washington Memorial Parkway, and the Laurel Highlands Trail in Pennsylvania.

American Discovery Trail

The American Discovery Trail is the nation's first coast-to-coast hiking corridor. While it still consists of a lot of roads (perfect for cycling), the trail continues to add actual footpath to its impressive length. Sponsored by *Backpacker* magazine and the American Hiking Society, this trail will eventually link existing scenic trails and backcountry byways. Winding through the nation's varied landscapes and towns, the trail begins in the Bay Area of San Francisco and ends in Delaware.

Canada, too, has a number of long-distance trails similar to those in the U.S. National Trails System. Here is a sampling of Canadian trails.

Bruce Trail

This trail system, which runs along the Niagara escarpment in Ontario, features about 500 miles of main trail and 125 miles of side trails.

Canadian Continental Divide

The Rocky Mountains continue another 850 miles from the U.S. border north into British Columbia. While the Canadian section of the Continental Divide Trail is not yet complete, there are currently a number of trails that can be linked together to hike most of the divide.

International Appalachian Trail

While most of this trail is complete, permission is still pending for the southern terminus section of the trail, which is to begin just south of Baxter State Park in Maine. From there, the trail heads northward 520 miles to Cape Gaspé in Québec.

Canol Heritage Trail

This is one of the most remote trails in the world. It runs more than two hundred miles from Macmillan Pass in the Yukon to Norman Wells in the Northwest Territories. Because it follows old roads cut to lay oil pipeline in World War II, the trail can be hiked or biked.

Trails on Federal Lands

National parks and national forests are the best known resources for backcountry trails on public lands. The National Forest Service boasts more than 120,000 miles of trails and the National Park Service has over 12,000 miles. These trails offer access to some of the nation's best known parks—the Great Smoky Mountains, Yellowstone and Yosemite—as well as many less appreciated areas such as the Idaho Panhandle National Forest or South Carolina's Sumter National Forest.

There are also thousands of miles of hiking trails (primarily in western states) on land managed by the Bureau of Land Management and (throughout the country) on national wildlife refuges.

The most popular national parks and even some national forests may require permits obtained in advance. Call as you begin making your plans to avoid disappointment later.

National parks in Canada also offer miles of hiking trails. In Banff National Park in Alberta, for example, there are more than one thousand miles of hiking trails.

State Parks and Forests

State forests and parks are also rich resources for hikers. They offer a variety of trails and there is often one close to home. To find out more about the parks and forests in your area, check the state government listings in your phone book and call the state or local headquarters for parks and forests.

GUIDEBOOKS

Once you decide on (or even simply dream of) the general area where you want to hike, you will want to get a guidebook. There are a multitude of guidebooks that show where to backpack in every state in the nation and most of the countries in the world.

A guidebook's contents can be as simple as a brief description of a trail's location and length, or it can be a more complex description of nearly every inch of the trail and it can include detailed maps and elevation profiles. You can find guidebooks at outdoor stores and even at chain bookstores, where they are usually stocked in the local interest section. If you want to go farther afield, check the travel section of your local bookstore for guides to foreign countries or distant states. And these days, there is always the Internet. See the index of this book for suggested sites.Choose your guidebook according to the amount of information you feel you will need, and it won't be long before you're making that first trek.

BACKPACKING TIP

If you are planning a trip, buy a guidebook early on. Not only will it help you decide which hike you want to take but what the trail will be like once you get there.

A good guidebook should include:

1. Current information. Make sure you check the copyright date.
2. Clear instructions on how to get to the trailhead, including road conditions.
3. Recommendations on which maps to purchase or copy.
4. Information on special regulations or permits required for the area.
5. A rating system for the difficulty of a trail, including information or charts on large elevation changes or potential hazards such as river fords.
6. Detailed trail descriptions.
7. The location, the reliability, and the purity of water sources.
8. Services available in the area (such as gas, food, and lodging).

TRIP LENGTHS

Short Hikes

A short hike is usually no more than three nights; anything longer than that usually qualifies as an extended hike. If it has been a while since you backpacked, or if you have not previously backpacked, a short hike is the best way to start. Short hikes allow you to test borrowed or rented equipment or get used to your own. You will also be able to practice many of the skills discussed later in this book: hiking technique, orienteering, setting up camp, and cooking a meal. In other words, you will do everything an extended or long-distance hike requires, but on a much smaller scale.

There is no prescribed mileage for a short hike. I've done everything from just over a mile to more than twenty for an overnighter. It really just depends on your goals.

In most places, you can find a short hike within an hour's drive of your home.

The previous Trail Destinations portion of this chapter outlined just a few of the limitless possibilities. Even really big cities and megalopolises often have places set aside—recreation areas, wildlife sanctuaries, and city parks—where backpacking is allowed.

Extended Hikes

Losing yourself in nature is one of the best reasons to get into backpacking, and extended hiking is one of the best ways to accomplish this. Heading off into the "woods" for a week or more provides you with experiences and perspectives that the day and weekend hiker may never have.

Anyone who has backpacked for an extended period of time gains a totally new outlook—a special regard for the simpler things in life. Many hikers coming off a long-distance trip rethink and subsequently change their lifestyles, intentionally avoiding the materialism of today's society.

Long-Distance Hikes

Each year nearly two thousand people set out to hike the length of one of the country's major long-distance trails—the Pacific Crest, the Continental Divide, and the Appalachian Trails are the most popular. If you are thinking about hiking an entire trail in a year, you may want to consider this first: only a small percentage of those who try to do so actually complete their goal; the others must leave their dreams by the wayside.

This happens for a number of reasons, but most often long-distance backpacking turns out to be more than people bargained for.

There are many long-distance trails that can be backpacked by just about any person with enough determination. Others—the Pacific Crest and the Continental Divide, for example—possess physical challenges that are too difficult for some people. Long-distance trails have been backpacked by the young, the old, and the handicapped; physical ability is not all it takes. We sometimes romanticize backpacking as an easy walk in the woods, but it is almost never easy, and it is never just a walk in the woods. The next chapter describes what it takes to plan a long-distance hike.

SPECIAL HIKES

Cold-Weather Backpacking

I slowly drifted awake to a soft blue light. Snuggled warmly in my sleeping bag, I reluctantly withdrew an arm to unzip the tent and its fly. Three inches of snow covered the ground!

I quickly pulled on pile pants and top over my long johns. Boots, gaiters, and rainsuit followed, and then I stepped out into a world quite rare to the South.

Walking through the forest that morning was like walking into the pages of "Silent Snow, Secret Snow" by Conrad Aiken. It was a quiet place of softly falling flakes and the almost silent crunch of footsteps.

Camped just off the summit, I climbed up to its rocky outcrop to survey the valley below. It glittered like a scene in a magic egg—the snow was spun sugar, a stream was a ribbon of black licorice, and a barn was a gingerbread house topped with a layer of thick white icing.

I returned to my tent for a warm breakfast and then carried my cup of coffee back to the summit. As the

sun burned its path through the sky, the clouds disappeared. In the forest, trees that had just blossomed with bolls of snow began to lose their icy flowers.

Twisting through pastures and fields, the stream was soon swollen with the snowmelt. Rows of cornstalks marched out of the drifts while shingles of white began to slide from the roof of the barn.

With a sigh, I returned to my camp and began to pack. I had retreated to the woods that weekend for a bit of solitude. I left having been part of a fairy tale.

Experienced hikers have learned that backpacking is not only pleasurable during the warm months. Cold-weather camping is possible in many parts of the United States and provides much more solitude. It is a way to experience the Earth during its darkest season—to discover a new world both physically and mentally.

In winter, you'll find the trails much less crowded—even in the South, where, contrary to popular opinion, it does get cold and it even occasionally snows. You can find snowy places throughout the country where you can hike and camp in peace. But don't just throw on your pack, seal your boots, and head out into the elements; cold-weather backpacking requires a little more forethought as well as preparation.

Depending on the type of cold-weather backpacking you intend to do, you will face a number of choices. One of the most important is the type of footwear you will use. If the snow is not deep (or if it is hard-packed) and the trail is over gentle or only slightly mountainous terrain, then boots will probably suffice. A pair of gaiters and well-sealed hiking boots will make the trip more comfortable. Avoid the hard, plastic, cold-weather, mountaineering boots that were designed for technical climbing; they are impractical for backpacking. On the other hand, if you will be traveling in icy conditions, or over steeper terrain or deeper snow, you will probably need to consider crampons, snowshoes, or cross-country skis, which are discussed later in this chapter.

Once you determine your method of transportation, you must pack your pack. If you're heading out into the snow, you'll need a three- or four-season tent, preferably one that is freestanding and has a waterproof floor. An added bonus would be a tent that offers a cook hole in its floor. (The cook hole, a zippered or gathered hole in the bottom of the tent, can be opened so that you can cook directly on the ground. A cook hole is preferable to cooking on the floor of your tent, which can catch fire easily if your stove tips over. See the Equipment chapter for more information on tents.) In the deep South, a three-season tent will probably suffice since the temperature rarely drops below twenty degrees Fahrenheit (but it can occasionally hit minus ten degrees so don't underestimate southern weather).

When pitching your tent in the snow, make sure you level the area and pack the snow down. If this is not done, it is very likely you will wake up when the tent collapses on your head. Leaving your pack on while you stamp the ground flat will give you some extra weight to make the job go more quickly. If you make the base wider than necessary, you'll be able to walk around your tent without snowshoes or skis, which will

BACKPACKING TIP

For early spring trips in high-elevation areas, seek out trails located at lower elevations on south-facing slopes. These areas shed their snow and dry out earlier than others.

16

be especially useful should nature call in the middle of the night.

Special tent pegs for snow camping can be purchased from most outdoor stores. Once your tent is pegged, try pouring some water on the pegs. Once the water freezes, the pegs really won't move. When breaking camp, pour warm water over the pegs to unfreeze them and pull them easily from the snow.

When camping during cold weather, you will also need a sleeping bag with a low-degree comfort rating— a zero-degree bag will do for most situations. If you don't want the expense of two sleeping bags, consider using a liner to make your three-season bag warmer. It should go without saying that you will need a mummy-style bag for winter camping; it will keep you the warmest, and if the temperature really drops, you can tighten the hood until nothing but your nose is showing. Some sleeping bags are available with extra insulation at the bottom of the bag to combat cold feet.

Since your tent may be pitched on top of snow or frozen ground, you will want some good insulation underneath you. While a three-quarter-length sleeping pad may do for three-season camping, you may want to consider a full-length pad for cold-weather camping.

Remember that layering your clothing is of utmost importance when backpacking during the winter. Begin with a layer of long underwear. Next, you may want to add a shirt and pants made of pile or fleece. You can top these off with a warm parka and waterproof, insulated pants if the weather is really cold, or with a lighter rain/wind suit if the temperature is only reasonably cold. Don't forget that you can add greatly to your warmth by donning a hat or balaclava.

If you are sufficiently bundled, the exertion of hiking should keep you warm. If you start feeling hypothermic, stop immediately, change into dry clothes if yours are wet, crawl into your sleeping bag, and drink some warm liquid. Make sure the stove you bring will light (as well as boil water) in frigid weather.

Cold-related hazards are discussed in detail in the first aid information found in the On the Trail section of this book. Remember that it is wise to wear sunglasses when hiking on snow because the reflected sunlight can burn your eyes. Snow blindness can occur even on overcast days. If you don't have sunglasses, cut eye-slits in something (a bandanna, for example) that you can tie around your head. Should someone become snow blind, treat them with cold compresses, a painkiller, and a lightproof bandage. Between eighteen and twenty hours later, the blindness should diminish.

All the equipment needed for cold-weather camping—warm clothes, four-season tents, sleeping bags, tent pegs, snowshoes or skis—is available through outdoor stores, where you will also find information on how to use the equipment.

Special techniques for cold-weather hiking will be discussed in the technique portion of On the Trail.

Crampons and Ice Axes

Some backpacking requires the use of crampons. Simply put, crampons are used for hiking on ice and hard snow. While not necessary for most backpacking trips, there are areas along both the Pacific Crest and Continental Divide Trails, as well as other trails that have high elevations or are located in northerly climes, where it would always be wise to carry a pair.

Crampons, which usually have twelve points or claws, strap onto your boots. They must be fitted properly—using loose crampons can be as, if not more, dangerous than hiking crampon-less across slick ice or snow. For backpacking, flexible crampons are a must. Consult an outdoor store that features climbing equipment when choosing a pair of crampons.

When hiking in winter conditions, an ice ax is another useful piece of equipment. It will help you cut steps in ice or snow, and it can be used as a brake should you start to slide downhill (see the information on ice ax self-arrest in the technique portion of On the Trail). The purchase of an ice ax should be discussed with your local outfitter.

Snowshoeing or Cross-Country Skiing

Which is best for you? How do you decide whether you

should look into what *Backpacker* magazine so charmingly calls a "webhead" or a "freeheeler"? Actually, it's pretty easy. If you like to take your time and explore everything there is to see when hiking, and if you've never been on a pair of skis plus you have little money to invest in them, then you probably want to opt for snowshoes. On the other hand, if you like going really fast, and if you have been skiing since you were a toddler and you have money to burn, cross-country skiing is your bag, baby. Of course, if you're anywhere in between, you can go for both. You can break into cross-country skiing slowly by renting gear, and the same goes for snowshoeing. With a little practice, you can become adept at both. Keep in mind that we're talking backpacking here. Carrying a pack on snowshoes or cross-country skis can be done, but it takes practice and it's more difficult than snowshoeing or cross-country skiing when you're unburdened.

Snowshoes   When it comes to gearing up, snowshoes beat cross-country skis both in price and in quick and easy use. They can be fitted to just about any pair of boots in just a matter of seconds. But even with snowshoes, most people manage to backpack no more than four hours a day in the snow.

Traditional snowshoes of wood and rawhide are still available, but most snowshoes today utilize technologically superior frames of aluminum and molded plastic and thongs of nylon and plastic.

When purchasing snowshoes, look for these five qualities:

1. Flotation—the greater the surface area of the snowshoe, the better its flotation. A backpacker will need more surface area because of the added weight of his pack.
2. Traction—the grip of the snowshoe. Traction comes from the cleats, or crampons, at the base of the snowshoe. The more climbing you intend to do, the more traction you will need.
3. Tracking ability—the shoe should be heavier in the tail than in the toe, and your boot toe should fit through the toe hole and dig into the snow.

4. Traversing ability—a narrow design of ten inches or less is best.
5. Weight—the lighter the better. There is an old saying that "a pound on the foot is equal to five on the back." That is very close to the truth.

Most backpackers who snowshoe prefer cleats at the toe, forefoot, and heel for climbing slick snow and ice. Cleats at least one inch long should provide the traction you need when carrying a backpack.

The bindings should strap easily to your boots and grip them tightly without cutting off your circulation. They should also stay securely attached whether you are striding, climbing, or negotiating blowdowns. And, most importantly, in winter weather you should be able to adjust the bindings while wearing gloves.

While you can actually wear any boots you want to when backpacking in snowshoes, there are now snowshoe-specific boots available on the market. These boots provide warmth, dryness, comfort and support . The best use Thinsulate for warmth and some form of plastic brace for ankle support.

A pair of ski poles are supposedly invaluable to the snowshoer (many backpackers use ski poles as hiking sticks as well). There are a number of books on the subject, including *Snowshoeing* by Gene Prater (from The Mountaineers).

Cross-Country Skis   If you are unfamiliar with cross-country skiing, depend on the expertise of your salesman to help you choose the right cross-country skis. In some areas of the country, it is possible to rent cross-country gear from local outdoor and ski-gear stores.

Basically, you have a choice between waxable, waxless, and climber skis. If you are just starting out, your best choice is probably a waxless ski that has a series of scales on the bottom to improve the ski's traction and glide. This ski requires no application of wax; you just put it on and go. Waxable skis are more efficient, which means you will move along at an accelerated rate, but you have to have some knowledge of wax application.

Another feature to think about is the sidecut of a ski. This is the change in width between a ski's mid-section and its ends. The deeper the sidecut, the easier it is to turn. Shorter skis also make it easier to turn, but with shorter skis, you sacrifice flotation. If you are a beginner, go with a ski that is 170 to 190 centimeters in length, depending on your height and weight. Once again, a salesperson will know how to fit you.

When purchasing skis, make sure you inform the salesman that you are interested in a ski that you can use for backpacking. As with most anything, you will have to make some sacrifices to find the ski that is perfect for you. For example, you may want skis that are ideal for turning but you will have to expend extra energy on level terrain because the skis will be shorter.

For more technical downhill terrain or expedition skiing, you will need wider and stronger skis that are made especially for alpine touring.

Once you have picked out your skis, you will need to choose the appropriate boots and bindings (unlike snowshoes, you have to buy boots made specifically for cross-country skiing). To be quite frank, boots and bindings are very complex. To put it the most simply, 75-millimeter, or three-pin, bindings adapt to more types of boots. On the other hand, the New Nordic Norm (NNN) bindings are lighter and easier to use than the 75-millimeter. You would just have to buy boots that are specifically made for NNN. Boot soles will have platypus-shaped toes if they are designed for 75-mm bindings, or a solid metal bar across the toe for NNN. Make sure you buy touring boots that rise over your ankles, not the lighter racing boots. Also look for leather uppers. And you want the boots to be large enough to accommodate warm socks—try them on with the thickest pair of socks that you have!

Finally, you will need ski poles. High quality aluminum or fiberglass poles are your best bet. Make sure that the poles have adjustable wrist straps and that the baskets at the bottom of the pole are four to five inches in diameter. Most importantly, make sure that they are the right length. How to tell? Standing in stocking feet, the pole should fit snugly in your armpit.

Learn more about how to snowshoe and cross-country ski in the technique portion of On the Trail.

Desert Backpacking

The sun was sliding behind the mountains to the West. Stretching and yawning, Peter and Janet hoisted their packs on their backs and hit the desert trail. Having taken a siesta during the heat of the day, they were now ready to put in a few more miles before night settled in too deeply.

As the sky changed from brilliant orange to midnight blue, they began to look for a place to camp. A full moon and millions of stars lit the path before them.

A rocky outcrop looked promising and, using a flashlight, Peter checked for poisonous snakes. Given the all clear, Janet pulled on her wool sweater and unrolled sleeping pads and bags while Peter fired up the stove for some herbal tea.

Sipping the relaxing liquid, Peter and Janet listened to the scurrying of night creatures and the occasional howl of a coyote. The theater of the sky played on—the man on the moon smiled down on them, stars twinkled, planets glowed, and comets flared against the backdrop of the Milky Way.

Janet named her cactus sentinels while Peter pointed out the constellations. The night air grew cooler, but their sleeping bags were warm and it wasn't long before they drifted off to sleep. They had set their alarm for 4 a.m., hoping to get in some pre-dawn hiking in an effort to beat the desert's vicious heat.

"In the desert, one is sensible of the passage of time. In that parching heat, a man feels that the day is a voyage towards the goal of evening, towards the promise of a cool breeze that will bathe the limbs and wash away the sweat. Under the heat of the day, beasts and men plod towards the sweet well of night, as confidently as towards death."

—Antoine de St. Exupery

If you hike often in the Southwest, it is likely that you will hike at times in a desert. Both the Pacific Crest and the Continental Divide Trails move through extensive sections of desert. Many hikers enjoy trips into the desert because, like winter camping, there is more solitude and an awesome beauty few people have the chance to experience. Unlike winter camping, you don't necessarily need a lot of specialized equipment, but because of the intense heat in the desert, there are several unique problems you face immediately—dehydration, hyperthermia, and sunburn. Dehydration and hyperthermia are discussed in detail in the On The Trail section of this book.

Fortunately, there are ways to avoid these problems. If you intend to do a lot of backpacking in the desert, you may want to use an external frame pack as opposed to an internal frame pack. Why? Because an external frame will hold your pack away from your body, allowing more air to circulate on your back thus promoting the evaporation of sweat and the cooling of your body.

Obviously, the best time to hike in the desert is during the winter. Avoid the summer months, if possible. If you must hike through desert in the summer, hike during the cooler hours. The sun often rises about 5:30 a.m. and it does not set until almost sixteen hours later. Three or four hours after sunrise temperatures peak and they do not fall until evening.

By rising just before or at dawn, hiking until the temperatures peak, and resting throughout the hottest part of the day, you can save yourself a lot of grief. Try to find some shade, if possible, under a tree or rocky outcropping. You may also want to try setting up a tarp. Unless your tent is highly ventilated, I wouldn't suggest pitching it because it will heat up like a furnace. Hiking in the early evening, when it's cool, is also a possibility. Use a flashlight, a head lamp, or if you're lucky, the full moon.

Sunburn is a potential problem even in cold weather because it can do extensive damage to your skin. Burned skin can retard sweating, a critical function that keeps the body cool, and constant burning can lead to

skin cancer. Therefore, sunblock is necessary no matter when you're hiking. The Arabs know what they are doing when they cover their bodies and heads with long, flowing material. Take a cue from them and wear loose clothing that covers you completely—at least wear loose, long pants and a loose but high-necked and long-sleeved shirt. When it comes to desert back-packing, light-colored clothes made of cotton are your best bet. Don't wear black out in the sun unless you want to bake. Also, wear sunglasses and a wide-brimmed hat. The bright light of the desert can burn your eyes as well as your skin. On the other hand, don't forget to bring along some warm clothes for night; the desert cools down in the evening except during the hottest part of summer.

For more information on sunscreen and sunglasses, see the information on toiletries in the Equipment chapter.

To keep from getting dehydrated, you must drink at least a gallon of water per day, and unless you have very reliable sources, don't count on just anyone's word for the location of water.

It is safest to carry your own water even though it's heavy. And, like they say, don't put all your eggs in one basket. If you carry a one-gallon jug and it breaks or leaks, you've lost one entire day's water supply. Instead, carry your water in several one- and two-liter bottles.

Also keep in mind that your appetite diminishes somewhat in the desert, so you don't necessarily have to carry a cook kit. Cold foods will be just fine. Besides, who wants a hot dinner in the desert unless it is eaten in the middle of the night?

Some desert food could include tuna and hard-cheese-stuffed pitas, fruit leathers, peanut butter, candy bars, pemmican, and beef jerky. While hiking in the desert, it is better for your digestion to eat a bunch of small meals rather than one big meal.

Read more about hiking in the desert in the technique portion of On the Trail.

Backpacking with Children
Some of my best childhood memories are of hiking and camping. My family spent a lot of time hiking around California's Lake Shasta. I remember one hike in which we found a clear pool, almost perfectly circular, filled by a small waterfall—icy runoff from the snowy mountains that towered above us.

On another trip, we stumbled on a ghost town and set up our camp nearby. It was the perfect stage for ghost stories that night.

Then there was the time we were caught in a hailstorm on a sparsely treed hillside; my siblings and I concocted musical instruments from nature's bounty and held a concert for my parents. Another hike through head-high (for a nine-year-old) weeds tripped us all so continually that we ended up soaked with dew, and we busted our guts laughing at our completely innocent Keystone Kops imitation.

Should you take your children on a backpacking trip?

Why not? Most children love the outdoors. My own vivid memories of hikes and backpacks have led to my continued love affair with nature.

I discovered my daughter's love for the outdoors when she was three months old. While attending a conference in San Diego, I found that Griffin fell asleep more quickly when I carried her around outside rather than in our room. Maybe it was all those long walks I took trying to induce labor when she was two weeks overdue, but she blossoms when the wind caresses her face and the sun shines on her head. She even loves the sprinkle of rain and overcast skies! After that conference and a subsequent tour of Muir Woods, Griffin graduated to a backpack and she absolutely loved her new vantage point. Now, she always carries her own pack and she can't wait 'til she's old enough to hike the Appalachian Trail.

Infants

The younger the child is, the more difficult the packing (except for ages four to six months when they have not yet learned to crawl). Children younger than four months old don't yet fit in a pack, and after six months, they take off as soon as they touch the ground. If it's possible to set up your tent before you put your child down, you have a handy playpen to hold the child until you've set up camp.

Until your child has been toilet trained, you must carry diapers—disposable or otherwise. You'll have to pack them in and out. Cindy Ross suggests cloth diapers; she and her husband, Todd, dry these diapers on the back of their packs so that they are lighter to carry. When your child has a bowel movement, you can simply bury her or his poop as you would your own, fold up the diaper, and carry it in a sealable plastic bag.

Because someone must carry the child, the amount of extra stuff that you can take on your trip is limited.

This means the length of your trip will probably have to be shortened, but there are ways to get around that. One option is to use the cache system and bury or hide extra diapers, food, and other items along the trail you plan to hike. Another option is to plan a hike where you can stop at stores often enough to pick up the items you'll need—more food and diapers. Yet another option is to send extra items to post offices along the way if you will have steady access to them. Finally, there is the option of enlisting a support crew that will meet you at road crossings with the extra things you need.

As for food, when your child has begun to eat some solids but food still needs to be mashed and smashed, your trip will be a bit more difficult. Try to plan meals that your child can partake of, and bring along a hand-operated grinder. Some health food stores offer dehydrated baby foods. Jars of baby food are a heavier option, and once a jar is opened, it will keep only a few days (often less) without refrigeration.

If your child is breastfeeding and is not yet on solids, you're in a perfect situation for backpacking because you don't have to carry formula and bottles. Although difficult, formula-feeding is not impossible. Bottles can be heated on your cook stove the same way they would be heated on your stove at home—by warming them in water in your cook pot.

As for clothes, you know your child. Griffin tends to stay on the warm side so we don't have to carry a lot of warm clothes for her when backpacking. Other babies stay cool, so parents bring extra layers of clothing for their child's comfort. Children can be layered as easily as adults. There are a lot of layering options for children. Many catalogs even offer miniature rainsuits.

Since my child was due in the winter, I was anxious to find some warm clothes in a newborn size. I'll admit there wasn't much available, but I was able to find some red, cotton long johns. Less than twenty-four hours after Griffin's home birth, I dressed her in those long johns for her first trip to the doctor. It was twenty degrees outside and the long johns were layered with a blanket sleeper and finally a fleece baby bag.

Keep in mind that there are many things infants under six months of age cannot do—such as wear sunscreen or insect repellent. If you are hiking in the sun with infants, they need a wide-brimmed hat or a screen on their backpack. If your infant will wear them, there are sunglasses available in infant sizes. While still an infant, Griffin successfully wore the Flap-happy Hat sold by Biobottoms of California. The baseball-style cap had a wide front brim and a protective "flap" of material that covered her delicate neck. Patagonia makes a similar hat for infants and children.

When it is time to bed down for the night, where do you put your infant? When Griffin was younger, I shared my bag with her, but she eventually outgrew that arrangement. I have yet to find an infant-sized sleeping bag although some companies make bags designed to

Tents can be used as playpens for infants and toddlers while the parents set up camp.

keep an infant warm that can work as sleeping bags. You may also want to try designing your own with a child-size down comforter or several blankets.

Some children, like Griffin, have no trouble falling asleep in a dark tent while others are distressed by total darkness. I always keep a flashlight handy should I need to comfort Griffin with a little light. Some children initially are disconcerted by the confining walls of a tent, but usually they get used to a tent after a night or two.

The tent size that you need will vary depending on the size of your family. A two-person tent will probably be too small for two parents with one child, but a three-person tent might suit them well for a long time.

As your family grows, things get more complicated. I have only discussed backpacking with one child at this point because if you have more than one young child, your backpacking will probably be limited to day hikes until some of your children can carry their own packs and hike entirely on their own.

Toddlers

You have basically the same concerns when backpacking with a toddler as you do with an infant, but there is one major difference—the child can walk.

This means that they'll be eager to escape their pack and they'll hit the ground running. Unfortunately, to a toddler running means two entirely different methods of movement: (1) literal running, which usually ends up with the child on her face, especially on unlevel trails; and (2) walking a few steps and then stopping to explore, walking a few steps then stopping to explore, walking a few steps . . .

Both of these methods can result in frustration for a parent, but they are absolutely necessary for the sanity of a child. As much as Griffin loved her pack, she still needed to get out of it every once in a while to stretch her new walking legs.

Once a child is out of the pack, they require at least one set of eyes on them constantly. The outdoors is great for growing minds but it also poses certain dangers, especially if a child is still teething. In the latter case, everything she picks up is likely to end up in her mouth; she needs you to keep her from eating poison ivy or oak, snails, deer droppings, and all the other things in her path.

Most packs built to carry a child will hold your toddler until he reaches thirty-five to forty pounds. After that, you will begin backpacking with . . .

Young Children

This will be a difficult stage, no doubt about it. Your child—even if packless—will walk a hundred yards (if you're lucky) and then start complaining, weeping, wailing that he is tired. Remember that this is the same kid who can easily run the length of three football fields while playing with his friends.

When your child is at this stage, it is best to take frequent breaks until you reach your destination. You are thus limited as to the number of miles you can pack each day. No problem—just tone down your trips for a while.

Your child can start with a fannypack or daypack and carry his own toys and clothing. As your child gets older and stronger, you can move on to bigger packs and add food and sleeping bag to the gear he is carrying.

Gear

For forty to one hundred dollars, you can purchase a child's sleeping bag up to forty-eight inches in length, in the mummy design, rated for fifteen degrees.

There are packs designed especially for children and packs designed to carry children. Tough Traveler, Gerry, and Kelty all make superb packs to carry your infant or toddler. Designed to hold kids up to thirty-five or forty pounds, all include a pocket to carry diapers and other essentials for your baby. An optional rain/sunscreen can be purchased with the Tough Traveler, as can extra pockets. Child carriers cost from fifty dollars to one hundred twenty dollars.

Children's packs are made by a number of manufacturers but the one most commonly available is from Camp Trails, which also designs a child's pack for REI. The pack costs fifty dollars and adjusts to the growth of your child.

Manufacturers offer children's hiking boots, too! Both Vasque and Hi-Tec make hiking boots for children starting at about children's size 10. You can even find little boots for toddlers, but make sure your child can actually walk in them before you purchase them—they may be absolutely adorable but too rigid for a toddler's intrepid step.

Motivating Children

How can you make backpacking fun for your children and avoid the "how much farther" syndrome? The following are a few suggestions:

➤ Revel in nature. Stop to point out interesting flowers, clouds, trees, and mushrooms. Enjoy water by throwing pebbles and floating sticks and leaves. Play in sand or mud or snow. Watch frogs hop, squirrels and chipmunks scuttle from tree to tree, insects going about their business, a deer standing stock still, a hawk drifting on air currents . . .

➤ Teach your children geologic and natural history. Tell them about the Indians that once hunted in these woods, mention that they are walking on what was once hot lava, describe the intricacies of the glacier that molded this valley . . .

➤ Answer your children's questions. Why is the sky blue? Are there still Indians in these woods? Will the volcano erupt on us? . . .

➤ Get out the toys and a treat. Give your children a break with some fruit leather or a muffin and their favorite toys.

➤ Promise a celebration for attaining a certain goal. You might offer some juice and a piece of candy, or if you're health-conscious a fruit-sweetened cookie, when you reach the top of the mountain or the next stream.

➤ Play games that keep you moving. On slight inclines play Runaway Train, running wildly to the bottom of the hill (only if your children are capable of doing this without falling on their faces). Continue the train theme by pretending your family is a train and by making the appropriate noises while walking. Next, try some other vehicle—an airplane, ship, racecar, or truck.

➤ Tell stories. Parents can tell stories of past but true events, they can make up stories, or they can even invite their children to tell a story. Asking questions of a child can also prolong their stamina.

➤ Sing songs. Let your children choose or take turns choosing.

➤ Play animals. Pick an animal and tell about it, make its noises, and imitate its actions.

➤ Give out gorp. A handful of gorp for every 5, 10, 15, 20 steps (or whatever your children are capable of) will keep them going for awhile.

At some point or another a child will pull the "I can't take another step without collapsing" trick. When a parent falls for this ploy and the child is carried to your destination, the child usually experiences a miracle upon arrival; her eyes spring open and she's off and running, and the poor, exhausted parents later have to beg her to crawl into her sleeping bag.

On the other hand, children do not recognize fatigue and will drop from exhaustion before they show

Older children can help with chores around camp. Here the author's daughter, Griffin, cooks dinner.

any true signs of tiring. Children are tough but not superhuman. Don't push them too hard. Chances are, if you're tired, so are they.

Limitations

You should be aware of your own limitations. If you can't regularly carry a sixty-pound pack, don't think that you can do it when you have a child to carry, too. If you normally carry a forty-pound pack and your child weighs twenty pounds, carry no more than twenty pounds in addition to the child. In fact, consider carrying even less. Remember, you have a life on your back now. Don't endanger it.

A Final Comment

Keep your expectations in check. Introducing your children to the outdoors early in life does not necessarily mean they'll become avid backpackers later on, so don't be disappointed if they eventually lose interest.

Backpacking with Dogs

Dogs can make great hiking partners, but there is a downside. Dogs are seldom welcomed by other hikers and they are often not allowed in state or national parks. Be sure to check the regulations before you hike, but the following are some general guidelines:

➤ National Parks. Dogs aren't included in any "pack animal" designation. Most national parks do not allow pets of any kind in the backcountry. Some campgrounds and public areas permit dogs under restraint.

➤ National Forests. Whether or not dogs are allowed depends on the supervisor of each particular national forest, although most that do allow dogs require that they be leashed or under voice control.

➤ Wilderness Areas. As a part of the national forests, they are governed by the same rules.

➤ Bureau of Land Management. There are usually no restrictions on BLM lands except in unusual circumstances such as habitat restoration or wilderness areas. Restrictions, in these cases, might mean only that you must leash your pet.

➤ State Parks. Most state parks do not allow pets, and if they do, the pets usually must be leashed.

➤ Always check ahead of time about particular regulations at your intended hiking destination.

Dogs tend to scare up trouble. They have been bitten by rattlesnakes, swatted by porcupines, and are keen on rolling on dead animals—not a pleasant odor. If you choose to hike with a dog, you won't see much wildlife. If you do bring a dog on the trail, make sure you keep it under control. We were chased by some dogs in New Hampshire who, a few minutes later, bit another hiker. The dogs were on a day hike with their owners.

Other reasons not to bring a dog include the rough-rock scrambling required on many trails and the intense heat of summer hiking. We witnessed the death of a dog who had overheated in 90-plus-degree weather on a day hike in Pennsylvania. The owner, though well-intentioned, had neglected to bring enough water for his pet. Consider the kindness of leaving your dog at home, especially when you intend to long-distance hike.

Once you do decide to take your dog along, there are preparations to undertake:

➤ Your dog should have all its inoculations, and they should be up-to-date. Some parks require proof of a rabies vaccination.

➤ Your dog should have obedience training and should answer to voice commands. It should be leash-trained as well, since many state parks require leashes (if they allow dogs at all).

➤ Overly aggressive dogs and dogs that bark a lot do not make good backpacking companions. In most places, a dog seen injuring a human, livestock, or wildlife might be destroyed or impounded.

Get a clean bill of health from your vet. Take your dog for a checkup and let the doctor know just what you have in mind for your pet. The doctor will be able to tell you whether or not your dog is capable. Once your dog has met these conditions, it is time to make some plans.

The first question you must ask yourself is whether or not your dog will carry a pack. If the answer is yes, this is nothing to feel guilty about as dogs have been "beasts of burden" for thousands of years. Before Europeans introduced horses to the Americas, Indians used dogs to help carry their loads. The Iditarod was developed from an actual event in which sled dogs carried some much-needed medicine to Nome, Alaska, when a snowstorm prevented all other forms of transportation. And, at that time, sled dogs had been in used for years.

Both Wenaha and Caribou make packs for dogs. Such packs are generally designed to hold the dog's food. Like humans, dogs will need more food when backpacking because they will be expending more energy. The pack fits over the dog's back like a saddle and is secured across the dog's sternum (and sometimes its chest) with easy-release belts. Packs range in price from twenty to fifty dollars, and come in different sizes.

Use these guidelines when fitting your dog with a pack:

➤ A dog should easily be able to carry about one-third of its weight.

➤ Outdoors stores usually offer a range of dog packs. Make sure that you purchase one that suits both your needs and that of your dog.

➤ Make sure the pack is comfortable on your dog. It should allow ventilation. It should not ride too high or hang too low on its back. Make sure that it is horizontal to the ground and that weight is distributed evenly.

➤ Make sure there is nothing on the pack (or hanging from it) that will irritate or chafe your pet.

➤ Be careful about what your dog packs as it will likely be rolled on, shaken, soaked, and perhaps even muddied.

Preparing for the trail:

➤ Don't assume your pet is in shape. Unless you take it out regularly for runs, it might need some cardio-vascular conditioning. At a minimum, you should

Dogs can carry their
own food.

let it break in its new pack before hitting the trail. This means starting with just the pack and gradually building to the weight your dog will carry.

➤ Break in its feet as you would break in a new pair of boots. Pads are not naturally tough and the added weight of a dog pack will add extra stress to the feet.

On the trail:

➤ Carry special items in your first-aid kit just for your dog. Make sure you have tweezers, peroxide, an antibiotic cream, cotton swabs, scissors, and even a pair of needle nose pliers for especially tough thorns or splinters. In the winter, petroleum jelly will prevent ice balls from building up between your dog's toes.

➤ Carry an extra leash in case the other is lost or broken.

➤ Carry an extra towel for your dog as he is likely to get muddy.

➤ The leg from an old pair of panty hose can be used as a muzzle, if necessary. Wrap it over then under the snout before tying it behind the ears. Do not tie it too tight.

➤ Should you meet up with another animal, such as a bear that becomes aggressive, let the dog go to improve both your chances of escaping unharmed.

➤ Never let your pet use the trail as its restroom. Should an accident happen on the trail, be prepared to move the mess off trail.

➤ Make sure your dog gets enough water. Dogs dehydrate too. Don't let them get to the stage where they refuse drink. I have given up my last canteen of water several times to dogs who were on the verge of hyperthermia. Even if the dog has to carry it, always make sure you have extra water for your pet.

Preparing for a Trip

Once you have decided where, when, and how long you are going to hike, you need to prepare for it. Regardless of how long your hike, here are some suggestions to consider when getting ready to go into the outdoors.

GETTING YOURSELF READY

So, you are seriously considering hitting the trail, but now you are worried that you've spent too long on the couch watching ESPN and the Travel Channel. Fortunately, you can prepare yourself for a short or long-distance hike. Unfortunately, the only way to prepare is by starting off slowly with the very thing you plan to do.

While it is true that participating in any cardiovascular sport—jogging, cardio-kickboxing, aerobics, and such—will put you way ahead of the game, the only way to practice backpacking is to carry a backpack.

If you haven't done any cardiovascular exercise at all or in quite a while, you will want to start off packless. The best exercise for backpacking is walking. Walking exercises the muscles of the legs and lower back, muscles you will use constantly when backpacking.

If you are just starting out, try walking in one direction for fifteen minutes, then turn around and walk back. Try to find someplace you can walk that features irregular terrain even if the terrain is gentle. Walking on a track is good practice only for road walks, and you don't find many of those in the wilderness. As you continue, gradually increase your mileage to five miles.

Once you are comfortable walking five miles, start wearing a pack. But don't immediately load your pack with your final or anticipated pack weight! Start out with an empty pack and gradually increase its weight. Carrying water is a good idea because you can dump out some of the water if the pack begins to tire you too much. When you reach your target pack weight (no more than one-third of your body weight) and feel comfortable with it, try going out for a short hike—maybe a twelve-mile loop trip.

While training, make sure you carry along snacks and water to keep your energy levels up and your body from dehydrating. And don't forget to stretch before you go out and train. Stretching your calves is just as important for backpacking as it is for jogging or any other sport.

Also, try to find a hill to climb as part of your regular training mileage. Level ground does not strengthen the lateral muscles, tendons, and ligaments of the ankles and feet. Work those ankles, but gently! Forget about the stair-climbing machine, though, it just doesn't exercise your legs the way they need to be exercised for backpacking.

There are two supplementary exercises you can do to help strengthen your legs:

1. The barbell squat. Done properly, this is an excellent exercise for strengthening the thighs. To do this, stand erect, hold a barbell across your shoulders and behind your head and squat down. If you don't have a barbell, try using a broom across your shoulders with no added weight if you are a beginner, or simply hold a few bottles of water. When you squat, make sure you keep your chin up and your spine as straight as possible. And don't squat below the comfort level. If you have knee pain, you are squatting too low.

2. The foot lift. This is a great exercise to help prevent knee pain. This exercise is done while seated. Place the leg to be exercised over the chair's armrest and let the foot hang free. Hang a small weight from your foot using rope or webbing. Slowly straighten the leg as far as it will go and then bend it again. Exercise carefully, beginning with very little weight. If you can feel your knee grating, then you are trying to lift too much weight. Reduce the amount of weight and hold your leg stationary rather than attempting to bend it.

Finally, improving your balance will also help you out on the trail. Simply stand on one leg and look ahead and upwards for at least a minute on each leg. When you can do that, try doing the exercise with your pack on. Why? Balance is essential on certain stream crossings (doing the tightrope on a log), when removing that tiresome pebble from your boot (you don't want to have to take off your pack), and when rock hopping up and down mountains or across streams.

PACKING FOR A TRIP

What to Carry in Your Pack

An easy-to-use rule of thumb is to never carry more than one-third of your body weight. On shorter trips, it is wiser to carry even less—one-quarter of your body weight is about right.

Some hikers swear that you should carry only one-fifth of your body weight, but that can be difficult to do, especially if you are hiking in winter or carrying a week's worth of food.

What if you pack your pack and it weighs 60 pounds and you weigh only 120? Unpack and look at everything very carefully. Items like your stove, tent, and sleeping bag are absolutely essential. But what about your clothes? You don't have to wear something different every day. People also often pack too many toiletries. If you must shave, deodorize, and shampoo, try to find sample size containers. Don't bring a radio unless it's the compact Walkman type. Flashlights that are "hiker-friendly" can be purchased readily these days. A small flashlight that uses AA batteries will serve you just as well as one that uses C or D batteries.

These are just a few examples of ways to cut weight. Look objectively at what you've packed: Are you sure you can't live without it?

Here's another consideration: There is nothing more frustrating than carrying out as much trash as consumables you brought in. It very definitely indicates a packing problem, although you can be commended for "packing it out." The only thing worse than having to pack out a lot of trash is having to see the same stuff littering the trail. I have followed trails of cigarette stubs and candy wrappers on numerous occasions.

Fortunately, there are things you can do to minimize your waste:

➤ Purchase food with as little packaging as possible. Bulk foods have the least packaging.
➤ Use the extra-tough freezer zipper-lock bags to repackage foods you carry. These can be used dozens of times (make sure you wash them between each use).
➤ Purchase a refillable gas stove as opposed to a butane cartridge stove as the cartridges must be carried out. If you do own a butane stove, write to the manufacturer and ask that they develop a way to refill the cartridges. Also, keep your stove as clean as possible to keep it in peak working condition.

- Plan your meals carefully, bringing just as much food as necessary. Packing out the leftovers is not fun, and it is ecologically unsound to burn or bury them.
- Use loose tea and a small strainer to avoid packing out used tea bags. Instant coffee avoids the problems caused by filter packs or loose grounds, which must be packed out as well.
- Matches, particularly waterproof matches, are a better option than lighters as most used lighters must be disposed of.
- Women should use reusable pads or applicatorless tampons to reduce the amount of waste to pack out.
- Finally, sort through your trash when you return home to determine ways you can further reduce bulk on your next trip.

Guns and Alcohol

Firearms are a controversial subject among hikers. Most hikers feel that guns are unnecessary, but a few do pack pistols or even rifles that break down and fit into their packs.

Carrying weapons into a national park is a federal offense, and firearms are outlawed on other sections of trail as well. The real question is, are they necessary? To find out, we talked to hikers who, collectively, have hiked eighty-thousand miles on the Appalachian Trail as well as thousands of miles on the Pacific Crest, Continental Divide and other trails, including some in Europe. The bottom line was this: there was neither a single instance where a firearm was brought out of a pack (if one was carried), nor a case of a firearm helping a hiker out of a jam. None of the hikers we talked to, though some had carried guns, thought that firearms were necessary.

Guns do have a place, but backpacking isn't one of them (unless, of course, it is hunting season, you have a license, and you are intentionally backpacking to a hunting spot). Animals, including humans, don't present enough danger to hikers to justify carrying firearms.

Though much less controversial, the merit of drinking alcohol on the trail is worth considering. I don't intend to preach because, personally, nothing tastes better to me than an ice-cold beer on a hot summer's day, but unfortunately, during the past decade, the drinking of alcoholic beverages on trails has gotten out of hand.

One hiker nearly died of hypothermia atop New Hampshire's Mount Mariah after drinking a fifth of vodka. Too drunk to know where he was, he stumbled off the trail and passed out. Fortunately, he was spotted by other hikers and a search-and-rescue team was able to save him in time. A hiker in Pennsylvania was forced to shoot another hiker in self-defense when that hiker attacked him with a shovel during a drunken rage. Some hostel owners we know came close to closing their hostel (which was adjacent to their bed and breakfast) when drunken hikers began using their front yard as a urinal.

Tales like these abound. Please don't add your name to the list of those who have destroyed good situations for other hikers. Keep your consumption of alcoholic beverages moderate, especially if you are hiking alone. You may want to keep your consumption of alcoholic beverages to those times when you are taking a break in town. Alcohol can be life-threatening in the wilderness (and in town, too, for that matter).

Fortunately, most hikers are considerate; but it is always the few who ruin things for all. Also remember, as Ray Jardine points out in his guide to the Pacific Crest Trail, drinking alcoholic beverages is seriously dehydrating, which can be dangerous in a sport where keeping hydrated can be difficult.

Packing Your Pack

Once you've bought a pack, where do you put what? You're going to want certain items to be handy. It's a good idea to lay out all of your clothes, gear, and food before you begin to pack so you can see exactly what you have. (You may even see one or two things that you can do without.) Now you're ready to pack. Any system that you come up with will work as long as you know how to get at those necessary items quickly.

Here's the system I use:

Rain gear, for example, will be something that you'll want to be able to lay your hands on immediately. It is not unusual to be caught in a sudden downpour, and if you have to drop your pack and dig through it to get at your raingear, you and all your gear may be soaked by the time you find it.

You will also need a means to carry water so that you can get at it without taking off your pack. Some hikers use holsters for their water bottles while others keep their canteens within easy reach in a side pocket on their packs.

It also is important to distribute the weight in your pack as equally as possible. For example, don't put all your food on one side and all your clothes on the other. Believe it or not, food will be a good third of the weight you are carrying.

Pack the heavier stuff toward the top of your pack to keep the load centered over your hips, particularly in an external frame pack. On the other hand, don't follow this rule to its furthest possible conclusion because an overly top-heavy pack is also unwieldy.

BACKPACKING TIP

One of the greatest inventions for hikers is the zip-locked bag. It can be used to repackage food, mask food smells, or pack out trash.

Sleeping bags are usually secured at the bottom of an external frame pack, strapped to the frame just below the pack sack. In an internal frame pack, the sleeping bag compartment is usually the bottom third of the pack.

Another suggestion: you will probably want your food more readily available than your clothes and cooking gear, particularly at lunch time. Nothing is more aggravating than to have to dig through your clothes just so you can satisfy your craving for gorp.

Loading Tips

➤ On gentle terrain, pack the heaviest items high and close to the back. Because the pack's center of gravity is about at shoulder level, it will take only a slight bend at the waist while hiking to align the weight over your hips.

- If balance is crucial (as in climbing, hiking off-trail or over rough terrain), pack heavy items in the center, close to your back. You may have to lean over more to offset the pack's weight, but balance is better because the pack's top-heaviness is reduced.
- Women have a lower center of gravity and do well to pack dense items lower and closer to the back.
- If you are carrying anything sharp in your pack, pad it well. The last thing you want is to be stabbed in the back.
- Color-coded stuff sacks are a great backpacking tool.
- Make sure that all fitting points are properly adjusted to your torso.
- Long items should be lashed to the pack frame.

ON TO THE TRAILHEAD

Trailhead Safety

If a parking lot is known to be used by hikers, someone may be tempted to break in to your car while you are away. Take these steps to improve the odds that it won't happen to you.

BACKPACKING TIP

Before heading into the backcountry, highlight the route of your hike on a map and leave it with a friend (or at a local ranger station).

- Contact the park or forest district office where you plan to hike and find out if there have been any problems at the trailhead.
- When possible, use formal parking lots instead of simple pull-outs as they tend to be safer. Also avoid parking lots near bars and restaurants as they could draw late-night visitors.
- Leave any valuables at home or lock them out of sight in the trunk. If you leave the trunk empty, fold the back seat down to show thieves that there isn't anything there to steal either.
- Never leave a note on a vehicle telling where you are or when you will be back. We occasionally see cars at trailheads with some note on them and marvel that they haven't been broken into.

➤ If your car is broken into, always report it to the appropriate police and/or park authorities. Trailhead theft is often repeated and the sooner it is reported, the sooner they can catch the culprits.

You can avoid this entirely by arranging for someone to drop you off and pick you up. The only disadvantage is that you have a set time to reach your take-out point.

To add some peace of mind before you hit the trail, you may want to write out an itinerary of where you hope to be when, just in case you get lost. That way folks back at home will have suggestions on where to start looking for you. You should also let someone know how long you intend to be gone. In other words, "If you haven't heard from me in two weeks, you better send out a search party . . ."

Car Shuttles

Dropping one car at the end of a trail and then driving a second car to the beginning is one option, but there is another if you have a large-sized group. When you want to hike in an area where loop hikes aren't possible, you can split your party in two, start hiking at opposite trailheads, and meet in the middle at a prearranged campsite. After camping together, you swap keys and continue hiking to opposite trailheads. Each group should carry a set of keys to both cars should something unforseen happen and the mid-trip key swap is a bust. Also, make sure you set up a post-trip meeting place ahead of time.

If you don't have a second car available for either version of the shuttle, you might try to hire someone to take you to the trailhead. Hiking clubs should know of people in your area who are willing to shuttle hikers for a small fee.

BACKPACKING TIP

When leaving a vehicle at the trailhead, place a hide-a-key somewhere on the car just in case your keys get lost. Also, make sure everyone in your group knows where the key is in case of an emergency.

Long-Distance Hiking

DECIDING TO GO

Why People Hike Long-distance

There is no one reason that draws people to hike a long-distance trail, but there does seem to be a common denominator. Most long-distance hikers are at some point of change in their lives—divorce, graduation from college or high school, retirement, marriage, or an anticipated change of careers. These are all typical times when hikers take to some long-distance trail to follow it from end to end.

"One might conclude," Bill Foot noted in *The Appalachian Trail Backpacker,* "that the trail is a great place to figure out where to go or what to do with the rest of your life."

Some years ago when Frank and I became unhappy with our jobs at a daily newspaper, we decided to hike the Appalachian Trail and search for a solution to our dissatisfaction—what were we going to do for the rest of our lives? The six-month trip confirmed the fact that we wanted to continue with writing and photography, but on our own terms.

"I go forth to make new demands on life. I wish to begin this summer well; to do something in it worthy of it and me; to transcend my daily routine and that of my townsmen . . . I pray that the life of this spring and summer may ever lie fair in my memory. May I dare as I have never done! May I persevere as I have never done!"

- Henry David Thoreau

It is with that spirit that many backpackers seek the solitude and simple life of long-distance hiking—to be dependent on no one but themselves for an extended period; to commune with nature day after day after day; and to have no other worry but where to camp and where to get water.

What it Takes to be a Long-distance Hiker

"Finishing the trail was all-important," said Sondra Davis, who hiked the Appalachian Trail with her husband, Craig. "But enjoying the trail was reason enough."

Phil Hall said, "It takes determination, flexibility, and endurance. Without all three, you probably won't make it that far."

"I started with the intention of finishing," explained Doug Davis. "I think a lot of the quitters only committed themselves to giving it a try. As I went along I would try to imagine finishing. It was hard. I also tried to imagine not finishing. It was impossible."

Davis sums up the way most long-distance hikers feel. It takes determination and goal orientation to finish the trail you have chosen. Flexibility is the key.

Before you begin to plan a long-distance hike, ask yourself these questions:

➤ Am I afraid of the outdoors—of insects, animals, sleeping outdoors night after night?

➤ Will completing my hike be worth being wet/cold/hot day after day?

➤ Can I wear the same dirty clothes for days on end?

➤ Can I go without a bath or shower, sometimes for as long as a week?

➤ Can I withstand the physical pain that often accompanies backpacking?

➤ Can I stand being away from my home and my family and friends for a month or more—perhaps as long as six to eight months?

➤ Is the idea of backpacking this entire trail my all-consuming desire? Am I willing for it to be?

Some of these questions may seem trivial, but all of them point to reasons that people quit their long-distance hike. Obviously, severe physical injuries and emergencies at home also are a factor, but these have nothing to do with the determination, flexibility, and endurance it takes to hike an entire long-distance trail.

What do we mean by flexibility, endurance, and determination? Consider this experience penned by Cindy Ross in her book, *Journey on the Crest,* about her hike on the Pacific Crest Trail.

"We're aiming for a reservoir that the guidebook suggests we camp by, where we can go for a delightful swim. The idea has been on our minds all day. When we spot the blue speck below, Todd takes off in a trot, hollering like a madman. He kicks up the chocolate brown dust and chases all the cows, who run away in their own frightened cloud. I lag behind, giggling at the sight."

"When we arrive, we stare in disbelief. The "lake" is four inches deep! It's a slime-covered mud hole! The water level is very low, so that the rocks that no doubt normally lie submerged are exposed. We step on them to get out in the water. Muddy ooze squishes from the pressure of our weight, disturbing billions of mosquitoes breeding in the slime. Immediately they cover our ankles

and begin sucking blood. Take a swim in this? Todd
begins the laborious project of filtering water. He takes
a sweaty bandanna and drapes it over a water bottle
opening, putting a shallow dip in the cloth to help the
liquid through. I swat bugs off him as he collects a gallon. We look at each other. "Let's get out of here!"

Cindy and Todd did not enjoy their problems, but
they also didn't think about quitting. Every hiker has at
least one day like theirs, usually many more. It's just
something you have to keep in mind when you intend to
hike long-distance. Like four to six months in the "real"
world, something is bound to go wrong occasionally.

PREPARATIONS

Mapping Out Your Route

When and Where to Start

Now that you have decided to embark on a long-distance hike, you will need to decide where you want to
hike. You may want to stick to an established trail for
your first backpacking trip or perhaps, you are more
adventurous and would prefer to string together some
trails on your own and create your own hike. The really
adventurous often bushwhack out into the wilderness. I
wouldn't suggest that as a first trip, though once you
are comfortable in the outdoors it is certainly a possibility. Where you decide to go may depend on the
weather as much as your flexibility. Obviously, where
and when to start depends on what trail you're hiking.
The shorter long-distance trails (75-400 miles) give you
a bit more leeway; they take less time to complete, so
changing seasons is less of a factor. However, it might
be folly to hike the Ice Age Trail in the winter, though
this is probably the best time to hike the Florida Trail.

Shorter long-distance trails abound in the fifty
states. Some of the more popular trails include
Vermont's Long Trail, the C & O Canal Towpath Trail in
Maryland and West Virginia, the John Muir Trail in
California, the Chilkoot Trail in Alaska, the Grand
Canyon trails in Arizona, the Horseshoe Trail in

Pennsylvania, Isle Royale trails in Michigan, the Long Path in New York, the Ozark Highlands Trail in Arkansas, and the Pacific Northwest Trail in Oregon and Washington. There are hundreds of short long-distance trails in the United States and many more in Canada and Europe. England is especially famous for its paths, which criss-cross the country. The Pennine Way is said to be England's Appalachian Trail.

Longer trails—such as the Appalachian, Continental Divide and Pacific Crest—are more limited as to when you can start. The majority of backpackers begin the Appalachian Trail between March and May and hike northward from Georgia. A few choose to begin in Maine during the summer months and hike southward. Most Continental Divide Trail hikers begin at the Canadian border in July and hike south to Mexico; and those hiking the Pacific Crest Trail usually begin at the Mexican border in June and hike north to Canada. The latter two trails are often hard to complete in one year due to weather conditions. Regardless of the trail, there are several ways to overcome seasonal challenges.

Getting lost is part of the adventure of long-distance hiking. Martin Ferwerda, Phill Hall, and the author try and figure out where they are.

Flip-flopping

Some hikers find that they are not going to be able to make it to their destination before the weather gets too rough to permit hiking. Others find they have arrived at a section of trail that is still snowed in. Instead of calling off their hike, they flip-flop, jumping to the end of the trail and hiking backward from there. This is not necessary on most trails, but on the Continental Divide and Pacific Crest Trails, in particular, many hikers flip-flop rather than complete the trail in one continuous journey.

For example, a hiker begins the Appalachian Trail at Springer Mountain in Georgia. When he reaches Harpers Ferry, West Virginia, in August (about halfway), he begins to worry that he won't make it to Mount Katahdin in Maine before the park closes on October 15. He then decides to travel to Mount Katahdin and hike south to Harpers Ferry so that he can complete his hike in one year.

Some hikers set out to flip-flop a trail because they feel it gives them more time. Others flip-flop because they cannot begin their hike until midsummer or do not wish to hike entirely south- or northbound. A good friend of ours started the Appalachian Trail from Harpers Ferry in June so that he could hike with that year's thruhikers. After making it to Mount Katahdin, he returned to Harpers Ferry and hiked to Springer Mountain in Georgia.

BACKPACKING TIP

For more information on long-distance trails and long-distance hiking, you can contact the Appalachian Long Distance Hikers Association and ALDHA-West—the nation's only groups for long-distance hikers. They both hold annual gatherings of long distance hikers each fall which feature workshops and slide shows from trails around the country.

Section Hiking

An alternative to hiking a trail end-to-end in one year is to hike it in sections. This means completing an entire trail over a period of two or more years. If you are unable to take four to six months off for one long hike, you can break a trail up into smaller sections to be hiked over several years.

The completion of a trail over many years can be just as meaningful, if not more so, as hiking the trail in one long hike. But it means a longer commitment and it can be a logistical challenge to get to and from the trail each year.

Blue-blazing

Before you begin your hike, you should make an important decision. What is the goal you are pursuing? Is it to hike the entire trail or is it merely to spend several months hiking in the Sierras, the Rockies, or the Appalachians? You should ask yourself this question because opportunities will arise to cut off sections of the trail to make it shorter, easier, or to provide faster access to towns.

The term for taking these shortcuts is blue-blazing. The name comes from the fact that many of the side trails you will intersect are marked with blue blazes. While the Appalachian Trail has one set route and hikers who stick to this white-blazed trail think of themselves as purists, most other trails offer "official" alternative routes. Both the Pacific Crest and Continental Divide Trails have variable routes because the weather changes so drastically on those trails.

If you decide ahead of time how "pure" you want your hike to be, you will have less trouble deciding later. We have discovered that once you begin to blue-blaze, it is harder not to do so again. An example of an extreme case of blue-blazing would be taking the Tuckerman Ravine Trail down from Mount Washington in New Hampshire to turn a 12.9-mile hike across the Northern Presidential Range into a less than five-mile hike downhill.

Making a distinction before you leave home will help you choose which trail to follow once you're hiking. Whatever choice you make for yourself, remember that you are hiking for your own reasons, with your own goals. Allow others the same courtesy. Don't view another's hiking style as wrong; it is only different.

Money Matters

How Much Does it Cost to Hike?

How much do you want it to cost? The main cost you will incur is the food you eat and the fuel for your stove. From there, what you spend is optional. Most hikers will splurge on restaurant meals when they go into town and they might pay for a night in a motel or hostel. A good rough estimate is a minimum of $1.50 a mile, not including any equipment you may need or transportation to and from your selected trail. This is not going cheap, nor is it extravagant. If you are careful, the trail can be a very inexpensive four to six months.

Other expenses might include:

➤ laundry and detergent
➤ entertainment (batteries for your Walkman, movies, dancing, books, magazines, etc.)
➤ replacement of gear (if you haven't already set aside a fund for emergencies)
➤ doctor bills (also an emergency fund item)
➤ miscellaneous items (batteries for your flashlight or headlamp, stamps, stationery, etc.)

Money on the Trail

Hiking with a thousand dollars in cash is a bad way to test your trust in your fellow humans. Most hikers choose the safety and convenience of traveler's checks. Traveler's checks can be cashed almost anywhere. We haven't heard of any store, no matter how small or out-of-the-way, that wouldn't cash a traveler's check. By buying the checks in denominations of $20 as well as $100, you can rest assured that you won't be caught carrying a large amount of cash at any one time. For added peace of mind and to help you stay on budget, it is a good idea to split your traveler's checks up into two or three groups, sending some ahead to your mail drops.

Automated Teller Machines have made their way to many trail towns and have become a reliable way to receive money. With credit cards or bank cards that are part of a nationwide network, such as Cirrus, hikers can obtain money in an emergency or as part of a scheduled withdrawal.

Whether or not you intend to use your credit card for cash withdrawals, bring it along. A major credit card can be a lifesaver if equipment breaks or medical problems arise. Telephone company credit cards are helpful in reaching family and friends from the trail and can be used to contact equipment manufacturers in an emergency.

Shelter Planning

For the most part, your home away from home will be your tent, but from time to time (and depending on the trail) you may be able to take advantage of other opportunities. A very few trails—the Appalachian and Long Trails, and those in Great Smoky Mountains National Park and the White Mountains—offer hikers some sort of shelter as an alternate to tent camping. Very few shelters are available on western trails. You may find a few along the Pacific Crest or Continental Divide Trails but they may not be in excellent condition.

You are more likely to encounter hostels, especially if hiking in Europe. A hostel can be as simple as the floor of a church or barn, or as elaborate as a hot shower, a warm bed, laundry facilities, and food. Hostels range in price from free (although a donation is always appreciated) to twenty dollars or more a night. They are generally run by the American Youth Hostel (AYH) group, churches, trail clubs or private citizens.

If you intend to stay in hostels during your hike, count on leaving at least a small donation (especially if they don't ask for it). Some hostels will let you work off your stay, but all appreciate a helping hand, even if you're paying. If the hostel is a business, you need only be courteous and you may stay as long as you are willing to pay for a room or bed. If it is run by volunteers on a donation basis, help out, and limit your stay to a night or two (unless it's an emergency). Prove that hikers are not the socially irresponsible crowd a lot of

people think we are. Try to clean up behind other hikers as well as yourself. A good attitude goes a long way toward improving relations along any trail.

AYH hostels require membership in their group before you can stay in one of their hostels. The group was created to provide inexpensive lodging for travelers. Be sure to look into this before you count on a stay at a particular hostel. For more information on AYH, write: AYH, Data Processing Department, P.O. Box 37613, Washington, D.C. 20013. They will send you membership information. Upon joining AYH, you will receive a handbook that includes a listing of AYH hostels in the United States.

The time to plan on staying in hostels is before you hike; many require reservations. It is up to you to look into whether there are any hostels available along the trail you plan to hike. The local trail club will be able to give you this information.

Trail Registers/Trail Names

Along some trails, you may find "trail registers." They are anything from a sign-in sheet in a national forest to a notebook or diary at a shelter or in specially-built boxes along the trail.

Started as a safety measure to pinpoint the whereabouts of hikers, trail registers have become an important link in a vast communications network. Trail registers offer hikers the chance to make comments to those behind them, and to get to know, sometimes intimately, those ahead.

A little common sense should be used when writing in trail registers. Profanity should be avoided because families hike the trail and read the registers; don't write anything you wouldn't want a second-grader to read.

With that said, remember how important other's entries can be to you. If you have something on your mind, don't be afraid to share it. After a tough day of slogging through the rain, a read through the register can be entertaining. On the other hand, entries that ramble on for more than a page often go unread.

To fulfill the registers' initial purpose of keeping tabs on hikers should an emergency occur, always give the date, the time of day, your name or your trail name, and where you are headed next.

Trail names are the nicknames used by hikers to identify themselves in registers. A trail name can become an important identifier even if you hike on the trail only a few days a year. For some reason, trail names are much easier to remember than given names. They are more interesting and often give you some idea of the person who bears the name. For example, when Ed Carlson began hiking, he was under a lot of stress and very high strung. He decided to take the name of Easy Ed, hoping that he would change to suit the name. In his case, it worked.

Names involving characters from the Tolkien novels are popular as are those playing off the slowness of turtles. The Grateful Dead have inspired numerous trail names. Of course, some people choose an aspect of their name or personality to draw upon.

MANAGING YOUR SUPPLIES

It's obvious that you aren't going to be able to carry all the food and supplies you will need on a long-distance hike, so you will need to plan ahead and determine

Repackaging store-bought commodities can reduce weight and make food supplies more manageable.

where and when you will resupply. One key factor in determining where you resupply is how much food you are willing to carry between supply points. The more food you carry, the less frequently you need to resupply. Some people have no problem continually carrying two week's worth of food on their back, whereas others strain under the weight of a week's worth. Know your limits. We often carry only a few day's worth when we know we'll be able to resupply frequently. Of course, the trail might also dictate where you resupply. Some trails, like the Appalachian, afford resupply points on the average of once a week. Others, like the Pacific Crest and Continental Divide, often force the hiker to carry as much as two weeks, of food.

With these things in mind, here are some alternatives for you to consider when planning your trip.

The author packages food for later use on the trail. These supplies will be mailed to pre-determined mail stops along the trail.

1. Mass mail everything you need to your resupply stops. The advantage: you don't need to worry about someone forgetting to mail you supplies. The disadvantage: your schedule isn't as flexible as it might otherwise be. If you fall behind, you might run out of food.

2. Have relatives or friends back home send you food on a prescribed schedule. This offers you more flexibility; as you hike, you can adjust when and where packages are sent in order to match your pace.

3. Buy food as you go along. This is the ultimate in flexibility, but it doesn't work in more remote areas.

4. Create food caches before you hike. This is good in extremely remote areas, and barring accidents, you know where and how much food you will get when. Of course, caches can get broken into, or

you might not be able to find them again. Caching also takes a lot of prehike preparation.

Regardless of which method you choose for resupplies, you may also want to have a general box that you send along in front of you. Long-distance hikers Bill and Laurie Foot combined the use of primary resupply mail drops sent in advance with smaller packages they sent ahead of themselves along the trail: "We sent ourselves large boxes every eight to ten days. When we picked them up, we would pack what we needed for four or five days, and put the remainder into a smaller package and send it to a post office five days ahead. This way, we knew our schedule better and avoided problems with arriving in a town when the post office was closed."

Frank and I agree that post office drops in expensive or poorly stocked towns are an immense help. Also, sending yourself "care" packages filled with goodies such as candy and nuts insure you'll have a high-calorie treat when you finally arrive at the post office. You can also send yourself dehydrated foods to add variety to your diet.

Mail Drops

Even if you don't intend to send your food ahead, you should plan a few mail drops. Sending hard-to-buy items such as film, guidebooks and maps, Sno-Seal and seam sealer is just one use for a mail drop. Friends and family can be given a list of post offices where you plan to check for mail. This usually produces a variety of letters and packages, making all your planning worthwhile.

Packages should be addressed to you, General Delivery, with the city, state, and zip code of the post office. By having the letters and packages marked "Hold for northbound (or southbound) (Name of Trail) hiker," you will ensure that the post office will hold them much longer than customary. Post offices that are frequented by hikers generally hold mail until that year's group of hikers stops coming by, then it returns them to the sender. Zip codes for post offices near the trail and distances from the trail to the post office can be received through the conference in charge of the trail you are hiking.

As nice as receiving mail can be, remember that mail drops can also be a nuisance. If you come in to a town after noon on Saturday, you will probably have to wait until Monday morning for mail. If the mail drop is not essential, you can leave a forwarding card and let the mail catch up to you later. Using a number of mail drops for food or any other essentials (e.g., money) means that you will have to schedule your hike around getting to town when the post office is open.

Spacing your post office pickups about 150 to 200 miles apart should be sufficient if you don't use them as your only source of food. Distances between post offices will vary according to what trail you are hiking.

Mailing Gear Ahead

One way to use the mail system to your advantage is to send equipment farther down the trail instead of home.

"One of the most helpful things I did for myself about a third of the way through my trip was to have a box that I continually sent ahead of myself," said Rob White. "I used the box to carry excess equipment up the trail for me. And when I decided to get rid of my tent and use the tarp, I sent the tent about a week ahead before I sent it home."

This technique can be used for extra food, contact lens solution, clothing, soap, re-sealable plastic bags, and more. The postage costs can add up, but if you're thinking of doing without some piece of equipment, it's best to try living without it for a few days first.

Insurance

No one plans on getting hurt, but it does happen. Unless you have a serious bankroll somewhere, setting out to hike a long-distance trail without medical insurance is risky at best, though many hikers, ourselves included, take this route. Relatively low-cost, short-term medical insurance is available through many companies. The short-term policies are designed for people between jobs and typically last no longer than six months. This type of policy is nonrenewable but it allows enough coverage for the duration of a long-distance hike. As with any policy, the higher the deductible, the lower the premiums will be.

THE AFTERLIFE

If you are not ready for a major life change, don't take a long-distance hike. Once you've hiked an entire long-distance trail, you will find that things will never be quite the same again. The trail's effect is different on each hiker, but no one is left unchanged.

"Too many things hit you," said Todd Gladfelter, who has hiked both the Pacific Crest and Appalachian Trails. "Bills, phone, cars, appointments."

After hiking the Pacific Crest Trail, Todd's wife, Cindy Ross, had so much trouble readjusting that she camped out in her backyard for awhile upon her return home and walked around sniffing sage from her mother's spice cabinet because it reminded her of the desert. These changes often lead to a change of lifestyle, and sometimes a change of career. Cindy and Todd have since built their own log cabin, grow their own vegetables, and do whatever it takes to be their own bosses.

Many others have settled down near a trail so that they can continue to be a part of the lifestyle they love so much. Teaching is a favorite career taken up by long-distance hikers because it allows them to hike during the summer months. Others have chosen jobs that allow them to work for awhile to raise enough money for a long-distance hike and then take off for four to six months. Folk singer Walkin' Jim Stolz has accumulated thousands of miles of hiking experience while maintaining his lifestyle by singing about his journeys.

Equipment

So, you've decided to hit the trail. What exactly do you need in order to head out into the woods? Well, first of all, before you invest in the myriad equipment you will need to take a backpacking trip, you might want to rent what is needed or borrow it from a friend. Backpacking gear can be expensive, especially when you've figured in the cost of tent, sleeping bag, stove, backpack, and boots—all essential to a backpacking trip (OK, maybe you can get along without the boots on a trial trip).

But, how do you even begin to go about choosing when there are so many different manufacturers out there, each offering numerous choices in terms of gear? Fortunately, when it comes to choosing gear, whether or not you choose one manufacturer over another is not a life or death decision. Choosing a K-Mart tent over a tent designed by The North Face won't be putting your life in danger although it very likely will add several more pounds to your pack. Keep in mind that part of the "fun" of backpacking is enjoying the outdoors. If you're toiling away beneath a heavy pack, you're good times will be diminished. The same goes for maintaining your gear between trips. The idea is to spend as little time as possible maintaining and repairing your gear on your trip. This book features a chapter on gear repair in the last section.

A number of outdoor retailers such as REI, Eastern Mountain Sports, and more offer gear rentals. But, read ahead first, and see why you need this gear and what it is used for before heading off. Then, if you like your first trip, this book can be your guide to finding the gear that is just right for you, that will help you plan the most comfortable trip possible.

BOOTS

Boy, have things changed in what people choose to wear when hiking. Twenty, thirty years ago, hiking boots weighed a ton and were all leather and that was that. Today, you have your proponents of lightweight, medium-weight, and heavyweight boots, those who swear by their cross-trainers or jogging shoes and those who will wear nothing but Tevas. And I bet there isn't a hiker out there who hasn't gaped, visibly, at those day-hikers stumbling down the trail in spike heels! I wonder how many sprained ankles rangers treat each year in our national parks. But are spike heels so unusual on the trail when you see tons of people trudging down those city sidewalks in hiking boots? What's the difference, really? It is definitely the age of wear what you want when you want.

Whether you choose to wear your running shoes or Tevas as opposed to good, old-fashioned hiking boots is up to you. I admit freely that there are times when it is just as easy to maneuver a trail in my cross-trainers as in my boots. And when it comes to stream crossings, there has been many an occasion when I have slipped on Tevas to both protect my feet and keep my boots from getting wet. But, I am going to concentrate on boots as the majority of backpackers still prefer to go traditional on the trail.

Almost every hiker can tell you a boot story—from dissolving uppers and disappearing soles to swamp rot and ulcerous blisters. Boots can both protect and destroy your feet. And, since backpacking usually involves being on your feet all day, well-suited boots will be your most important gear acquisition.

Boot Weight and Height
Your selection of boots will depend on where, when, and how often you want to hike. Lightweight boots are ideal for day hikes and backpacking on easy terrain. For example, most of the trails along the east coast can be hiked in lightweight boots. Rock scrambling and rougher terrain call for medium-weight boots, which are better suited to that kind of stress. Heavyweight boots are designed for those who intend to do intensive backpacking in mountainous terrain, including snow and ice hiking. Both the Pacific Crest and Continental Divide Trails, among others, involve this type of hiking.

You also have a choice between differing lengths of upper—above ankle boots, ankle high boots, and below ankle boots. Above ankle boots offer the most support and are usually only found in heavyweight boots made of leather. They are great if you need to carry a big pack in the backcountry. Just make sure you allow yourself plenty of time to break them in. Ankle high boots are cut just at or just under the ankle. They are good for moderate loads and are fine for most trails. These can be found in both lightweight and medium-weight styles. Finally, below ankle boots are usually only lightweight in style and are best for very light trail use. If you wear them for tougher trips, you risk blisters and insufficient ankle support. Because so many trails are made hazardous by rocks and roots, conventional wisdom sides with having some type of ankle support, though in the end, it's as much a matter of preference as necessity.

Lightweight Boots

Lightweight boots usually weigh less than 2.5 pounds per pair and are generally made of a combination of leather and a "breathable" fabric. Lightweights have been around for only a decade, but it would be impossible to hike any trail without running across someone wearing a pair. Beyond the fact that they don't weigh your feet down, lightweights rarely require a breaking-in period. If they do, you're probably wearing a medium-weight boot or you've purchased the wrong size or brand. This type of boot is more flexible than the medium-weight and heavyweight and it has shallower lug outsoles.

There are disadvantages to lightweights. Your feet will get wet quickly when it's raining or when you're walking through dew-soaked grass or leaves. On the other hand, they dry out more quickly than other boots.

They offer less support than heavier boots, particularly in the ankles, and they don't last as long. Taking that into account, they usually cost a lot less than heavier boots.

For all their disadvantages, lightweight boots are still the best choice for day trips and light hiking. Be sure to look for a fully gusseted tongue when purchasing a pair of lightweights. Gussets, the extra material sewn between the upper and tongue, help the boots shed both moisture and trail debris (dust, leaves, twigs, etc.).

Although Frank lost the soles of his lightweights, it is usually the seams that begin to fall apart. We know one hiker who burst the seams on four pairs of lightweights. That was an extreme, though.

Medium-Weight Boots

For most hiking conditions, medium-weight boots have replaced the heavyweight boots of yesterday. Weighing between 2.5 and 4 pounds, medium-weights are almost entirely, if not all, leather, although you will see some stronger fabric/leather combinations in this category. Higher uppers offer better ankle support and

more protection in snow and on rocky terrain. Wider outsoles and heavy-duty midsoles, combined with a half-length to three-quarters-length steel shank to strengthen the sole, help to protect your feet from bruising stones. It usually takes medium-weights longer than lightweights to get wet, and conversely, longer to dry out. Make sure you break your medium-weights in before setting out on a backpacking trip.

Top priority for medium-weight boots is fit. You must try them on before you buy them, or purchase them through a mail-order house with a liberal return policy.

Heavyweight Boots

Heavyweight boots usually weigh more than four pounds and are designed for technically demanding hiking such as on ice with crampons or on snow and alpine rock.

Heavyweight boots are made of thicker, stiffer leather than medium-weights, and sometimes of molded plastic. They have close-trimmed soles and a half- to full-length steel shank in the sole. Some heavyweight boots offer a padded, insulated inner boot for protection against the extreme temperatures involved in mountaineering.

Which Boot is for You?

One way to determine which type of boot you need to look for, is to figure out beforehand what kind of hiking/backpacking you will be doing. There are basically five categories to help you decide what you will need:

Trail: If you are interested in light overnight hikes or day-hiking from a basecamp, below ankle or ankle high boots are a good choice. Basic trail hikers combine fabric and leather or split-leather construction. They also usually have multiple seams, which allows for more moisture to enter your boots and thus dampen your socks. If the boot doesn't have a waterproof/breathable liner, you'll need to purchase some Gore-Tex socks or apply some waterproofing and carry along some gaiters for "just in case." These lightweight boots have stiffer soles, more stability, and better traction than running or walking shoes, but they can be unstable on slippery or rocky terrain.

Technical Scrambling: Both lightweight and midweight boots can be designed for basic boulder scrambling and light trail use. They are usually below ankle and ankle-high boots that hug the foot closely. They have sticky rubber soles for traction as well as anti-abrasion toe rands. They provide enough support to carry a light backpack on well-maintained trails, but if you plan to do major miles with a heavy pack, you'll want a more substantial boot.

Rough Trail: Medium-weight boots made from a leather/fabric combination or split-grain leather are perfect for easy, short backpacking trips when you are not carrying a too-heavy pack. Some of these boots have waterproof/breathable liners and others are porous and well-ventilated for desert hiking. They tend to have tapered plastic midsoles or half-length shanks which provide enough sole rigidity to protect your feet on rocky trails but still allow good flex at the balls of the feet.

Off Trail: These are heavyweight boots designed for bushwhacking across unknown terrain (unknown to you, at least). They are made with full-grain leather, above-the-ankle support and rigid sole stability. They are best for long backpacking trips because they offer plenty of protection beneath heavy loads, yet provide enough flex at the balls of your feet to be comfortable. If you put enough miles on these boots, they will eventually become very supple but it can take a long time for the sole and the heel-cup to soften. Off-trail boots also offer excellent waterproofing and durability because they have a minimum number of seams. Because of new boot technology, many of these "heavyweight" boots are now a lot lighter. Some models have a lip on the welt of the sole to handle step-in crampons for glacier travel or the new snowshoe bindings.

Mountaineering: High, cold, and mountainous terrain requires the Arnold Schwarzeneggers of boots—heavy, tough, and rugged. With full-grain leather uppers, minimal seams, excellent traction and sometimes even insulation, mountaineering boots are ideal for the toughest of trips. They rise well above the ankle and

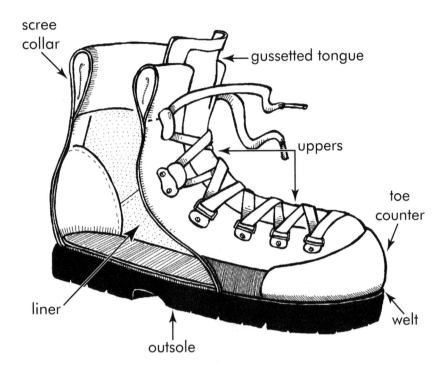

scree collar

gussetted tongue

uppers

toe counter

liner

welt

outsole

accept binding-style crampons. They have full-length shanks or stiff nylon midsoles and are usually too rigid for normal backpacking. Before you plan a trip, though, make sure these boots are fully broken in because the blister potential is phenomenal. Look for rockered (curved) soles for a more natural stride, minimal heel slippage, and rubbers along the welt for durability and waterproofing.

Boot Construction

Uppers

There are numerous types of uppers—that is, the portion of the boot above the sole—including full-grain leather, split-grain leather (a portion of the inner hide split off from the waterproof and supportive outside), Nubuk leather (sanded full-grain leather), synthetic fabrics (often used in combination with leather), Gore-Tex and other proprietary waterproof/breathable membranes (which are added inside the leather or fabric upper), and plastic. Because of its support, breathability, comfort, protectiveness, and ability to be waterproofed, leather is most often used when constructing uppers. The highest quality boots feature an all-leather upper because there is less stitching for water to leak through and fewer seams to burst. Multiple-piece leather uppers are your next best option because they cost less than all-leathers and can be waterproofed.

➤ Combination fabric/leather uppers use leather to reinforce canvas or nylon; the leather not only helps the boots resist abrasion, it increases their ankle support. Only the leather pieces can be waterproofed because the fabrics will not take waterproofing treatments.

➤ Uppers made of plastic are used only in heavy-weight mountaineering boots. Although light, warm, strong, and waterproof, plastic uppers are too rigid for most terrains.

➤ Uppers also include cuffs or scree collars that are stitched to the ankle top of most boots to provide some protection against the inevitable invasion of pebbles and twigs. Internal cuffs are better than external because they last longer.

➤ The tongue of the boot should be gusseted for the best protection against moisture and debris. The gusset is a thin piece of leather or other material sewn between the boot upper and tongue. The best protection is found in a bellows tongue, which has a full-length gusset that covers the entire tongue opening. Overlapping tongues also provide a nearly watertight closure. Well-padded tongues are more comfortable, offering some protection against tightly laced boots.

➤ The protective piece of leather sewn over the back seam of most boots is called the backstay. Because it is next to impossible to replace, look for a backstay that is narrow. It will be less vulnerable to abrasion.

➤ Toe and heel counters are also part of a well-made upper. These are stiffeners built into the toe and heel areas to provide some protection against rocks and roots.

Leather

Hide straight off the cow is too thick for even the heaviest of boots. All leather is split into sheets of varying thickness. Full-grain leather, the outside layer of the hide, is the highest quality leather—resistant to abrasion, the most waterproof, and the stiffest. All others layers are called "splits." The quality of splits varies but only the layer beneath the full-grain can be used in boots and it must be specially treated to make it resistant to water. Once the hid has been split, it must be cured before it can made into a boot.

There are several different methods used to cure the leather that makes up the hundreds of boots designed for hiking, backpacking, and mountaineering. Tanning immediately comes to mind. This initially involves curing leather by placing hides in a rotating drum containing a solution of chromium sulfate. Formally called chrome tanning, all leather undergoes this first process, which takes the skin or hide of an animal and protects it against decay while making it supple. Some leathers then undergo a vegetable process that involves tanning with plant derivatives. This step gives the leather extra body and solidity. Some leathers are put through a step called fatliquoring in which the leather is cured with either oils to make it softer, or waxes to make it firmer.

Most manufacturers use full-grain leather in their uppers. Because of the battering hiking boots receive, many manufacturers will turn the full-grain leather inside out before stitching it to the sole. This way, the water-resistant side is facing inward and is less likely to receive nicks and scratches from rocks and roots that will allow water to seep into your boot. How can you tell which way the full-grain is facing? The outside of the boot will be smooth if the top layer is out, rough if the top layer is facing in. Boots designed for easy hiking often have the top layer facing out.

Soles

The outsole, midsole, and steel shank make up the sole of the boot. The outsole, often a Vibram brand these days, usually has either shallow or deep lugs to provide traction. Good traction is particularly important if you intend to do some rock scrambling or if you will be gaining and losing a lot of elevation while carrying a heavy pack. While shallow lugs are designed for easy to moderate terrain and are usually paired with light-weight boots, deeper lugs can be found on medium-

weight and heavyweight boots and provide the traction needed for most backpacking trips.

The style of tread varies from boot to boot. All seek to ensure good traction regardless of terrain.

Between the outsole and insole of the boot is the midsole. The thickness of the midsole varies with the boot but is designed to provide extra protection, extra support, and cushioning between your foot and the ground. Even lightweight boots feature a midsole, often of EVA or polyurethane, for added comfort.

Most boots have a steel (or plastic or nylon) shank that ensures that the sole of your boot flexes at the ball of your foot. Except for plastic boots, which have an inherently rigid sole, shanks range from quarter- to full-length. The lightweight boots usually require only up to a half-length shank while the medium-weight to heavyweight boots need at least a half- to full-length shank for optimum rigidity.

The Welt

The importance of the welt (or how the upper is fastened to the sole) never occurred to me until Frank lost the soles of his New Balance Cascades outside of Elk Park, North Carolina. Hiking sixty miles to the next town with his soles duct-taped to his uppers was pure torture, but what if a friendly hiker hadn't had the tape? A bare-footed jaunt to the next road carrying a forty-pound pack was unthinkable. So, a plug for carrying duct tape (probably one of the better modern inventions along with WD-40—just ask MacGyver) and a strong suggestion to check out the welt on the boots you plan to hike in. Welts are usually made with stitching and/or cement and affects both the strength and flexibility of the boot.

The Goodyear welt is built with two rows of stitching. A horizontal stitch joins the upper to both the insole and a strip of leather. This strip of leather is then vertically stitched to the soles. This welt is very flexible and is often used in lightweight hiking boots. Both the outer and midsole can be replaced on boots using this welt.

The Norwegian welt also uses two rows of stitching—a horizontal stitch to join the upper and lining to the insole and a vertical stitch to attach the upper to the midsole. While not as flexible as the Goodyear welt, the Norwegian welt is much stronger and is often used in medium-weight and heavyweight boots. Outer and midsoles can also be replaced on this boot.

Another type of welt is called the "inside fastened,"

Scarpa's Edwardo uses the strong Norwegian welt.

the "Littleway," or the "McKay." This welt is achieved by rolling the upper between the insole and midsole and then stitching all three together from the inside. This is both a flexible and durable welt method and is often used on lightweight hiking boots. Like the other methods, both the outer and midsoles can be replaced.

Because they are not intended for heavy use, lightweight boots often have cement-welted soles. A narrow outsole is required, which can be a drawback. Advances in technology have produced strong adhesives, but boots with soles that are attached with an epoxy take a bit of extra care (i.e., common sense). Don't dry them out too close to a heat source because the epoxy could melt and a few miles down the trail, the sole could separate from the upper.

Fit

Select your boot carefully. Backpacking is an activity that involves spending the entire day on your feet with an extraordinary amount of weight on them. The strongest welt, the toughest leather, and super-traction soles will mean little if every step is agonizing because of improper fit. You may be proud of your small, shapely feet, but buying a boot because it enhances your appearance is foolish and may amount to a face lined with anguish by day's end.

The most important consideration when purchasing a boot is whether or not it is comfortable. Boot sizing is notorious for its inconsistency. You might normally wear a size 6 in tennis shoes but a 5 or a 7 in a boot, so don't just buy a boot outright without trying it on. When trying on the boot, wear hiking socks. A boot might feel comfy over a thin cotton crew, but slip it on over a thick polypropylene and suddenly your foot feels like a sardine. Also, if you intend to wear insoles, which give you extra cushioning and arch support, bring them along when you are trying on boots because insoles also affect the way a boot fits. Make sure that the

BACKPACKING TIP

When determining the best boot fit, try this technique: Push your foot to the front of an unlaced boot. If you can just slide two fingers in between your heel and the boot, you have found a good fit that will allow the little extra room you need without giving too much play.

boots are not only long enough for you but wide enough as well. Unlike typical, off-the-rack tennis shoes, boots do come in several widths: find the one that's right for you. Don't be surprised if you can't find a perfect fit. With more than 132 potential foot shapes, no manufacturer can fit everyone. After finding the closest fit, the boot can probably be altered with orthotics or broken in to fit.

Here are some tips for finding the perfect (or near perfect) boot:

➤ Always look for boots late in the day. First thing in the morning, your feet won't have swollen to their normal size. And believe me, after a day on the trail lugging a heavy pack, your feet will swell.

➤ Always wear the socks you will wear hiking or something similar when trying on new boots. Their thickness will determine how well a boot fits.

➤ Always measure your feet on the off chance your feet have spread (widened) since the last time they were checked.

➤ Lace your boots up securely, and determine if any part of the boot is uncomfortable. Pressure should be even all over your foot, which contains more than twentysix functional bones. Tell the salesperson what you feel. Is there unusual pressure at the instep? Let him or her know. They'll probably suggest a boot that will suit you better.

➤ Always walk around the store to see how the boot feels. If the store has an incline ramp, use it to see if your heel lifts on the uphills or your toe jams into the front of the boot on the downhills.

➤ And always find a solid post or wall and kick it a few times to see if your toes hit the front of the boot. If they do, relace and try again. If they still do, try the next larger size, yet another lacing technique, or a different model of boot.

How do you know if the fit is big enough but not too big? Is there a thumb's width between your toes and the tip of your boot? Can you wiggle your toes for good circulation? Take all the time you need to get a good fit.

While my first pair of boots didn't give me blisters, they were too short. On the downhill, my feet slid forward into the toe of the boot, resulting in painfully numb toes that throbbed all night long. Not even aspirin could dim that pain. Long-distance hikers often lose toenails. A boot that is long enough will help alleviate that problem. On the other hand, make sure your heel doesn't slip. This could lead to blisters. The heel should be snug but it shouldn't pinch you.

Waterproofing

If your boots have any leather in their construction, they need waterproofing. Sno-Seal and the newer Aquaseal are two popular brands of sealant, although there are a number of others. Devoutly follow directions for the waterproofer you purchase. It really does help to have dry feet! If you purchase boots that are Gore-Tex, the Gore-Tex is already waterproofed, but if the boots are both Gore-Tex and leather, you will have to waterproof the leather.

Unfortunately, sealing your boots is not a one-time deal. It must be done periodically, and the more you use your boots, the more often you must seal them. For hikes of more than a week or two, you may want to carry sealant along with you. If you plan to use mail drops, send some sealant up the trail.

Taking care of your boots will ensure a longer life span (for your boots, that is). After every backpacking trip, brush off dirt and debris before storing your boots. If your boots are wet, try stuffing them with newspaper to soak up the inside moisture and let them dry in a cool, dry place. Don't try to dry them quickly by setting them near a heater, an oven, or an open flame. It could mean the death of your boots. Once they are dry, reseal them with waterproofer. Seams and welts and the leather used in lightweight boots require a special sealant. All boot sealants can be purchased in outdoor stores.

Laces and Lacing

While leather laces used to be popular, their tendency to stretch when wet has been their demise. Nylon has replaced them as the standard lace for hiking boots. The durable, soft-woven, unwaxed nylon laces also hold knots best.

Hiking boots usually feature three different methods of lacing—grommets, D-rings, and hooks. Lacing using only grommets is probably the sturdiest; grommets usually last well past the lifetime of the boot. The only problem with an all-grommet boot is that it can be difficult to lace, particularly when your hands feel like blocks of ice. Many boots have grommets in the lower half of the boot and hooks at the top. Instead of grommets, my boots have D-rings on the lower half and hooks above. They are very easy to lace, even with numb fingers (it's the knot I have trouble with when I can't even feel the laces).

BACKPACKING TIP

It is not uncommon for one leg to be slightly longer than another. A two-centimeter or more difference can lead to knee and hip pain. Heel lifts can help, but first ask your doctor to measure your legs to see if heel lifts will do the job.

There are a few tips to keep in mind when lacing your boots. If the upper knot of your boot rubs against your shin, lace your boots to the top then back down a few notches and tie the knot midway down your boot to prevent a painful bruise. Another advantage of this method is that it keeps the knot from loosening under the pressure of your constantly bending ankle.

If your toes are feeling cramped, try loosening up the lower laces a bit, tie a knot, and continue lacing the boot tightly. Unfortunately, this won't work when you're going downhill because the loose laces will cause your toes to slide painfully into the front of your boot. In this case, you might want to try the opposite approach.

Breaking in Your Boots

The single most important advice when it comes to boots is "break them in." Any experienced hiker will tell you (and it cannot be stressed enough) that boots must be broken in if you intend to hike more than a mile or two in them.

Once you find a pair of boots that fit comfortably and you have sealed them properly, it's time to break them in. Start by walking around your neighborhood. Wear the boots to the store and on short errands. If you start to get a blister, put moleskin on it immediately—don't wait. If you catch a hot spot before it becomes a blister, you'll save yourself a lot of pain.

The next step is a day hike. Wear your boots for an entire day without a pack on your back (you can combine this with walking exercises to break yourself in!). If this goes well, you're ready for the next step—hiking with a pack. If not, continue to day-hike until the boots are comfortable.

If you intend to use these boots only for day-hiking, you will want to try hiking with a day pack to see if they are still comfortable with weight on your back. If they are, your boots need no further breaking in.

Backpacking requires more breaking in. No matter how comfortable your boots are without a pack, that could change once you add thirty or more pounds to your back. A lot of weight on your back changes the way weight is distributed over your feet and it could change the way your feet feel in your boots. One of the strangest feelings in backpacking is taking your pack off after a long day. Suddenly, it feels as if you're walking on air.

When you can backpack five to ten miles in your boots without creating any sore spots, your boots are ready for extensive backpacking.

Inserts

Some hikers find that they can make their boots more comfortable, and more supportive, by adding special insoles. Also, the insoles and arch supports that come with your boots begin to wear down after a while. Adding insoles that provide additional arch support can extend the life (and comfort) of your boots. They can also provide extra warmth and insulation. Insoles for boots can be purchased at most outfitters or department, discount, and drug stores.

Extra Shoes

Should you carry an extra pair of shoes with you when you hike? Well, that all depends on the distance you're hiking. For day trips, you probably don't need an extra pair of shoes, especially if you're wearing lightweight boots. Weekenders must decide if they want to carry the extra weight on such a short trip. It really is a matter of preference. Some people can't stand to be in boots once they've made camp.

If you are going to be out for more than a few days, you need to seriously consider additional footwear. We've seen all kinds—tennis shoes, espadrilles, flip-flops, Nike Aqua Socks, and sandals.

There are a number of reasons to carry additional footwear. Picture this typical scenario: You've been hiking all day in the rain; your boots are soaked, your socks are soaked. You arrive at your campsite, make camp, and prepare to bed down. Keep in mind that this entire time you've been sloshing around in wet boots. Because you're no longer hiking, your feet are getting cold. You cuddle up in your nice, warm sleeping bag . . . then nature calls. Do you really want to put those freezing cold, damp boots on your feet just to make a quick run into the woods?

Another example: It's a wonderful, warm, and sunny day and you have to ford a stream. Because of sharp and slick rocks, there are very few times when you have the option to remove your boots and cross a stream barefooted. But you don't really want to get your boots wet. A second pair of shoes is a great alternative in this case.

Also, hiking boots are tough on campsites. Another pair of shoes (soft-soled) is an ecologically sound alternative. If you're hiking long-distance, it can be nice to wear a spare pair of shoes into town to purchase food, wash clothes, et cetera. And because many trails are not entirely routed in the woods, you may want to wear another pair of shoes on road walks. Asphalt wears down the tread on hiking boots.

These are all good reasons to bring along a second pair of shoes. But choose wisely: the last thing you need is an extra burden.

Footcare

Hardening your feet before setting out on a hiking trip is not an easily accomplished task. There is nothing like carrying a thirty- to sixty-pound pack to quickly break in your feet. But there are some things you can do to make the transition a little easier. Wear your boots as often as possible before you set out on a backpacking trek, and for a week prior to your trip, rub your feet each day with rubbing alcohol or tincture of benzoin to help toughen them up.

While backpacking, continue to use the alcohol or benzoin each day on your feet. Airing your feet out during breaks will also help keep them tough, as will sprinkling your socks with foot powder prior to putting your boots on. And most importantly, don't forget that as soon as you feel a hot spot on your foot, cover it with moleskin!

CLOTHING

The late French film director Francois Truffaut once remarked that he could not believe Mrs. Dean wore a different outfit every day of the Watergate trial. How could anyone feel sympathy, he said, for a man whose wife could afford so much clothing. As Americans we are notorious for our overabundance of luggage when traveling, and for buying inexpensive, poor quality clothing in order to fluff our wardrobe. When hiking, you do not have to carry a backpack full of clothes to be prepared for all types of weather. Shorts, T-shirt, long johns, pile jacket and pants, and rain gear can all be layered to add warmth.

Buying a few, high quality garments will see you through many backpacking trips. Style doesn't matter on the trail—comfort and quality do. Fortunately, there are many reputable manufacturers of backpacking clothing, and you can purchase quality along with style. One good pair of Patagonia shorts, for example, will last as long as, if not longer, than five cheap pairs of shorts. Clothing is undoubtedly a matter of personal preference, but there are some tips that could save you a lot of frustration. The most important tip is the famous Boy Scout creed—"be prepared."

Layering

When we found ourselves camping at an elevation of 9,000 feet recently, I was glad that experience had already taught me to be prepared for any type of weather. Although it was late May, at that elevation in Utah's Bryce Canyon, the weather turns chilly pretty quickly once the sun starts to set. Fortunately, we were all able to bundle up in our pile pants and jackets and really enjoy the small campfire we had built rather than huddle around it for heat. In the morning, with the temperature hovering near freezing, we pulled the pile back on over the long johns we had slept in, fired up the stove, and were soon sipping hot cocoa as the sun gradually rose and warmed the day. By the end of day, I was wearing shorts and a sleeveless T-shirt beneath the hot desert sun.

The ability to layer clothes when backpacking can be a lifesaver.

Take the time to select your clothes carefully and think about layering. Buy an ensemble that can be adjusted to fit the circumstances.

Layering allows you numerous options, and the clothes involved in layering can be lighter and more durable to allow you greater physical flexibility. The layering system works better than other methods (such as a separate outfit for each weather condition or, for cold weather, one large coat), especially when you get wet or sweat. It is important to layer with the right pieces— long johns, pants or shorts, a wool or pile garment, and a waterproof shell. Layering cotton long johns under blue jeans may keep you warm at first, but as soon as the garments are wet with rain or sweat, you'll be miserable.

When you are layered correctly, you can adjust easily to a change in temperature. If you are sweating, take off your hat first. Because you lose most of your heat through your head, removing your hat or hood will act as a kind of air conditioning. If you're still hot, unzip your rain jacket collar, and loosen the sleeves (buy rain gear that allows the sleeves to be cinched tight) to let the air circulate.

Remove and add layers as you get warm or cold. This may seem tiresome and time-consuming, but you'll be much more comfortable for the bother.

Depending on the time of year, you may be comfortable in a pair of loose pants or tights instead of shorts. And one of the better backpacking options is the convertible pant, which offers several options when traveling. Not only are these pants made of quickdrying material, the legs can removed to give you the option of wearing shorts, and a zipper along the leg seam allows you to pull the pant legs off without removing your boots.

Another great option for women these days is the sports bra. Many companies make a version of the sports or jog bra that can be worn under a T-shirt or alone when things get really hot. Many sports bras are made of Cool Max as well, and wick the sweat away from your body in addition to drying more quickly.

Fabrics

Choosing the fabric of your clothes is as important a decision as choosing what clothes you will bring. But glancing through the pages of an outdoor store catalog can be a mind-boggling experience! Synthetics with names such as Supplex nylon, Polartec polyester, Thinsulate and PolarGuard polyesters, Taslan nylon, Lycra spandex, Cordura nylon, Tactel nylon, Orlon acrylic, Hydrofil nylon, Capilene polyester and Ultrex nylon make you feel like you need a degree in chemistry to purchase your clothes. Fortunately, it is not as overwhelming as it seems.

Innerwear

Acrylics: Fibers polymerized from acrylonitrile are called acrylics and are rarely used in their "pure" form in clothing except maybe in underwear. Acrylics such as Orlon are often found as a blend, especially in socks.

Cotton: This ancient fabric is not the best choice in outdoor clothes. When wet, cotton conducts heat rapidly away from the body, causing it to cool, and in extreme instances, leading to hypothermia. (This quality, however, does recommend cotton for hotter climates.) For this reason, clothes that might serve you well at home will not do as well on a backpacking trip. The best example is blue jeans. Not only are they constricting, but when they get wet they double or triple in weight.

In general it's wise to avoid cotton long johns, socks, sweaters, and 100 percent cotton T-shirts.

Cotton blends offer an alternative to 100 percent cotton clothing. For instance, Patagonia Baggies (shorts) are made of a nylon-cotton blend and are favored by many hikers because they are lightweight, roomy, and water-resistant. Many manufacturers make pants and shorts of nylon-cotton blends. T-shirts made of cotton and a synthetic are the most popular hiking shirts because they allow freedom of movement and dry more quickly than all-cotton T-shirts. For day hikes in pleasant weather at moderate altitudes, a cotton T-shirt is a good choice.

Duofold Coolmax: This is a unique four-channel design that creates 20 percent more surface area than ordinary fibers. This makes for faster evaporation and greater dryness against your skin. Coolmax comes in a number of different weights for everything from summer to winter wear.

Lycra Spandex: This is a very stretchy, strong synthetic used extensively in clothing—from cuffs and waistbands on jackets to bras, socks, running tights, and shorts. Tights made of a blend of polypropylene and Lycra are especially popular because they keep you warm and conform to your figure allowing you a lot of freedom of movement.

Nylon: Because it's one of the easiest synthetics to manufacture, you will find many nylons on the market. Nylon is inexpensive, durable, abrasion-resistant, strong, and dries quickly. There are hundreds of types of nylon, from the rough-textured Taslan and the super-tough Cordura to the supple, softer nylons such as Supplex, Taslan and ripstop.

Polypropylene: This petroleum-based synthetic is a lightweight fabric that keeps you warm when it's wet. Unlike wool, it dries out quickly. This is because it is non-absorbent. It will not retain moisture, wicking it away immediately. When used as your first layer of clothing, it keeps your skin dry by transferring moisture to your next layer. Polypropylene is primarily used in long johns and socks. One drawback to polypropylene is that it absorbs the scent of perspiration and must be washed in a special detergent to remove the odor. It is also renowned for its pilling, which can be annoying, especially to the fashion conscious. Polypropylene must be line-dried to prevent shrinkage.

Silk: This one of the lightest fabrics and is often used in long underwear. Although silk is a strong, flexible fabric, it tends to be less sturdy than synthetics, giving way at the seams more quickly. It does give you warmth without the bulk, and it provides an effective first layer. Silk must be hand-washed and line-dried.

Supplex: This fabric, made by DuPont from nylon, offers the durability of nylon with the supple feel of cotton. It is quick-drying, wrinkle resistant, and can withstand most abrasions, punctures, and tears.

Thermax and Capilene: Thermax is another synthetic used in garments designed to keep you warm. Like polypropylene, it draws moisture away from your body, and its hollow-core fibers trap air to provide insulation. Thermax can be machine-washed and tumbled dry, and it does not retain the odors of perspiration.

Capilene is a polyester fiber and is similar to Thermax in its attributes—it is odor resistant and can be machine-washed and dried. Both Capilene and Thermax are said to be softer than polypropylene and provide a lot of warmth for their weight.

Outerwear

Fleece: This polyester fabric, sometimes constructed with a nylon, Lycra, cotton, or ceramic blend, is generally lightweight and breathable with a high warmth to weight ratio. Some fleeces may also have wicking properties.

Gore-Tex: Gore-Tex fabric actually consists of two layers of material—a nylon or polyester fabric that's laminated to Gore-Tex membrane. This is designed to be waterproof, windproof, breathable, and durable.

Gore-Tex Windstopper: This fabric—actually polyester fleece laminated to Gore Windstopper membrane—is windproof and somewhat breathable.

Gore-Tex Activent: This material consists of a membrane laminated to various fabrics for windproofing breathability. It is also generally very lightweight.

H2NO Storm HB: Patagonia's proprietary waterproof, breathable membrane is actually a three-layer laminate. This three-layer laminate can be used with almost any fabric, such as nylon or polyester. It is primarily used to make waterproof, breathable outerwear pieces. H2NO Storm HB is also used in conjunction with another proprietary technology—The Deluge DWR water repellency treatment system—and this makes for an unbeatable combination.

Hind Drylete and Arctic Drylete: This is a technically effective moisture transfer material for a variety of weather conditions. A combination of polyester, hydro-nylon and Lycra spandex, the fabric rejects sweat; the interior polyester transfers moisture away from your body to the exterior or hydro-nylon, where it can evaporate quickly. The material can be used as either an inner or outer layer. The Arctic Drylete is a multi-task thermal fabric that siphons perspiration away from the skin. It is made of a soft non-pilling nylon/Lycra knit exterior and a non-pilling low-pile polyester fleece interior.

Omni-Tech: This is Columbia's proprietary waterproof, breathable technology. It can be coated or laminated to nylon or polyester fabric. It is primarily used for mountaineering, backpacking, and skiing outerwear, or in inserts in gloves and footwear.

Polarplus, Polarlite, Patagonia Synchilla: These bunting or pile materials are good insulators. Polarplus is a double-faced pile of fine-denier Dacron polyester (a denier is a unit of measure for textile fibers). Polarlite is said to be a lighter and stretchier version of Polarplus. Synchilla is Patagonia's well-known, double-faced synthetic pile. Comfortable jackets and pants made of these fabrics are bulky and heavy, but may be worth the extra bulk and weight on a cold night. For day hikes to higher altitudes, these insulating materials provide good protection from wind and cold when you stop to take a break. The materials are generally far too warm to actually hike in, but are said to be warmer per pound than wool and to dry more quickly than the natural fabric.

Although Polarlite is supposed to be lighter than Polarplus and Synchilla, it appears to weigh approximately the same, if not more, when used to fabricate similar garments. As with food, you may want to inspect a little more closely anything termed "lite."

Polartec Windbloc: This polyester fabric with windproof, breathable membrane is designed to protect from weather, wind, water, and abrasion.

Sympatex: This is a windproof, waterproof, breathable fabric made out of nonporous polyester. It is also produced as a nonporous membrane of hydrophilic film that can be laminated onto another fabric. Sympatex comes as three-ply laminates, linings, and inserts for outerwear, footwear, gloves and other accessories.

Triple-Point Ceramic: Lowe Alpine System's proprietary waterproof breathable coating technology. It is a twin-coated, high pressure coating that can be applied to a variety of fabrics, including polyester or nylon. The combination of the coating process, fabrics, and durable water repellent finish all play into the specific windproof, waterproof, or breathable function of each specific garment.

Wool: This used to be your best bet for winter wear, but it is rapidly being replaced by pile products. The new synthetics—the "Polars" and Synchilla—are giving wool a run for the money. When wool is blended with polypropylene or other synthetics, it makes good socks. Wool keeps you warm when it's wet.

Rain Gear

Donning rain gear once meant putting on that heavy rubber yellow slicker, and in some cases, the matching pants. In all cases, you felt like a fireman on the way to a three-alarm fire. That, or the Gorton fisherman!

Thankfully, the era of yellow slickers has given way to more sophisticated apparel that not only boasts durable waterproof/breathable fabric, but features like vents, articulated sleeves, and ergonomically correct hoods.

First of all, decide if you need a waterproof breathable piece or simply a jacket that will protect you from the wind and light squalls. You can literally spend hundreds of dollars on outerwear. A top-of-the-line Gore-Tex jacket can easily cost four hundred to five hundred dollars. Add a pair of pants to your outfit, and you've thrown away a round-trip ticket to Hawaii. There's no sense in forking out big bucks for a waterproof coat if you just need to have something lightweight for summer hikes, or simply for blocking a stiff breeze on the trail.

Regardless of your choice, you should definitely take some rain gear. Some hikers refuse to fight the battle of staying dry, opting to get wet by hiking in the rain in just shorts and T-shirt. That's all well and good when it's steamy outside, but what about when it's cold or even just a bit chilly? Wet clothes can lower your body temperature to the danger point, but if you have some rain gear to put on when you get chilly, you will at least be able to keep warm if not dry.

If you are climbing and hiking in places like the Rockies, or camping on Washington's Olympic Peninsula, you should definitely consider a waterproof/breathable model. But if most of your primary activity will be hiking barrier islands or taking short hikes along the Appalachian Trail, you might want to consider some of the newer fabrics that place more emphasis on wind-blocking and breathability.

What to Look or in Rain Gear

Fabrics and Construction: Hands down, the most common name in shell material is Gore-Tex. It is also true that you will pay more money for that designer label. A decade ago, Gore-Tex was the only game in town for waterproof/breathable protection. Nowadays, there are literally dozens of similar fabrics, such as Sympatex, Triple-Point Ceramic, Omni-Tech, and H2NO Storm HB, that offer relatively similar performance. Rather than asking for a Gore-Tex jacket when you walk into the store, tell the clerk you are interested in a waterproof/breathable shell. Sure, Gore-Tex should be one of your options, but if it is the only thing you are shown, go to another store.

Rather than sweat the manufacturer of the waterproof/breathable laminate or coating on the fabric, focus on features instead. Check for meticulously taped seams with no bumps or bubbles, perfect stitching, and a good fit.

The advantage of buying a Gore-Tex or Sympatex jacket is that both companies mandate that the manufacturers who use these products make sure that the garments adhere to a minimum standard of performance. Because of these standards set by the makers of Gore-Tex and Sympatex, other companies follow suit and make sure that their garments have the same quality controls as well. Also check the warranty of the jacket. Some companies, like The North Face, offer a lifetime warranty on the product—your lifetime, not the coat's. It's rare, but sometimes something can go wrong during the manufacturing of the fabric or coat. Make sure the company you are buying from guarantees the jacket will live up to its advertised performance.

And again, keep in mind that by gaining waterproofness, you lose breathability. If you are planning on carrying heavy loads, or are into trail running, you might want to forsake complete water protection for added breathability. Many of the new microfiber fabrics and laminates (of which Gore's Activent is the best known) allow for a generous flow of air, they break wind, and they still shed a nominal amount of water. They also are softer, lighter, less bulky, and cheaper than most waterproof/breathable shells.

Linings: Remember that layering is the name of the game. A heavy-duty shell with a permanent lining is great if you are expecting arctic weather, but it is too heavy and hot for most high-aerobic activities. Your best bet is a shell with a zip-out liner, or simply a shell that is large enough to accommodate a fleece jacket or wool sweater underneath. However, sometimes you just want to put on a warm jacket without a bunch of layers. The insulated shell may not be as versatile, but it can be more convenient in cold weather.

One cautionary note—the new Windbloc or Windstopper fleece apparel is great for a top layer, but inappropriate for a second layer under a waterproof/ breathable shell. Since the windblocking material trades breathability for wind management, it works like a sweat chamber if layered under another not-so-breathable garment.

3-ply versus 2-ply: Sorting out the drawbacks and advantages of 3-ply versus 2-ply shells is worse than the debate over whether 2000 or 2001 is the first year of the new millennium. The systems work the same, though 3-ply usually costs more. Two-ply jackets have a mesh lining, which adds weight, but may move more easily when layered over fleece or wool. Three-ply shells are generally higher, and considered top-of-the-line, since the material is more expensive than 2-ply.

Ventilation: Anyone who has walked uphill knows how fast you can work up a sweat. The fabric of your jacket may breathe better than a good Pinot Noir, but you'll still need built-in vents to accommodate the heat you create during rigorous activity. The most common ventilation systems are underarm zippers that can be opened to allow air flow when you are in danger of overheating. "Pit zips" are a priority feature on waterproof/breathable jackets, and less important on shells designed merely to thwart wind. Many companies still persist in adding overkill closure measures such as a Velcro flap over the pit zip. Unfortunately, the Velcro inevitably sticks shut when you want it open, defeating the vent's purpose. Look for a coat with sealed zippers and no Velcro.

To test the workability of a pit zip, grab the tip of your left jacket sleeve by the fingers of your left hand. Stretch your arm above your head, keeping a hold of the sleeve. With your right arm, reach over, grab the zipper, and open or close the vent. If the zipper doesn't slide easily with this single-hand method, look for another coat. Some jacket designs come with chest zips and mesh-lined pockets, both of which add ventilation. The advantage of chest zips is that they are convenient to open and allow quick access to the breast pockets of your second layer of clothes. The downside is that they can be mistaken for pockets themselves, which can lead to lost car keys and wallets.

Lately, manufacturers have been making increasing use of back and chest yokes for ventilation. While these always-open flaps (sometimes with a mesh inner lining) do provide additional breathability, they aren't appropriate for cold weather or high wind use, since they can't be sealed shut.

Hoods: The weak link of most jackets is hood design. Look for a model that will tuck away when not needed, so you don't always have it flapping in the breeze. Zip-off hoods are an option, especially if you don't plan on using the feature. However, you run the risk of reaching for it in a downpour and realizing you left it in a drawer back home.

A common downfall of hoods is that they cut off peripheral vision and hinder breathing when they are zipped into position. A well-designed hood should swivel when you turn your head and allow for adequate breathing space when zipped. Check the adjustment straps on the hood. Will your hair get caught in the toggle cords? Can you see out of the face hole when the hood is up or do you look like a turtle peering out of its shell?

Snow Skirt: If cross-country skiing or snowshoeing is your primary pursuit, consider a rain jacket with a snow skirt (an inner flap of nylon around the hips that can be cinched down to prevent powder snow from sneaking up to your soft, warm underbelly). Snow skirts add significant warmth on cold days, but their need is precluded if you wear bibs. If your jacket is for multi-season use, the best advice is to do without the snow skirt (you'll save weight) and to plan on wearing shell bibs for powder days.

Other Items to Consider: When searching for rain gear, you might find crotch straps on the bottom of some waterproof/breathable jackets. Obviously these are to keep your jacket from pulling out of your rain pants. Are they comfortable? I don't think so, but if you don't mind that type of thing it may be a plus for you. Also, if your jacket of choice has a drawcord at the waist, check to make sure it doesn't interfere with the waist belt of your pack.

Check the durability of the zippers: Large-tooth zippers seem to hold up better than standard coil zippers. It is interesting that Gore recently altered its standards to accommodate new waterproof zipper technology, a standard used exclusively on Arc'teryx and Wild Things Jackets. Also scrutinize the zipper pull and end tags for reinforcements, since these areas are the most likely points of failure.

Look at the cuffs on the coat: Velcro closures here are good, since they can be tightened to seal out water and worn loose for added breathability and comfort.

Remember to test the coat with any and all accoutrements you might be wearing with it—packs, harnesses, gloves, and secondary layers. Your jacket will ideally be part of a system that will keep you warm, dry, and comfortable, so make sure all components work together to meet that goal.

If you are female, keep in mind that there are an increasing number of jackets on the market that are made specifically for women. These coats are cut shorter in the sleeves and torso, wider in the hips, and narrower in the shoulders than men's/unisex models. You can expect the same features and durability from a women's jacket as a men's design; however, many companies don't make their top-of-the-line performance coats in anything but men's small, medium, and large. Although a women's coat may fit you better (as it could a small-framed man), don't limit your selection to women's only. Women with large shoulders and a more athletic build might well find a better fit in a unisex model, so take advantage of the opportunity to try on all available styles.

Jacket Maintenance and Care

All waterproof/breathable jackets have durable water repellent (DWR) finishes, which eventually wear off. When this happens, you can apply products like Nikwax, ReviveX or Zepel to restore the DWR finish. You'll know you have lost your DWR when the coat appears to be absorbing water. It is not the fault of the waterproof/breathable membrane (i.e., Gore-Tex or Sympatex) but the fact that the DWR finish is no longer causing water to bead on the fabric's surface.

You can revitalize your DWR a number of times before you have to replace your garment. First, try machine-drying your garment on medium heat (unless the manufacturer warns otherwise). If that doesn't work, try ironing it (once again, unless the manufacturer states otherwise). Make sure you iron only the outer layer of the garment on a medium setting. Also, before you turn the iron on, clean the iron sole plate with denatured alcohol to make sure you don't transfer anything to the material. If your garment no longer responds to these steps, you may want to try a reconditioning treatment. You can purchase DWR treatments (as mentioned above) in spray or liquid. Look for fluropolymer treatments like 3M Scotchguard or DuPont Teflon Fabric Protector. Wash-ins, like Nikwax TX-Direct, can be used unless the garment has a free-hanging, wicking liner.

Unless the manufacturer tells you to, you should never dry-clean waterproof fabrics because the solvents used could ruin the coating.

Ponchos and Umbrellas

The least effective of all rain gear options, most back-packing ponchos are designed to cover both you and your pack. Ponchos do shield you from a lot of the rain under ideal conditions, but in the wind they are practically useless. While a minority of hikers favor ponchos, most hikers dispose of them during their hike.

And yes, you will probably happen on those happy few who are content to sing in the rain as long as they have an umbrella over their head. Some people highly recommend umbrellas, particularly Ray Jardine, author of *The Pacific Crest Trail Hiker's Handbook*. Jardine even offers instructions for umbrella modifications in his book. He and his wife, Jenny, won't leave home without theirs and only recommend not using them in fierce storms and gale-like winds.

Hats

Because much of the body's heat is lost through your head, hats are an indispensable part of your backpacking outfit. For example, putting a hat on your head will do more toward warming cold feet than adding an extra pair of socks. Another pair of socks might actually make your feet colder by making your boots too tight and constricting the circulation in your feet.

A wool cap with a polypropylene liner will keep your head warm while wicking away perspiration. Thermax hats are also good for the same reason. If you will be doing a lot of coldweather backpacking, you may want to invest in a balaclava. This hat covers your head and neck and most of your face and is much lighter to carry than an extra shirt or sweater!

While not as warm, baseball-style caps are great for keeping the sun off your head and face. They are also great worn under your rain jacket hood to keep the hood from dripping rain on your nose and to help the hood move with your head. Many types of baseball caps are available, including those that offer a neck flap for extra protection against the sun.

For those of you who go for the high-tech products, Sequel offers the Desert Rhat Hat. An adjustable chin strap keeps the hat on your head even in high winds, a large bill with a black underbrim provides sun protection for your eyes and face, a breathable lining of Tex-O-Lite metallic film shields the top of your head from the sun's intensity, a removable white cape reflects the sun, and a terrycloth headband absorbs the sweat.

Socks

It used to be that you needed to wear several pairs of socks with your hiking boots just to be comfortable. Fortunately, the way boots are made these days, all you really need is a pair of liner socks and a pair of hiking socks. There was a time when there was only one type of sock to wear with your hiking boots—it was wool or nothing. Now there are so many options, it's hard to decide. While wool socks are still very present in the sock market, they are giving way to synthetic blends designed especially for backpacking.

Wool, cotton/wool blends, and cotton socks are not as good for backpacking compared to the wool/ polypropylene or nylon blends and the Orlon acrylic/ nylon blend of Thor-Lo socks. Wool socks retain foot odor while cotton socks do not retain their shape. The Thor-Los were designed specifically for sports and include designs for running, hiking, climbing and backpacking.

Vapor Barrier System

The vapor barrier system is the quickest way to get warm when you're really cold. It uses an impermeable barrier such as a plastic bag to retain both your body's heat and moisture. Although not exactly comfortable because you stay wet, it is extremely effective.

Vapor barriers can be used in sleeping bag liners and in clothes such as pants, shirts, socks and gloves. You can purchase garments made for this purpose, or you might choose to rely on Ziploc bags.

Some people believe in using vapor barriers in all cold-weather situations while others would rather die then submit themselves to the agony of the vapor barrier. Try it before you decide. I am from the school that believes vapor barriers are just fine when it's freezing cold outside and there is no other way to get warm. I have used plastic bags a number of times to warm up my feet, especially when my boots have failed to dry from the previous days of rain and it is raining again.

Whatever material you prefer, you will need to consider both the liner or inner sock, and the outer sock. Liners are important because they wick away the perspiration and help keep your feet dry. Liners are made of silk, nylon, polypropylene, Thermax, or Orlon. Keep your liners clean. At least rinse them out often so that they don't "clog up." Socks can be hung out to dry on the back of your pack. (You can use clothespins or safety pins to fasten drying clothes to the back of your pack.)

Choose your outer pair of socks wisely. Most experts suggest a blend of wool and nylon or wool and polypropylene. Cotton is never suggested because, unlike wool, it will not keep you warm when it's wet.

Some socks are made with added padding at the toe and heel as well as extra arch support. These socks are usually a nylon-Orlon-polypropylene blend; liners are not necessary with them. Try several brands and find out what's right for you. I've discovered that mostly wool socks retain too much foot odor for my likes, but Frank has absolutely no complaints with his wool-polypropylene blend.

Gloves

My hands get cold easily, but I find that when hiking I rarely need gloves. Cold, wet days are the worst, especially once I've made camp. I've used glove liners without the gloves fairly successfully—they are easier to maneuver your fingers in because they don't have the bulk of leather gloves. But for those days when sticking your hands in your pockets just won't do (what if you take a tumble with your hands in your pockets?), there are a number of glove/mitten options available. From wool mittens with a Gore-Tex shell to gloves of wool, wool-blends, Thinsulate, pile and other synthetics, you should be able to find a pair of hand warmers that fits your needs.

Keep in mind that you can also purchase glove and mitten liners (usually very lightweight and made of silk or synthetics used in the manufacture of thermal underwear) for extra cold days. If you're desperate, use plastic bags as vapor-barrier-style gloves. The vapor barrier system is explained in the box at the end of this information on clothing.

Bandannas

In the backpacking world, you're not a true hiker unless you have at least one bandanna on your person. Bandannas are wonderfully versatile. I use them as headbands, hats, and handkerchiefs. They can also be used to strain water before filtering and to cool hot necks (dip the bandanna in water and loosely tie it about your throat). Similarly, they can be used as a cloth for washing or as a towel for drying (your body and your dishes). I always carry several with me when I am backpacking.

Gaiters

Hiking gaiters are made of water-resistant materials. They fasten below the knee and extend to cover the upper portion of your boots. Their purpose is to keep water and snow out of your boots so that they remain dry.

Gaiters come in a variety of heights, from ankle-height to just below the knee. Some hikers wear the ankle gaiters to keep dust and leaves from working their way into their boots. Gaiters are also useful when hiking through wet brush, grass, leaves, and poison ivy and oak.

Unlike pack covers and rainsuits, gaiters are not essential rainwear for any hike. However, they may make your hikes more comfortable and are worth looking into, particularly for hikes in the snow.

Town Clothes

If you intend to spend more than a week on the trail, and especially if you're going to be long-distance hiking, you may want to consider bringing along "town clothes." All this means is that you stash away one shirt that you will wear only when hitching or hiking into a town. Your appearance and your attitude will determine how you are treated when you go to town. Some female hikers carry broomstick gauze skirts. They pack down small, they're light, and they're supposed to look wrinkled anyway.

Caring for Your Clothing

While backpacking, caring for your clothing will be limited to a bit of rinsing here and there. On short trips (unless your clothes get really awful), you can wait until you get home to clean your clothing according to the tag's instructions.

While hiking, I rinse out my nylon shorts every other day(or every day, if I have really sweated). I simply rinse them in a cookpot and hang them to dry on a branch or rock if it's a dry night. If it's wet outside, I take them to bed with me, stuffing them at the bottom of my sleeping bag. If they are not dry by morning, I just wait for body heat to dry them out while I hike (or for my sweat to wet them even more).

T-shirts and socks can be rinsed in the same manner and cleaned once a week using a biodegradable soap. Some synthetics require a special detergent to rid them of their perspiration odors. Read labels and know what to do before you go. Never, never wash your clothes in a water source—even biodegradable soaps leave suds and a bad taste. Always dump dirty wash water far from any water source. If you are on a long-distance hike, you will hit an occasional town where you can wash your clothes in a laundromat.

On the trail, if you don't want to hang your clothes over a branch or rock, you can use your rope to form a clothesline. Lightweight clothespins are available at outdoors stores or you can center your rope around a tree, twist it tightly, tie it to another tree, and then pull apart a twist to hold your clothes. You may want to carry a thin, lightweight line just for this purpose.

SLEEPING BAGS

Most people know that a third of their life is spent sleeping, but what many beginning backpackers don't realize is that there are times when you will spend even more than a third of your day in a sleeping bag. There come times, particularly on extended backpacking trips when inclement weather, most likely vicious thunderstorms or snowstorms, will send you burrowing into that bag to wait it out. This possibility makes choosing a comfortable bag all the more important.

It's probably wise not to go for an extreme bag unless you plan to buy several. Sleeping in a zero-degree bag (see the information on Temperature or Comfort Ratings) on a muggy summer night in Arkansas can be as much torture as having only a forty-five-degree bag when you're snowed-in in the Sierras.

Important Features of Sleeping Bags

I won't even begin to recommend a bag because they really are a matter of preference (as are most pieces of backpacking equipment) and there are so many options available.

Choosing a bag really isn't as daunting as it may seem. The first consideration is how much you wish to spend (sleeping bags can be purchased for under one hundred dollars, for more than five hundred dollars, and at every price in between). Next, decide on the temperature rating, fill, and weight. From there, you can narrow down your options by taking into consideration bag shape and shell material. The trick is to find a balance point between comfort and practicality. Care, cleaning, and the bag's construction should also be kept in mind.

BACKPACKING TIP

Keep yourself warm by wearing a hat, drinking plenty of liquids, and warming yourself up with a few jumping jacks before climbing into your sleeping bag.

Temperature or Comfort Ratings

A comfort or temperature rating is assigned to most sleeping bags by the manufacturer or retailer. The rating, basically, is the lowest temperature at which the bag remains comfortable.

Unfortunately, most comfort ratings are overly optimistic and vary widely between manufacturers. They assume you are an average hiker under normal conditions. The problem lies in trying to define who is "average," what conditions are "normal," and what is considered "comfortable." What it really means is that you are neither fat nor thin, you are not overly fatigued, you are using a sleeping pad, and you are not sleeping out in the open. These ratings do not take into account whether or not you are using a bag liner or overbag, what type of sleeping pad you are using, and what you might be wearing. You'll be a lot cooler sleeping in the nude and a lot warmer wearing long johns, for example. Whether or not you are hungry or well-fed, hydrated or dehydrated, whether you just hiked one mile or twenty, and how hot you run (your metabolic rate) also add to the equation. Keeping all this in mind (you know yourself the best), comfort ratings can be helpful when comparing one sleeping bag to another—a ten degree bag will keep you warmer than a twenty-degree bag.

Before deciding on a comfort rating, determine the range of temperatures in which you will most often be hiking. If your hiking will take you through both cold and hot weather, you may want to consider layering a sleeping bag with a bag liner (see below). For example,

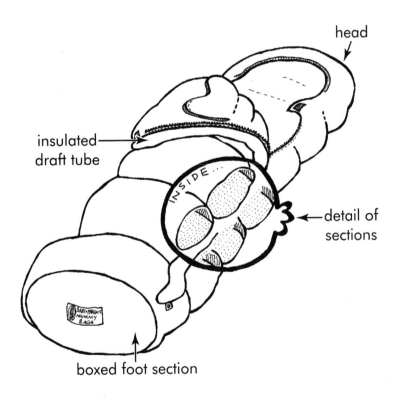

head

insulated draft tube

INSIDE

detail of sections

boxed foot section

you may want to buy a twenty-degree bag for use in moderate weather, and add a bag liner, lowering your bag's temperature by as much as fifteen degrees, for cold weather. Of course, if money is no object, you may prefer to buy several bags with ratings ranging from zero to forty-five degrees or so. A simple rating range is: forty-plus degrees for summer camping, twenty- to forty-degrees for spring, summer, and fall (three-season camping), and twenty -degrees or lower for winter. These are general guidelines. Geography, elevation and even unusual weather can cause temperatures to fluctuate dramatically.

To take this a step further, a twenty-degree bag is adequate for three-season camping unless you live in Alaska. But if you get cold easily, a twenty-degree bag may be a bit chilly when the temperature dips below freezing. It is better to buy a warmer bag (or at least, a bag liner or overbag) than to face a twenty-mile day after a cold and sleepless night. If it's too warm to slip into your bag, you can always sleep on top of it!

Some people choose to cut down their backpack weight by carrying a blanket (and in one case we know of, a table cloth) instead of a sleeping bag. Whether hiking on the West Coast, East Coast, or anywhere in between, it is unwise to forfeit your sleeping bag for the sake of weight. Any meteorologist will admit that weather is unpredictable, seemingly changing at whim from hot and muggy to cold and stormy within twenty-four hours. During my backpacking career, I have had both my coldest and hottest days in Pennsylvania in June. I definitely recommend that you purchase a sleeping bag, even if you only intend to make overnight trips. It could be the difference between life and death.

Fillings
Fillings are the heart and soul of the sleeping bag; they give the sleeping bag its temperature rating. Hard as it might seem to believe, sleeping bag—filler technology advances almost daily. Regardless, there are six main categories into which these stuffings have been delegated—

down, the old synthetics, the new or short staple synthetics, the continuous-filament synthetics, pile or fleece, and proprietary synthetics. The filling characteristic that should influence your decision the most is its effectiveness to warm you should it get wet.

According to tests conducted by Recreational Equipment Incorporated (REI), "a synthetic bag will lose about 10 percent of its warmth while gaining about 60 percent in weight" when the sleeping bag gets wet. Conversely, they said a water-soaked, down-filled bag "will lose over 90 percent of its warmth, gain 128 percent in weight, and take more than a day to dry."

What this all means is that your ability to keep a down bag dry is a major factor when deciding to purchase a bag. All six fillings have strong proponents. When purchasing a bag, decide how much trouble you want to go through to keep your bag dry. Stuffing your sleeping bag into a plastic garbage bag before putting it in a stuff sack will keep it dryer. And if you will be fording a stream or are expecting hard rains, put the stuff sack into another bag for extra protection.

Other characteristics that may effect your decision include weight, compressibility, and loft.

Down: Down has long been lauded and is still number one when it comes to providing maximum warmth and comfort for minimum weight and bulk. Down sleeping bags breathe better than polyester fiber bags and are less stifling in warmer temperatures than their synthetic counterparts. But when a down bag gets wet, it loses almost all of its ability to warm and gains much more in weight than synthetic bags. However, if you are hiking in areas that have little precipitation, down bags are a good bet. Down bags also mat and clump worse than synthetic bags over time, creating cold spots, and they are notoriously bad for hay-fever sufferers. If you're allergic to feather pillows, you'll be allergic to down bags. They do however compress tightly, therefore using less space than synthetic bags.

Both goose down and duck down are used as fillings and the difference between them is discernible only under a microscope, but goose down is generally considered structurally superior. In addition to its comfort rating, a down bag is rated for its fill power or loft. That infamous tag (Do not remove...) called the bedding or law tag will inform you of the bag's loft. The number you see represents the number of cubic inches one ounce of down will expand to in a twenty-four hour period after it's compressed. For example, 600 cubic inches is considered to be a superior loft, 500–550 is very good, and so on. The greater the loft of the bag, the warmer it will be or the higher its comfort rating (or maybe that would be lower as in it will keep you warmer at lower temperatures!). By the way, the consumer is allowed to remove the law tag once the product has been purchased.

Quallofil and Hollofil or Hollofil II: You can find these synthetic fills in the budget bags these days although at one point in not too distant backpacking history they were considered state-of-the-art. While they will keep you warm when they get wet, these fillings are a lot heavier and bulkier than the newer synthetics.

The fibers of the Quallofil filling are hollow, each with four microscopic tubes that allow for good insulating ability and more surface area. This polyester filling, which is as soft as down, is non-allergenic, and retains most of its loft when wet. (In this case, loft is the thickness of the filling.) So, when Quallofil gets wet it doesn't become thin and hard or lose its ability to warm.

Also polyester, Hollofil fibers are about two inches long and must be sewn to another backing to prevent clumping; this leads to cold spots in a sleeping bag. Similar to Quallofil, Hollofil has a single hole in the fiber; but it allows for more "air" per ounce and thus provides more insulation. The insulation is gained at a price because the backing materials used for the filling adds weight. Like other polyester fills, Hollofil loses only about a tenth of its warmth when wet. The newer Hollofil II has silicone added to make the fibers easier to compress, so the bag fits more easily into a stuff sack.

Lite Loft, Micro-loft, Primaloft, Primaloft 2, Primaloft Lite, Thermolite Extreme: These short-staple synthetic fills come pretty close to matching down's warmth and softness. They are also a good deal lighter and more packable than the natural filler. But, unlike down, heavy-duty use reduces their loft.

Thinsulate Lite Loft by 3M is the warmest synthetic insulation available for its weight. Its microfine polyester/olefin fibers make it lightweight, even when wet, and easily compressible. Microloft is made by DuPont and boasts the smallest of the micro fibers. These tiny fibers enable Microloft to trap more heat and remain soft and supple. The Primalofts mimic the structure of goose down with tiny fibers interspersed with stiffer fibers. Unlike down, Primaloft is water repellent and retains its warmth when wet.

Polarguard, Polarguard HV and Polarguard 3D: These long, continuous-filament synthetics are more durable than the short staple synthetics. The fibers, which are long and interwoven, don't become matted, which eliminates the need for a backing to prevent cold spots. Polarguard HV also retains its loft—and thus its warmth—when wet. The new Polarguard HV is 20 percent warmer than the old Polarguard, and Polarguard 3D is even better than its older siblings. While Polarguard 3D seems to be used in most bags these days, it does tend to be bulkier and heavier than the short-staple synthetics.

Pile or Fleece: This fabric is really only used in some ultralight warm-weather sleeping bags.

Proprietary Synthetics: These are synthetic fills produced by the manufacturers of some sleeping bags to fill their own bags. Quality varies according to manufacturer.

Weight
The lighter your bag the better. Unfortunately, the lighter the bag, the more it's going to cost. Try not to buy a bag that weighs more than five pounds. A bag in the two to four pound range is probably your best bet for cost-efficiency and warmth.

Weight is related to the comfort rating and the filling. Usually, the lower the comfort rating, the more the bag weighs. Fillings other than those mentioned above weigh a lot more than you'll be willing to carry, even on overnight trips.

Keep in mind that it is likely that the bag you buy will eventually get wet, and that will increase its weight somewhat.

Shape

Sleeping bags come in three basic shapes—mummy, rectangular, and semi-rectangular. Most backpackers choose the mummy-shaped bag because it offers the most warmth and space for the least weight. Most bags have what is called a draft tube behind the zipper to prevent air from leaking into the bag. If you intend to use your bag in windy or even cool weather be sure that the bag you choose has a draft tube.

Mummy: Formed to the contours of your body, the mummy has the least amount of air to warm and takes less material to make (so there's less to stuff) This saves on weight as well. The mummy's "head" is designed to draw down over and around your own on cold nights, limiting your body's heat loss. Most mummy bags also feature a "boxed" foot section which keeps the insulation in place over your feet so that they stay warmer. But like everything, the mummy has its drawbacks. There is absolutely no room to turn around in it. You either toss and turn the entire bag or sleep in one position through the night. Also, the short zippers hamper ventilation.

Rectangular: This is the roomiest and the heaviest of sleeping bags. Three sides of the bag are zippered allowing you to ventilate to the point of making the bag a blanket. Room and ventilation become the bag's drawbacks on cold nights because there is more air to heat up and no hood to prevent heat from escaping through your head. This bag is more appropriate for warmer climes.

Semi-rectangular: The taper of a mummy bag without the hood, this design saves some on weight, provides good ventilation because it, too, is zippered on three

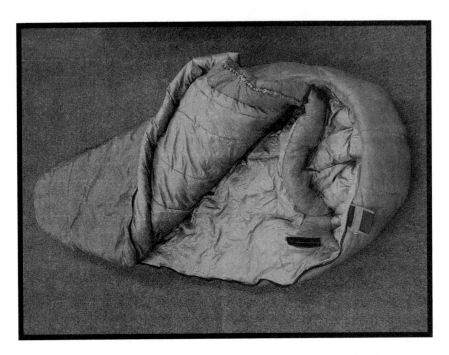

Typical mummy-shaped bag with boxed foot section, draft tube and draft collar.

sides, and has a bit less air to heat up. Like the rectangular bag, there is no hood for cold nights. It is a good choice for large-framed hikers who don't mind carrying the few extra ounces.

When purchasing a sleeping bag, make sure it fits. A bag that is too narrow or too short will affect the quality of your sleep. Because a mummy bag follows the contours of your body, make sure that it is not too tight in the shoulders and around your head. If you are planning extended backpacking and/or cold-weather trips, you may want to buy a bag with extra room at the feet. The extra room will accommodate water bottles, boots, socks, or any other things you may want to keep from freezing.

Shells

Another important consideration when buying a bag is the shell or outer covering. Although there are numerous materials to choose from, you will want to consider only shells made from Dryloft, Microfiber, Ripstop, and Taffeta.

Dryloft is made by W. L. Gore and is a highly breathable and water-resistant fabric. This is very similar to Gore-Tex and will hold wind, condensation, and light rain at bay. In a sleeping bag with a Dryloft shell, you can sleep under the stars or in a snow cave without having to worry about waking up cold and wet.

Compared to the new quarterback, Dryloft, Gore-Tex is pretty much second-string now, although it is still often used in bivy sacks. Even Gore doesn't recommend Gore-Tex shells anymore because they are not as efficient at allowing moisture to escape, which in turn causes the insulation to lose its loft.

Microfiber is a tightly woven nylon or polyester fabric that is usually more supple and lighter than Dryloft. It is, on the other hand, less resistant to water than both Dryloft and Gore-Tex, but it does repel wind and breathe well.

Ripstop nylon and polyester feature heavier threads interwoven in the fabric every quarter inch or so in a checkerboard or diamond pattern to prevent rips from running down the bag. It also forms a web of reinforcement to reduce stress. Strong for its weight, ripstop nylon is also wind resistant. On the other hand, it does not repel water and therefore gets wet easily—although it dries quickly.

Taffeta is a flat-weave fabric that is softer than ripstop but isn't as strong or as resistant to wind. It, too, gets wet easily. Nylon taffeta is often used as an inner lining.

Added Features

Some extra features you might want to keep in mind when purchasing a sleeping bag include

Brushed inner lining: This fleecy lining feels soft and cozy on cold nights. On muggy nights, this lining can wick away the perspiration from your body, but some people claim the lining holds in too much heat.

Insulated draft collar: This is a puffy yoke or collar that can be cinched closely around your neck (usually with a drawstring) to keep the warm air in the bag and the cold drafts out of it. A draft collar makes a huge difference in how warm you stay on a cold night.

Hood: As you probably already know, most of your body's heat is lost through the head. That's what makes wearing a hat so important in cold weather, and similarly, that's what makes having a hood on your sleeping bag so important in frigid conditions. Look for a hood with a contoured cut that is snug but not too tight and that features plenty of insulation. Some hoods use elastic to snug the hood, others a drawstring.

Pocket: Some sleeping bags feature a zippered pocket at chest level to provide you with handy storage for things you might want to keep close by, such as contact lenses, a flashlight or headlamp, and lip balm. This works well for those who can maintain a single position throughout the night.

Storage bag: This is a big, breathable cotton bag designed to prolong the life of your bag when you are not using it. If you cram your bag into its stuff sack and forget about it for a few months, it will lose its loft.

Zipper options: This essentially means that you can choose whether or not you want a right-handed zipper or a left-handed zipper or whether or not the zipper can be mated with another sleeping bag.

Insulated zipper draft tube: This is basically a draft collar for your zipper and is a wonderful option. The tube should hang from the top of the zipper so that it stays in place over the teeth.

Woman's model: Some sleeping bags are designed with a woman's needs specifically in mind. What does that mean? Usually that they feature extra width at the hips and less at the shoulders, more insulation in the foot box, and less overall length.

Mated Bags

For couples interested in hiking, some sleeping bags may be zipped together. Many sleeping bag manufacturers offer bags with right and left zippers.

If you intend to buy mateable bags, you may want to consider buying one lightweight (approximately 40-degree) and one heavier (about twenty-degree) bag. That way, if it's warm, you can use the cooler bag on top—and vice versa. Of course, if you're trying to mate mummy bags, you probably won't be able to use them in this manner; you can zip such bags together, but you can't open them flat enough to use one bag on the bottom and the other on top.

Caring for Your Bag

Synthetic sleeping bags can be washed by hand or in a commercial washer with warm or cold water. They should be cleaned with a mild soap such as Ivory, and, if not air dried, they should be dried at a low setting in your dryer. When air drying any bag, make sure it is well supported. Never hang it by one end because the weight of the wet filling may tear out the inner construction and ruin the bag. Supporting the bag on a slanted board is a good option. Don't wash your sleeping bag after every trip. That stresses the fabric and reduce its ability to warm. Rather, wash it only when it is really dirty.

Down sleeping bags should be hand washed. If washed in a machine, your bag could lose its loft because the detergent breaks down the natural oils of the goose down. Down bags should not be dried in a household dryer; rather, they should be drip-dried for several days. The bag can then be placed in a commercial dryer on low heat to fluff it. Throwing in a clean pair of tennis shoes will break up matted down.

Sleeping bags should not be stored in the tiny stuff sacks that they are normally carried in on a hike. A big, loose bag is the best container for keeping your bag in good condition when you're not on the trail. Stuffing your bag into a small sack every day while hiking is all right because you're taking your bag out almost every night. But if you store it that way at home, the filling becomes packed together and it is hard to restore its loft. Never roll your bag up neatly because this compresses the insulation. Stuffing the bag into its sack assures you of a different pattern of compression each day, which is better on the loft.

Another way to increase the life of your bag is to wash up each night before crawling into it. The dirt and oil on your clothes and body will find its way into your bag's fill and inhibit its ability to insulate. If you can't wash up, change into clean clothes.

How can you sleep more peacefully?
Try these time-tested tips:

➤ Make sure your bag fits you. If the bag is too tight, then the insulation will compress and will be unable to do its job. And, if it is too loose, you will expend extra energy trying to heat up the addi-tional space, draining your energy reserves before dawn breaks. If possible, wear whatever you intend to sleep in when trying out bags. And don't even think about sleeping naked when it is cold!

➤ Don't forget to cinch the draft collar and your hood (if you have them). This will keep you much warmer.

➤ Keep your bag from getting wet at all costs. Store it in a waterproof stuff sack and carry extra garbage bags to store the stuff sack in on wet days. And never, ever, climb into a sleeping bag wet. As a matter of fact, if you're facing hypothermia, it is better to crawl into your bag naked rather than with wet clothes on. But, make sure you change into dry clothes as soon as possible.

➤ Keep some extra clothes nearby along with a hat (if you are not already wearing one) to slip on should you start to get cold during the night.

➤ Make yourself an old-fashioned foot warmer with a Nalgene or other leak-proof bottle filled with warm or hot water.

➤ Eat well before heading off to dreamland. This helps keep your energy level high enough to ward off the chill. Also, keep a snack nearby in case you need to replenish yourself in the middle of the night.

➤ Empty your bladder before you crawl into your bag. Believe it or not, it takes energy to keep that liquid warm.

➤ If it looks to be a cold night, do at least twenty jumping jacks (or other calisthenics) before heading into the sack. If you get cold during the night, crawl out of your bag and do some more.

Bag Liners

Purchasing a bag liner is a good way to warm up your bag without adding much cost or weight. There are three types of bag liners—overbags, vapor barriers, and plain inner liners.

Overbags: The overbags slide on over your sleeping bag and have a filling that increases the warmth of your bag by as much as twenty degrees. They cost approximately fifty to one hundred dollars and weigh about two to three pounds—kind of bulky for extensive backpacking but not too bad for short, cold-weather trips. They can also be used as a sleeping bag in and of itself in really warm weather.

Vapor Barriers: These liners are inserted inside your sleeping bag and can raise its temperature by as much as fifteen degrees. Basically, you're sticking yourself inside a plastic bag. They are constructed out of coated nylon or other materials and weigh only five to six ounces. Also, they cost much less than the overbags— approximately twenty to thirty dollars a bag. The draw- back to the vapor barrier is comfort; they are designed to make you sweat and use your own warmth to keep you warm. Vapor liners are recommended for tempera- tures well below freezing.

Plain Inner Liners: For five to one hundred dollars, you can purchase simple bag liners made of flannel, cotton, breathable nylon, synthetics, or down and weighing three ounces to two pounds. The degree to which they warm your bag varies and should be clari- fied by the salesperson before you decide to purchase such a liner. They, too, can be used as warmweather sleeping bags.

Sleeping Pads
Sleeping pads are a necessity. If you don't sleep on a pad, you lose a lot of warmth to the ground. Although the padding is minimal, pads are more comfortable than the hard earth. Fortunately, as with all things back- packing gear—related, there are plenty of pads to choose from and you are sure to find one that meets your preferences.

Types of Pads
Closed-cell foam: This type of pad features tiny plastic bubbles squeezed together in a honeycomb-style. These are both inexpensive and lightweight and they shed water to boot. Closed-cell foam is also pretty durable. Its drawback? It needs to be relatively thick to block out

those roots and rocks, and of course, the thicker the pad, the bulkier.

Open-cell foam: This is the opposite of the closed-cell pad. Think rolling waves of foam so that the texture is on the outside rather than the inside and you get the general idea. This type of pad always reminds me of the inside of an egg carton. This pad offers excellent comfort and contours, is inexpensive and packs down small. Unless it has a waterproof coating though, it becomes a sponge in the vicinity of water.

Self-inflating pad: Who hasn't heard the one about the boastful hiker who was like a Therm-A-Rest? That's right! Self-inflating! This is an open-cell foam pad encased in a watertight, airtight cover. Fitted with a valve all you have to do is roll out the pad, unscrew the valve, and wait while the foam rebounds to its original shape. You can blow in more air for a stiffer feel if so desired. This pad provides the best comfort available. But of course, it has its drawbacks too. It is expensive, it is on the heavy side, and it is susceptible to puncture. Still, it is far and away the type of pad favored by most hikers.

Other materials: Other pad options include those filled with heat-reflective materials and those filled with down.

After deciding which type of pad you want to purchase, you might also want to look into the different features available in pads these days. One of the most popular

---

Pillows

Some people cannot sleep without a pillow. Whenever I hike, I use my pile jacket as a pillow. I carry it anyway so there's not the added bulk of a camping pillow. I consider camp pillows needless weight even on short backpacking trips, but for those of you who wish to carry the extra half-pound, you have the choice of a small (10–12 by 16–20 inch) synthetic stuffed pillow or an inflatable pillow. Relatively inexpensive, backpacking pillows are a matter of preference. But remember, your body can only carry so much weight.

pad features is the ability to convert to a chair. Some pads have buckles and straps that allow you to turn your sleeping pad into a camp chair. You can also buy a conversion kit that will turn any pad into a chair.

Some pads come with what are known as integral compression or roll straps. These make shrinking and packing your pad a bit easier. The straps also give you more options when it comes to attaching the pad on the outside of your pack.

Pads with multiple chambers allow you to over-inflate one section without creating an annoying bubble elsewhere. Another bonus: should the pad get punctured, only one chamber will deflate rather than the entire pad. The insulation on these pads is affected by the seams between pads, though. Cold air can creep through at these junctures.

Some closed-cell pads feature a molded surface that is dimpled or ridged. It is preferable to the flat models because it is less slippery, provides better cushioning, and weighs less.

A new gimmick to save on weight and bulk is the mummy-shaped pad. The main drawback is that you need to be one of those people who sleeps soundly and doesn't move around a lot in your sleep; otherwise you might find your feet slipping off the tapered bottom section.

Another cool feature is a no-slip surface. A brushed or sticky surface on your sleeping pad helps your sleeping bag maintain the traction it needs to stay on your pad, especially on uneven campsites.

Some pads come with an attached pillow but these tend to be bulky and most hikers can do with a rolled up jacket or sweater beneath their head.

Two other features you might want to look for and purchase are the repair kit and stuff sack. The former is particularly important because a few patches and fix-it glue might make the difference between a good night's sleep and waking up on the wrong side of the sleeping bag. A stuff sack is just added insurance against trail grime and possible puncture if you have a self-inflating pad.

When it comes to determining the thickness, weight, and length of your pad, your own preferences are the best judge. You know how much padding you need and how much weight you can carry. Your height, too, will affect how long your pad needs to be. Another consideration is where you intend to do most of your hiking—desert, beach, woods, or granite mountaintop. That is, what type of terrain will you be buffeting your body against?

STOVES

It was a beautiful spring day in the Nantahalas. We passed through a tunnel of rhododendron and after a short climb found ourselves on a rocky summit with a scattering of hardwoods. It was the perfect spot for lunch. We pulled out our Outback Oven, fired up the stove, and in less than half an hour, we were feasting on pesto pizza. As we were finishing the small pizza, a couple of backpackers passed by and glanced at our feast with obvious envy, no doubt dreading their lunch of gorp or Little Debbie snack cakes.

It is true that using a campstove while backpacking is almost mandatory now because there are so many areas where fires are prohibited. Gone are the days when gobs of dough were roasted on a stick over a blazing campfire. In areas where fires are permitted, the woods around shelters and campsites have often been picked clean of downed wood by other hikers. Fortunately, stoves are now lightweight and efficient, as well as inexpensive. And with the advances in stove technology, backpacking cuisine doesn't have to be synonymous with macaroni and cheese. There are now many options when it come to trail cuisine.

What Type of Stove Is Right for You?

So how do you decide what stove will best suit your needs? Backpacking stoves tend to be categorized by the type of fuel they burn. These fuels have different advantages and disadvantages. Some heat food very efficiently, others are available worldwide, and some (those available in canisters) are very easy to use. Choose the fuel best suited to your needs. Most fuels are either gases that come in disposable canisters, or they are liquids that need to be placed in refillable containers. Liquid fuel stoves nearly always have a separate container although there are a few models that have a small tank that is permanently attached next to, or underneath, the burner. There is one stove available (the Primus Multi Fuel System 3288) that features special attachments that enable it to use both canister and liquid fuel.

Types of Fuel

Here is a brief description of your fuel options.

Auto Gas: A number of stoves can now use the unleaded gas you use in your automobile, but most manufacturers still recommend you use it only as a last resort when white gas or kerosene is not available. I have had to use it in an emergency and it does tend to clog up the jets more quickly. If you must use auto gas, choose the lowest-octane, unleaded gas available. Make sure you cook in a well-ventilated area because with some stoves there will be an increase in smoke, soot, and noxious fumes.

Alcohol: Very few backpacking stoves use denatured alcohol for fuel. While it is both a clean and non-volatile fuel, the petroleum-based fuels burn much hotter and more efficiently than alcohol.

Blended Fuel Canisters: Blended fuels are usually comprised of propane and butane. Occasionally, isobutane will be added to these fuels to help maintain a steady output of heat until the fuel has been used up. These types of canisters are harder to use in cold weather at high altitudes unless you can warm the canister or your stove already has a built-in component that heats the fuel line and aids vaporization.

Butane Canisters: Unless the butane has been blended with propane, it does not have the heat output that produces the hot flame of other canister fuels. Butane canisters also tend to lose their heat output in temperatures below forty-five degrees Fahrenheit. Butane does tend to be very reliable, though, and it can have excellent flame control in warm weather. Butane is a particularly popular European fuel.

Isobutane: These canisters can be hard to find but they provide a quiet, clean, and controllable flame when the temperature is above forty degrees Fahrenheit. Isobutane has a slower boil time than the blended fuels but it will burn consistently until the canister is completely empty.

Kerosene: This is probably the most internationally available of all the fuels. It is also the least expensive and it burns hot as well. If this sounds too good to be true, recognize that kerosene does have its drawbacks—it produces lots of smoke, soot, and noxious fumes, and its ability to clog is second only to auto gas. If you do use kerosene, stick with K-1 as opposed to the diesel if possible. Although kerosene will not ignite readily, it also does not evaporate quickly. Kerosene stoves can sit directly on the snow, but like white gas, all kerosene stoves require priming.

The Yellow Stove Lite Trail by Primus and the Giga Power Stove by Snowpeak on the opposite page are examples of stoves that use disposable fuel canisters.

White Gas: This has long been the liquid fuel of choice. Usually found under the name of "Coleman," it comes in gallon cans and can be found just about anywhere in North America. The flame it produces is hot, reliable, and relatively clean in almost all weather conditions but only if you keep your stove properly primed and the fuel tank well pressurized. White gas evaporates quickly, but the spilled fuel is very flammable, and self-pressurized stoves using white gas must be insulated from snow or cold.

Wood/Solid Fuel: There are a few backpacking stoves that use solid fuel (Pyromid and ZZ Manufacturing are the only two I can think of, offhand). These are fine to use in places where an open flame is allowed and finding fuel is not a problem (Pyromids can use coal), but otherwise you have to carry your own wood or fuel. You also need to keep a close eye on your stove to make sure the fire stays stoked.

Some stoves come with an attached fuel reservoir or a fuel bottle, which is included in the purchase price. If

you don't want to bother with finding your own fuel bottle, this might be a good option for you.

If you need or want to buy more, there are a number of manufacturers of fuel bottles. The most common fuel bottles are made by MSR, Sigg, and Nalgene. The MSR fuel bottles can be purchased in three sizes: eleven, twenty-two, and thirty-three ounces, though the latter is quite large and is probably not necessary for most hikes. Sigg offers sizes ranging from 8 to 48 ounces. Both brands are made of noncorrosive aluminum and are relatively inexpensive. Fuel faucets are available for both the MSR and Sigg bottles. The screw-on cap allows you to turn the top to pour and to turn it again to seal the bottle without a leak. Nalgene bottles, which do not fit the MSR stoves, can also be purchased and range from 16 to 32 ounces.

MSRs Whisperlite 600 International and Peak 1s Apex II on the opposite page use fuel bottles that can be refilled with white gas and other fuels.

A twenty-two-ounce container generally lasts seven to twelve days. In the winter, because fuel consumption is slightly higher, you can count on no more than a week's worth of fuel from any 22-ounce container.

Stove Accessories

There are a number of other features that you may want to consider before purchasing a stove.

Depending upon the type of backpacking trips you intend to make, one option is to purchase a stove with a double burner. This allows you to cook two pots of food and/or liquid simultaneously. The major drawback with the two-burner is that it adds a significant amount of weight to your pack.

Another option, though not exactly an important one, is whether or not your stove comes in a hard-shell (plastic) case or in a stuff sack. Personally, I prefer the stuff sack as I tend to carry my stove nestled inside the cook kit anyway. The hard-shell case is more difficult to pack but you can always remove it from its case and carry it in a stuff sack or in your cook kit.

Push-button ignition or "piezo ignition" is another option you will find. This means that you can light your stove with the push of a button. Keep in mind though, that the piezo can short out in the rain and too much heat can actually melt the button. As long as you have a back up plan, i.e. matches or a lighter, you shouldn't have to worry too much if that happens.

Some stoves come with a repair kit, and for others, you must purchase this item separately. Either way, it is always a good idea to carry along a repair kit for your stove no matter how trustworthy you feel it is.

Most stoves come with some sort of windscreen, either a stand-alone, wrap-around aluminum barrier that keeps the wind from affecting the flames on your stove or a small, half-inch band of metal that circles the stove's burner. The latter is less effective in high winds.

Tips for Operating Your Stove

➤ Practice setting up, starting, and taking apart your stove before you hike.

➤ Pre-filter any low-grade fuel you might use to avoid clogs and repairs later. Most manufacturers offer filters for their stoves, and Coleman sells an all-purpose, 1.5-ounce aluminum filtering funnel.

➤ Don't fill white gas stoves more than three-fourths full. The extra air space allows pressure to build up and make your stove work efficiently.

➤ Unless you have a butane stove or a wood burner, you will probably have to prime your stove before you can start it. What does this mean? Priming is simply a way of preheating your stove before you start burning the fuel for the use of cooking. Most stoves are primed first by pumping the fuel tank to build up pressure and then by allowing a little fuel to seep into the priming well, lighting it, allowing it to burn out before turning on the gas and relighting the stove. With butane stoves, you need simply turn on the gas and light.

➤ If you can't prime your stove directly, carry an eye-dropper. You can extract the fuel from your fuel bottle with the dropper, and that's much safer than pouring fuel from the bottle into the priming well. This produces much less flaring.

➤ A foam beverage insulator can be slipped onto butane cartridges to keep them warm.

➤ Always use a heat deflector and a windscreen, even on still days: they help to keep your flame steady and reduce fuel consumption. If you don't have a windscreen, use a piece of doubled aluminum foil.

➤ To conserve fuel, keep a lid on your pot whenever possible.

➤ When cooking on snow, make sure there is some sort of insulation beneath your stove so that it doesn't sink. Old license plates work well for this.

➤ Carry a repair kit from your manufacturer should something break or need adjusting in the field .

➤ Most importantly, don't forget to pack out your empty fuel cartridges.

Stove Safety

The following tips will help ensure the safe and efficient use of your fuel:

➤ Never heat your fuel canisters with a candle flame or lighter: the results could be disastrous. Instead, warm the cartridge in your hands or keep one in your sleeping bag at night for easier lighting in the morning. You can also set the canister in a pan of shallow water. As long as the water is warmer than freezing, it will warm up the canister. An activated chemical hand-warmer is another way to warm up that cold canister on frigid days.

➤ Never use a piggyback-style canister stove with baking oven and hood. The hoods reflect too much heat onto the canisters and can cause flare-ups.

➤ Unless the fuel cartridge is self-sealing, do not remove it while your stove is inside your tent. The escaping fumes can be dangerous.

➤ Since most stoves get very hot once lit, never set the stove directly on the floor of your tent. You can use the vestibule of your tent as a kitchen but make sure you set your stove on a non-burnable pad such as a ceramic tile or a flat rock. Also, make sure your stove is firmly set before lighting to avoid a tip-over.

➤ Never light a white gas/kerosene or other liquid-burning stove inside your tent. Flare-ups are very common and tent/sleeping bag materials are susceptible to flames as are your hair, eyebrows, beard, and clothing.

➤ If you must cook in your tent, make sure it is well ventilated or try cooking under the vestibule. Stoves use up oxygen and produce carbon monoxide—a sure way to a quick death.

Tips for Maintaining Your Stove

➤ After each trip, empty the fuel from your stove. What you can't pour out, burn. Fuel left in stoves leaves residues that will clog your fuel jets and filters.

➤ Once a year, burn a cap of Gumout Carburetor Cleaner along with a half tank or half pint of gas to help dissolve residues.

➤ Just as residues build up in your stove, residues also build up in your fuel source (e.g., your Coleman fuel can). If your fuel is getting old (if you haven't used it in a year), get rid of it. Don't put it in your stove. You can hold on to your Coleman fuel longer if you store it in individual fuel bottles rather the original gallon container. The fuel will stay cleaner longer, and thus it will burn hotter and leave less soot on your pots.

➤ Keep your stove in a dust-free environment (such as a fabric sack) when it is not in use.

On Going Stoveless

Other not-quite-so-popular options are to eat only cold foods or to build fires. I've met only a few hikers that depend on cold meals during their backpacking trips. It is not an impossible option, although most hikers can't live without their morning coffee, and hot liquid is vital in cold, wet weather. Hikers who opt to go stoveless subsist for the most part on sandwiches—both cheese and peanut butter—along with toaster pastries, tuna, and cereal.

I have never met any hikers who depend only on fires to cook their food. While some solid fuel stoves might be easy to start in the rain, I often have trouble lighting campfires in wet weather. Cooking over camp-fires creates other problems, including instability; hikers can lose their meals to the flames when an unbalanced pot tips over into the fire! Campfires are wonderful for the warmth they produce, and their smoke is indispensable during mosquito season, but stoves are the best option for cooking when hiking.

Although I recommend using stoves to cook your food, it is still in your best interest to be able to build a fire if necessary. A time may come when you just can't get your stove to work and you desperately need a fire for warmth, drink, and food. Remember to check local U.S. Forest Service, National Park Service, or state park regulations concerning fires before you go on a hike.

Most outdoors stores offer a number of gadgets that will help you start a fire in inclement weather. I always carry windproof and waterproof matches along with my trusty butane lighter—the simplest of solutions. Also available are fire starter kits containing waterproof matches, tinder and fire starter sheets; fire sticks that will light even when wet; fire ribbon (a fuel paste); and magnesium fire starter that uses magnesium shavings as a flame source. Another alternative is to carry a few votive candles; once lit and set in the tinder, they last a lot longer than matches.

If you are one of those people who wish to carry everything for every situation, you could carry a cake pan to build a fire in and a small grill to go on top of it to hold your pot. Unfortunately, if you carry everything you might possibly desire, your pack will end up weighing more than you do.

If building a fire is absolutely necessary, balance your pot by using large, flat rocks for support. A trough between the rocks contains either the fire or the coals from an adjacent fire.

Another option is to cook your meal over the fire by hanging your pot from a stick suspended between two other Y-shaped sticks wedged in the ground. The disadvantages to this method are numerous. There are many places where you will either not be allowed to cut down limbs to form your suspension system or you will not be able to find limbs to cut at all. From experience, it is very difficult to get the two y-shaped limbs embedded in the ground. You must also keep the weight of your pot in mind. Your supper could end up all over the ground if the horizontal limb is not strong enough to bear the pot's weight. The crossbar must also be wet or green enough to keep from catching on fire.

Building a low-impact fire, one that leaves little testimony of its presence, is a very important consideration. There is nothing uglier in the wilderness than the scars left by fire rings. If you must build a fire, try to build one in an established fire ring. If there is not a ring available, try building a fire in a pan or keep the fire small and remove its traces as much as possible. Obviously, if it is an emergency, you will be more concerned with getting a fire lit than the impact it will have on the environment. So, once again, don't build a fire unless (1) it is an emergency and/or (2) there is an established hearth or fire ring.

Fire Safety

If you must build a fire, there are a number of precautions you should take:

➤ Never build a fire on pine needles or leaves. The fire can smolder for days (even if you think you've extinguished it) before bursting into flames and torching an entire forest.

➤ Make sure you build your fire in a well-cleared area, so if sparks fly, wood pops, or ashes take sail, there is nothing for them to light on as they fall to earth. (The need to clear the ground is yet another reason for not building a fire unless absolutely necessary.)

➤ Always build your fire in a clearing with no overhanging branches. The rising sparks can ignite the leaves and small branches in dry weather.

➤ Should you decide to build a fire, a ring of rocks or a formal fire ring is an absolute necessity because it will contain the fire and keep it from spreading. Don't use damp or wet stones when building a fire ring. Some stones will explode when dried and heated by the fire's warmth.

➤ Never leave your fire unattended, even for a second. Unless you have someone to watch the fire for you as you search for downed wood, collect all the wood you will need before you light your fire.

➤ If it is a windy day and the area is under a fire hazard (that is, it is dry and fire could spread easily), don't even think about lighting a fire.

➤ Don't use wood that causes a lot of sparks; the sparks can start forest fires not to mention put holes in your tent or sleeping bag. Soft woods like pine burn quicker but cause more sparks; use hard woods to keep the sparks to a minimum.

➤ Never chop down a tree for a fire—always used downed wood.

➤ Never build a fire against a large rock because the black scar left by the fire will last for centuries.

➤ Finally, make sure your fire is completely out. Stir the ashes to make sure no coals remain and then drown it with water and cover it with dirt.

If you're a smoker, don't be surprised if you are not allowed to smoke in certain areas while hiking. Some forests are routinely under a fire hazard during much of the year, usually summer and fall. Often, hikers are sent on a detour around a forest because it is on fire. The ensuing roadwalk is miserable—hot asphalt, exhaust fumes, and hundred-degree heat—and all because someone didn't properly extinguish a cigarette!

COOKWARE AND UTENSILS

What Pot is Right for You?
The cooking pot may seem innocent enough, but it is one of the hiker's most important tools. It is a multiuse vessel, employed to boil water for drinks and meals, to gather water from a nearby source, to eat out of instead of a bowl, and even to hold your stove while hiking.

Pot Construction
These days, there are even several options when it comes to choosing which material your cookware is made of:

Aluminum: Lightweight and generally inexpensive, aluminum is more prone to denting and scorching than steel. If you want to purchase aluminum, buy pots with a nonstick coating.

Stainless Steel: This metal is more durable than aluminum but it is also heavier. Because of its slick surface, it is easier to keep clean.

Titanium: This amazingly lightweight, strong metal may cut ounces but it is also expensive and prone to scorching.

Composite: These pots are usually made of aluminum and stainless steel fused together with the stainless on the inside to minimize sticking. While they offer a nice balance of weight and durability, they are more expensive than plain aluminum or stainless steel.

Other features you might consider find when searching for the perfect cookset are bail or swing handles, a black exterior finish, a nonstick finish, a lipped rim, and rounded bottom edge.

A bail handle works fine on large pots, but be careful if it falls against the side of the pot: the handle will conduct heat pretty quickly, and unless you have a pot holder, you could be in a for a nasty burn. Oddly enough, swing handles, designed to address this very problem, can get hot too. Swing handles swing out from the sides of the pot, but even the rubber-coated handles get pretty warm. Swing handles also make it hard to use a windscreen and make it difficult to nest your pots. Your best bet: avoid pots with handles. Instead, buy a handleless pot and use a pot grabber or potlifter instead. The latter items can be purchased separately and cost very little. Not only will a potlifter keep you from burning your fingers, it can also help you avoid spilled meals.

A lipped rim is essential if you intend to use a pot grabber. Not only does it give the pot grabber something to hold onto but it makes your pot stronger and less prone to warping. Pots with rounded bottom edges encourage the even distribution of heat up the sides of the pot and make cleaning a bit easier.

Pots that have been given a black exterior finish tend to absorb heat faster and boost the boiling time on your pot. Another option is to spray a pot you already own with flat black paint. You will achieve the same effect. As with your home cookware, camping pots with a nonstick finish make cooking and cleaning that much easier. A nonstick finish is a must if you intend to bake.

Pot Size

Backpackers use a variety of pot sizes when they hike. You should choose your pot depending on your menu and the number of people in your group: you don't want to go too small nor too big. I've met many hikers who have found that the one-quart (or one-liter) pot tended to overflow during cooking, and the food that boiled over the side was much harder to clean. Improperly cleaned pots can lead to an uncomfortable hike: they increase your chance of food poisoning and serve as an irresistible lure to hungry animal neighbors in the night.

Still, if you hike solo and eat small meals, the smallest, 1-liter pot, will probably be fine for you, although only the smallest of stoves will nest in the pot. Probably the most ideal size for solo hikers and the smallest for couples is the 1.5-liter pot. Most stoves will nest in this pot and it can accommodate enough pasta for two (or one really hungry hiker!).

Most couples I know carry nesting pots, the 1.5- and 2-liter pots nestle perfectly and you can carry your stove in the 1.5-liter pot. If your stove doesn't fit in the 2-liter pot, it is too big. For our family of three, we use one pot to cook our dinner and the other to mix drink (or to warm the drink when it's cold outside). A 3-liter pot is really only necessary if you are cooking for a group of four or more. Many stove manufacturers offer special cooking pots to go with their set-up.

Preparing Your Cookware for the Wilderness

Before you head out into the woods with your new pots (or old ones), you might want to make some modifications to make cooking in the backcountry that much easier. If you have pots without a nonstick finish, try

notching the inside walls of your pot at commonly used intervals such as 1-cup, 2-cup, 3-cup and so on. This will help you measure the correct amount of water for rice or other meals that can be ruined by approximation. If you have a nonstick finish on your cookware, try painting a line on the outside of your pot.

If you use a frying pan and it doesn't double as a lid, you may want to try soldering a heat diffuser to the bottom of the pan. This will spread the heat more evenly across the bottom of the pan. Heat diffusers can be bought at most outdoor stores but you can even use a tuna fish can to create some separation.

As I mentioned before, you can give your pots added power by spray painting the outside black if they don't already have a black finish. This, too, diffuses heat and keeps food from scorching.

Utensils

When it comes to carrying utensils, hikers opinions are split. I usually carry a spoon, a bowl, and a pocket knife. Some hikers prefer a fork, spoon, and a pocket knife, and they use their cooking pot as a bowl. Couples usually carry bowls, and almost no one uses plates.

Cups are a matter of preference. I have carried the Sierra-style cup that features indentations showing measurements, but I don't really like them. Now I have switched to the increasingly popular thermal travel mug.

A three-inch lock-blade pocket knife or a Swiss Army knife will prove adequate for most hikes, though hikers usually say they aren't used often.

Extras, such as grills and coffee pots, are rarely used on longer hikes. They may be worth their weight and bulkiness on short trips if you drink a lot of coffee or intend to grill the fish you catch or the steaks you brought. And the coffee press is rapidly replacing the old-style percolator. For extended trips, most hikers stick to instant coffee and eat their steaks when in town to resupply.

Baking on the Trail

It used to be that if you wanted to bake something while backpacking, you were going to have to carry along several pounds of stove. Traveling Light has made baking while backpacking an actual option with its Outback Oven. With the Ultralight, which uses your own cookpot for baking, you need only add seven ounces to your pack weight.

The Outback Oven uses the circulation of hot air in a convection dome to concentrate heat around the baking pan. Hot air vents out a hole in the top, and a thermometer can be viewed through the hole to monitor the baking temperature. A riser bar separates the pan from the heat to prevent scorching, and a stainless steel diffuser plate disperses heat from the stove. Finally, a reflector collar directs heat upward to boost the stove's efficiency.

Does it work? Yes, actually. As I said earlier, it is a great way to add a gourmet touch to your camping trip. Should you take it on a backpacking trip? Sure, if the trip is short. But on an extended trip, it might be just a bit too much trouble and the food mixes just a tad too expensive.

BACKPACKS

Backpacks are as much an extension of personality as they are a way of transporting your gear whether you're in the dog-eat-dog world or on a two-day or multi-month commune with nature. If you are the type who needs to be prepared for every possible situation, then chances are you'll purchase the biggest backpack possible. If you don't mind getting by on a wing and a prayer, then your backpack may more closely resemble a day pack. Some hikers would rather die than carry an external frame pack but you might find that nothing suits you better. It really doesn't matter what backpack you choose as long as it suits you.

As I mentioned in the Introduction, if you visit any major National Park—Bryce Canyon, Great Smoky Mountains, Yosemite, Yellowstone—you will be appalled by the number of poorly clad and unprepared tourists trodding the shorter trails. But sling on your pack and head out onto even a slightly less-used trail, and within a couple of miles you'll have left the crowds behind and you'll be convinced you've entered another dimension. Sound like *The Twilight Zone?* Actually, in some ways it is very similar. Sometimes when you leave the crowds behind and you're surrounded by acres of forest or desert and not a car or human is in sight, you have to wonder if you're still in the twenty-first century. The peep of a frog, the skittering of a lizard, the cry of an owl have replaced the incessant noise of pagers, cellular phones, and automobiles. You could be convinced it was the eighteenth century if it weren't for the luxury of your internal frame pack, ten-degree sleeping bag, dome tent, and small but powerful camp stove. Unlike the pioneers, you won't be sleeping under the stars and cooking over a fire. Within half an hour, you'll have purified some water from a nearby stream with a few strong pumps on your water filter, and you'll be feasting on three-cheese lasagna. Then, with the pots washed and the bear bag strung over the nearest accommodating tree, you can crawl into your sleeping bag, and by the light of your headlamp, you can update your journal before drifting off to dreamland.

This experience would have been impossible without your backpack. Gone are the days of blanket rolls and heavy, shapeless canvas bags. Today, selecting a pack is almost as tough as finding a pair of boots. Dozens of manufacturers offer hundreds of options.

Advances in technology have made backpacking easier on hikers, but as with other types of equipment, you face choices. You first must choose what type of packing you'll be doing and on what terrain. This will influence your choice of pack frames. The internal frame is designed for rugged, mountain backpacking; the external for gentle to moderate terrain. (The frameless rucksack is experiencing a comeback as well, and a number of manufacturers offer these packs for hikers who like to travel light.)

External versus Internal Frame Packs
Both frame designs have their pros and cons. The basic differences: the external frame is designed to distribute weight equally, it has a higher center of gravity (perfect for established trails), and it tends to be cooler; the internal frame pack is designed to custom-fit each wearer, it has a low center of gravity (popular for off-trail hiking and mountaineering), and it is built to carry heavier loads. Here are some more specifics on both styles of packs.

External Frame Packs
External frame packs come in top-loading, front-loading, and combination models. A top-loading pack works like a duffel bag attached to a frame, whereas, front-loading packs give you easier access to your gear. Most manufacturers now design their external packs with both top-loaded and front-loaded sections as well as front and side pockets.

The most important feature is the pack's hip belt. The hip belt carries the bulk of the weight, so that a properly fitted pack allows you to drop one shoulder out of its strap without a significant change in weight distribution. The hip belt should be padded, well built, and snug fitting. Many companies offer optional hip belts that are larger or smaller than the standard adjustable hip belt. If you're planning a long-distance hike, keep in mind that because of weight loss, the hip belt that fits you when you begin may not fit you later in your trip.

Hip belts are prone to breaking because of the amount of stress they receive. If this happens, manufacturers are usually great about replacing them free of charge. Keep the manufacturer's telephone number (usually toll-free) handy in case you need to order another hip belt or have one replaced.

Manufacturers of external frame packs boast that the frame keeps the pack away from your body and thus is cooler in the summer. A good external frame pack will have a mesh back band that will allow for circulation of air. This band should be tight and well adjusted for your comfort.

Features to look for in an external frame pack include:

➤ A welded tubular frame, preferably of aluminum because it is lightweight and strong
➤ A coated nylon packcloth (although not waterproof, it is water resistant—a pack cover is needed to waterproof your pack)
➤ Thick, padded shoulder straps
➤ A mesh backband to allow the air to circulate in warm weather
➤ A thick, foam hipbelt with an easy-release buckle
➤ Outside pockets on the pack bag

Internal Frame Packs

Rather than purchase two packs, many people are turning to the internal frame as the option that best suits all their needs. Unless you hike easy trails exclusively, an internal frame will suit you well on all trails.

As an example, I had an agonizing time climbing through Maine's Mahoosuc Notch with my external frame pack. The .9-mile stretch of tumbled boulders requires squeezing in and out, over and under. My

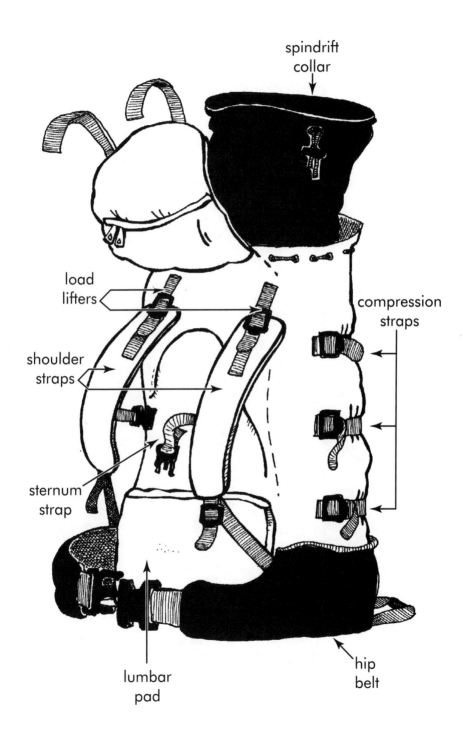

spindrift
collar

load
lifters

compression
straps

shoulder
straps

sternum
strap

lumbar
pad

hip
belt

external frame continually threw me off-balance, leaving me quaking in my boots and near tears. At that moment, I would have done anything for an internal frame. Another thing that irritates me to no end is hitting my head on the frame. Every time I fall while wearing an external frame (I've never met a person who hasn't fallen while backpacking), I bang my head on the frame. Adding insult to injury is the knot on my head.

Internal frames were designed to alleviate these problems. Because they hug your body and have a lower center of gravity, they provide excellent balance and allow more upper-body mobility and flexibility.

Whereas the external frame pack gets its support from the aluminum frame, internal frame packs uses metal bars to create support. These come in two basic designs—two parallel bars or X-shaped bars—which are sewn inside the packbag. The internal frame is fitted to your body by a number of straps attached to the packbag. The internal frame's major drawback stems from the fact that the load is contoured to your body; this is often not as comfortable as a load carried in an external frame.

Typical examples of external frame packs. Dana Designs K2 and Kelty's Trekker.

Most internal frame packs are top-loading but manufacturers have begun to offer panel-loading and hybrid-loading packs as well.

Top-loading: This type of pack has a big top opening into which you dump what will fit, pack it down, and load some more. OK, you're not supposed to do it that way. Really, for a top-loading pack, you need to be very organized. That way, not only do you know where all your stuff is, exactly, but you can also more evenly distribute the weight. Many top-loaders have extension tubes to provide additional volume and a floating lid to cover it all. These packs are more water resistant than other packs because they either have no zippers or just one zipper around the sleeping bag compartment.

Panel-loading: These internal frames have one or more zippers on the front so you don't have to dig through all your stuff to get at whatever is on the bottom of the pack. On the other hand, having more zippers makes the pack a bit harder to load because you risk bursting zippers and it is less waterproof. If you do go for a panel-loader, make sure the zippers are really

Typical internal frame packs. Gregory's Banshee, North Face's Perseverence and Dana Design's Bombpack.

tough and make sure that there are at least one or two compression straps over the zippers to relieve some of the pressure (not to mention to hold things together should a zipper burst).

Hybrid-loading: Just about the best of both worlds because you can load from the top but also unzip to remove something near the bottom without unpacking everything. Once again, though, make sure the zippers are tough and make sure that there is compression-strap backup. Also, like the panel-loader, this pack is more susceptible to water-leakage. But, really, no matter what type of pack you get, you should always carry a pack cover.

Internal frame packs are equipped with harnesses, straps, and other adjustments so that the pack may be formfitted to each wearer. The hip belt on the internal frame pack is form-fitted, as well, and is part of the pack. Although it is adjustable and is offered in several sizes, it is not optional or easily replaceable. Some pack manufacturers are beginning to make inter-changeable parts for internal frame packs.

Things to look for in an internal frame include:

➤ Contoured aluminum stays to help distribute weight to your hips
➤ Thick, padded shoulder straps and hip belt
➤ A lumbar pad that will help support a heavy load and enhance ventilation
➤ Compression straps to keep smaller loads from shifting
➤ A reinforced bottom to resist abrasion
➤ A lot of lash points and loops to carry gear outside the pack
➤ A slim profile with either outside or add-on pockets
➤ Cinch straps at the shoulder and waist to keep the load close to your back

Internal frame packs are generally more expensive than external frame packs.

Pack Capacity

Knowing the capacity of a pack gives you a good idea of what length trip the pack is intended for, though your own tendency to travel light or heavy will also affect how far you can go with a given pack. The numbers below reflect external frame capacity; because sleeping gear must be carried inside the internal frame pack instead of attached to the frame of an external pack, add 1,000 cubic inches to the numbers below. The following is a rough guide:

2,500 to 3,000 cubic inches: This pack will handle the minimum needed for a warm-weather overnighter as long as you have a partner to share the task of carrying a small tent, cooking gear, and stove. This could also be a heavy-duty day pack.

3,000 to 4,500 cubic inches: The perfect pack for three-season weekend trips when you're carrying warm clothing and once again, sharing gear. If you keep it simple, you can make a slightly longer trip with a pack this size.

4,500 to 6,000 cubic inches: This is the perfect size pack for nearly all backpacking trips. You can head out for a weekend (alone or with a partner) or take off for a five-month trek of the Appalachian Trail, if you like. This pack will handle the load with ease.

6,000-plus cubic inches: This pack is big enough for all the gear you'll need for a cold and snowy winter camping trip, a long expedition, or if you're the main load-bearer, a family outing.

Pack Construction

Put some mileage on your pack and soon it will begin to wear out. The frame, seams, and zippers are especially subject to wear. Frank had a pack whose frame literally exploded off his back when it finally died. I lost an adjustment strap on my hipbelt, a relatively minor inconvenience compared to the number of miles I've put on that pack.

Before purchasing a pack, check the pack frame (if you are looking at an external frame) for sturdiness and clean welds. Check the seams for even stitching and reinforcements, especially at the stress points. Make sure that there is sufficient room between the stitching and the edge of the seam and fabric because this is a likely place for it to separate. Feel free to tug and pull on the pack as much as you like—better to have it fall apart in the store than on your first trip out hiking. Buy a pack with heavy zippers. They are more durable. Also, if it is a front-loading pack, make sure there are compression straps to take the pressure off the zippers once loaded.

Fit

Before buying any pack, you should test it first. The best method is to rent a pack and try it out on a weekend hike. Some stores even offer rent-to-buy programs. If you can't do that, see if you can't load up the pack you're interested in and try it out in the store. Many stores have sand bags on hand for this purpose.

Also, keep in mind that torso length is more important than overall height. For example, if a pack is suggested for someone six feet tall, it may also be appropriate for a shorter person with a longer torso—another reason to try on a pack before you buy it.

The hip belt should fit snugly around the top part of your hips and should not catch your legs when you're hiking uphill. The belt should be heavily padded for comfort, durability, and stability. Most importantly, make sure the hipbelt has a durable, easy-release buckle. There are times when you may have to get out of your pack quickly.

Tips for Fitting an External Frame

➤ When fitting your pack make sure that the shoulder straps are level within an inch or two above the shoulder. Shoulder straps should not pinch your neck nor should they slide off your shoulders. Mounted too high they put too much of the wait on your shoulders; too low, on your hips.
➤ The mesh back band should fit snugly, but comfortably, against your back and the hip belt should ride on your pelvis.

➤ Move the hip belt up and down the frame to prevent the lower end of the frame from making contact with your lower back.

➤ If the pack comes with load-lifters, they should join the frame at ear level and attach to the shoulder straps over your collarbone. Weight can be distributed from shoulders to hips with these straps.

➤ A sternum strap will help hold the pack more closely to your back.

Accessory features in packs include ice ax loops, crampon patches, ski holders, accessory pockets and camera rings. On some packs you will find that these features are standard rather than optional.

BACKPACKING TIP

When fitting your pack, make sure the pack is loaded with the amount of weight you intend to carry. This will allow you to adjust the pack properly.

Tips for Fitting an Internal Frame

➤ Once the hip belt is fastened, make sure that the pack's stays protrude two to four inches above your shoulders. If the stays are less than two inches above your shoulders, look for a larger pack. If they are more than four inches, look for a smaller pack.

➤ If the padded ends of the hip belt overlap in front, the belt is too big. If they rub your belly, you'll need a larger belt.

➤ The pack fits you in the shoulders if the shoulder straps join the pack about two inches below the tops of your shoulders. The lower ends of the straps should be a hand's width below your armpits.

➤ Load-lifter straps should join your frame at ear level to comfortably divert pressure to the front of your shoulders. The buckles for these straps should be positioned over your collarbone. Weight can be distributed from waist to shoulders with these straps, and for the most comfort, you should vary the position as you hike.

➤ If the pack hugs your back like a child holding on for a piggyback ride, you have a proper fit.

➤ If the waist belt is distorted by the way you cinched your stabilizing belts, the pack needs readjustment. Always make sure the pack is cinched tightly.

Pack Features

Adjustable torso length: Some packs features shoulder straps that move up and down to accommodate varying torso lengths. This is a great perk because it allows you to adjust the pack for a perfect fit. Make sure, if you go for this feature, that you know whether the pack has interchangeable suspension components or a fixed suspension. You'll have less adjustability with a fixed suspension but a more stable ride. Because the shoulder straps on an adjustable frame aren't locked into the frame, the harness can become wobbly when fully loaded.

Divider between main compartment and sleeping bag compartment: This feature is offered in some packs and allows you to remove the sleeping bag separately from the rest of the gear in the bag. Some packs have a removable divider, as well.

Day-pack conversion: Some packs offer a removable lid or pocket that can be converted into a day pack or fanny pack.

Hydration bladder and feeder tube: If you would rather suck water from a tube than stop and pull out a bottle, this pack option is for you. Packs that come with a "hydration system" usually include a bladder, a bladder sleeve or pocket, a feeder tube, and a slot for the tube to exit the pack.

Interchangeable suspension parts: A system which offers you interchangeable shoulder straps and hipbelts to offer a more personalized fit.

Shovel pocket: Once a feature for the cross-country skier's snow shovel, some manufacturers now offer this pocket as a convenient place to store rain gear or a jacket.

Spindrift collar: This is similar to a turtleneck on a shirt. Basically, the bag extends or stretches to contain gear that can't be fitted into the main compartment of the pack. They are particularly useful if you have a floating top lid and they also help keep out rain, snow and dirt.

Water bottle holsters: Small pockets designed to hold your water bottle so that it is within easy reach—assuming of course, that you're not drinking from a tube.

Women's components: An interchangeable suspension system designed with women in mind. This helps conform a man's pack to a woman's body.

Women's model backpack: Some manufacturers have gotten the radical idea that women might actually appreciate a pack designed with the female form in mind. These packs typically feature narrower shoulder straps, smaller hipbelts, and shorter torsos. Imagine! Believe it or not, not all manufacturers offer women's packs and those who do seldom offer more than a single model. Lowe offers the most options with nine women packs out of a stable of about twenty-five. Maybe that's why I love my Lowe Sirocco.

Other Pack Options

Frameless Rucksacks
These approximately 2,500-cubic-inch packs are regaining their popularity. For those backpackers who can travel with the bare minimum and don't need the support and suspension of a framed pack, the rucksack is an option. Most manufacturers carry frameless packs ranging in price from less than one hundred to two hundred dollars.

The Overnight or Two-day Pack
Some hikers can live leanly enough to make long trips with the overnight or two-day type pack. The advantages of the two-day pack are obvious—not only do you carry less weight, but stress to your body is lessened. The approximately 2,000-cubic-inch internal frame packs are definitely not for everyone.

Before you purchase a smaller-than-average pack, decide how much you can do without and still enjoy your hike. Two-day/overnight packs range from under twenty-five dollars to two hundred dollars. Gregory's "The Two Day" is especially popular.

Day Packs

Most day packs are made in the same teardrop style, so look primarily at how well the pack is made. Inexpensive day packs can be purchased at any discount store, but if they are poorly padded and have little support, you won't have hiked a mile before you regret the purchase.

Leather-bottomed packs are the most durable and carry the load better, supporting the weight rather than collapsing beneath it. Make sure the shoulder straps on your day pack are very secure because this is the first place that such packs fall apart. This occurs because you are carrying the weight on your shoulders as opposed to your hips. To prevent ripping, a number of day packs have extra reinforcement where the shoulder straps connect to the sack. Another feature to look for is padding at the back of the pack. The more reinforced this section, the less likely you'll be poked and prodded by the objects inside the pack.

Features to look for in day packs include:

➤ Convenient loading through the top or the front panel
➤ Pockets for smaller items (some day packs feature a special loop to hold keys)
➤ A waist strap to keep the back from bouncing against your back
➤ Padded shoulder straps
➤ Lash points for extra gear

Day packs are usually less than one hundred dollars and most manufacturers feature a variety to choose from.

Fanny Packs

Another way to keep things handy is using a fanny pack in conjunction with your backpack. Many hikers use these miniature packs in reverse, snug across their bellies with the strap fastened in the small of the back. Cameras, water, snacks, data books, maps, and guides—whatever you need quick access to—can be carried by this method.

BACKPACKING TIP

A daypack can by handy for side trips and do double duty as a stuff sack for your sleeping bag.

Fanny packs are not as comfortable as day packs because they do not distribute the weight as well, and they often cannot carry as much as you might like to bring. They can be used along with a day pack or alone (if you have a partner carrying a day pack).

When purchasing a fanny pack, make sure the belt is well padded for comfort and the sack is sturdy enough to carry the load you intend for it. Some fanny packs are designed to carry only very light loads and will sag if heavy objects are placed in them. Also, if the fabric is thin, you may get poked and prodded by the objects inside.

Pack Covers

Although all backpacks are made of water-resistant material, moisture will seep through seams and zippers and saturate your gear if your pack is left unprotected. A pack cover can be anything from a heavy duty garbage bag, which will keep your pack dry when camping (and protect it from the dew at night), to a specially designed cover made for that purpose. These coated nylon or Gore-Tex covers, when their own seams are properly sealed, fit over your pack but still allow you to hike. They are usually fitted to your pack by elastic or a drawstring.

No matter what kind of pack cover you purchase (and you do need to buy one), you will still want to carry a heavy-duty (BIG) garbage bag to keep your pack covered at night because pack covers are not designed to protect the straps and back of your pack. A plastic garbage bag is indispensable when you are forced to camp in a downpour but don't have room for your pack in the tent.

The poncho-style pack covers work under ideal conditions only. The poncho is designed to be one-piece rain gear, covering both you and your pack at the same time. Not only do ponchos tend to tear easily, but they work only when the wind is not blowing hard. If the

wind whips up, so will your poncho, and both you and
your pack will soon be soaked. For added insurance,
anything you don't want to get wet can be slipped into a
plastic bag before being stored in your pack.

TENTS

It was cold on the Serengeti and the wind was blowing
the smoke from a savanna fire right into our faces.
Fortunately, our tent offered some protection from the
smoke and, with an occasional cough, we managed to
drift off to sleep. Several hours later, we were awakened by the eerie laughing of hyenas as they foraged
among the extinguished cooking pits searching for a
stray bit of food. Listening to the peculiar bark they
make only when frightened and which had earned
them the moniker "laughing hyenas," I was seriously
thankful that I was hidden within my tent and not sleeping out under the stars. A little while later, the scream
of some wild cat, probably a serval by the size of the
paw print we found the next day, caused me to whisper
yet another prayer of thanksgiving that I was safe within
the confines of the tent's walls.

Now, as cold and scared as I was that night on the
African savanna, I wouldn't trade that experience for
anything. Had I been in one of the Serengeti's lodges,
not only would I not have heard the hyenas and serval,
but I would not have experienced that tingle of fear and
the enormity of being so very, very close to nature.
Thanks to the tent, I was a bystander instead of dinner,
and those thin nylon walls presented me with the
opportunity for a very memorable experience.

While it is always possible (because it seems nothing is impossible) that a griz might try to enter your tent
one-way while you're quickly exiting through the newly-
made backdoor, in my experience that borders on
urban legend. For the most part, you're safe in your
tent. Heck, even the folks in *The Blair Witch Project*
remained safe as long as they stayed in their tent!

Most hikers can tell you of a time they were glad
they had their tent. They can also tell you of a time they
cursed it. Whether you decide to use a tent or some

alternative—shelters, tarps, a tent's smaller cousin, the bivy sack, or nothing at all—depends on how much uncertainty and potential discomfort you're willing to withstand. And there are some parts of this country (and this world) where a tent is an absolute necessity just to separate the predators from the prey!

Strictly speaking, a large piece of plastic and some rope is all it takes. When asked what type of tent they prefer, backpackers will give you a range of answers—from ten-dollar tarps to roomy dome tents that cost in excess of five hundred dollars.

For most hikers, a tent is the most practical means of staying dry on a rainy night. Tents keep out the rain and bugs, they are warm on cold nights because your body temperature warms the tent (sometimes by as much as ten degrees), and the tent itself dulls the force of the wind. When it's cold, wet, and buggy, tents are invaluable.

When you are making your tent wish list, remember that you will have to carry the tent. When questioned, most hikers say that the weight of a tent is its most important feature. It is often the major reason cited for carrying a tarp or a sleep screen instead (options discussed later in this chapter).

Carrying more tent than the trip calls for can be almost as much of a mistake as not having an adequate tent. As a rule of thumb, try not to carry more than four pounds of tent per person (three pounds is better). If two people are splitting the load, you will be able to carry a roomier tent. You might have one person carry the poles and fly while the other carries the rest of the tent. Alternately, you might have one person carry the whole tent and the other person carry the cooking gear and more food.

Important Tent Features

Shape
Backpacking tents are designed in a variety of shapes, each with its own benefits and drawbacks.

A-frame: This classic shape is also known, in smaller

form, as the pup tent. Roomy and easy to set-up, A-frames tend to be stable except in the wind. They are usually inexpensive but they are rarely self-supporting, and many models have a support pole in the middle of the entrance.

Modified A-frame: This is an A-frame with a center hoop pole, ridgeline pole and/or curved end poles; this eliminates the tent pole in the entrance and allows for a lot more space on the inside as well as more structural stability. Some modified A-frames are freestanding tents.

Dome: The dome is probably the most popular back-packing tent because it solves the limitations of the A-frame: It's freestanding, roomy, stable, and taut in the wind. The dome also offers plenty of head and elbow room and maximum space for its weight. Consequently, its price runs a bit higher than the A-frame. Domes tend to be a bit heavier as well, and some dome tents do not fit easily into a pack. While they come in a variety of shapes and sizes, with numerous configurations of poles, all domes are based on a geodesic design. Because of this, they offer poorer ventilation than the A-frame because there are no natural doorways, and the floor plan is often a little odd.

A note from experience—dome tents are stable in the wind only if there is something inside weighing them down. They make great kites if left empty on a windy day, especially if the door is open.

Pyramid or Tepee: This typically consists of a waterproof rainfly that drapes over a single pole (or walking stick) and stakes out to create a cone-shaped shelter. Some pyramid tents come with detachable floors. These tents are really only good for temperate climates because they are dependent on good staking, prone to condensation or frost in cold weather, and provide little protection against bugs.

Tunnel or Hoop: The tunnel tent is gaining in popularity because of the relation of floor space to the overall size (and weight) of the tent. Much lighter and more compact than other tents because of its "covered

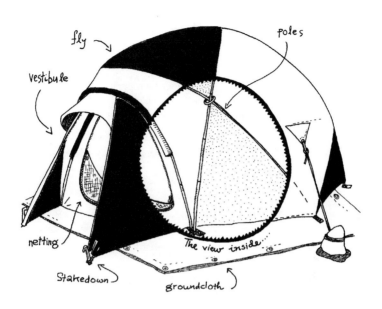

Labels on image: fly, poles, vestibule, netting, Stakedown, The view inside, groundcloth

wagon" look, hoop tents are rarely free-standing and must be pitched in the right position to provide optimum stability in wind. Sleeping in an unstaked tunnel tent is similar to bedding down in a bivy sack—it keeps you out of the elements. Some of the newer models offer a third or middle hoop and numerous guy points to improve their stability.

Ultralight or Bivy: As noted above, it is the barest minimum of tent in the tunnel design. The lightest and most compact of tents, the ultralight or bivy is not for the claustrophobic. As a matter of fact, some people classify the bivy sack as a sleeping bag rather than a tent.

Here are two related terms that you should know.

Freestanding: Dome tents and some modified A-frames do not require that you stake them down to keep them from collapsing once you've pitched the poles. Not having to stake down your tent is often convenient; it makes relocating, cleaning, and drying your tent much

147

BACKPACKING TIP

When setting up a tent, never shake out the shock-corded poles to snap them together. This will shorten their life-span and cause nicks to form at joints that will tear your tent-pole sleeves.

easier (though if it is windy out, you'll want to stake it down anyway). At times, particularly if you are camping in a place where you can't stake down a tent (on granite, for example), a freestanding tent is a necessity.

Single wall construction: This means only that the tent does not have a rainfly. These tents are usually made of a fabric that is both waterproof and breathable. Because they are made of high tech materials, they are often more expensive. But they are also lighter and easier to pitch. While the walls are designed to vent moist air while keeping the inclement weather at bay, most are susceptible to condensation in all but the driest of conditions. Seam-sealing is a must.

Room/Capacity

The second most important thing to look for in a tent is roominess. Are you tall? Is there enough room to stretch out to your full length? What about headroom? Do you have enough room to sit up comfortably if you so desire? Decide how much room is important to you before purchasing a tent. Also, will you be cooking inside your tent vestibule? On cold mornings, it isn't unusual to see steam rising from beneath the vestibules of tents as hikers heat water for coffee and oatmeal. If you think this is a possibility (something I never planned on but ended up doing countless times), make sure the vestibule has enough space beneath it so that it won't ignite. Whenever possible, place a flat rock beneath your stove for further insurance.

If a tent claims it holds one to two people, it means exactly that. Two people will be a tight fit without gear, one person will fit with gear. Keep that in mind when considering how much you want your tent to hold.

Ventilation/Floor Space/Layout

Ventilation is another important tent feature. On hot, buggy nights there is nothing worse than being stifled in

148

a poorly ventilated tent. Many tents these days offer plenty of no-see-um netting for cross ventilation as well as protection from bugs. If you are planning only cold-weather camping, this feature won't be necessary. On the other hand, if you intend to hike in every season, a good fly will compensate in cold weather for the extra ventilation needed in hot weather.

The multitude of tent designs today ensures you have many options regarding floor space and layout:

Hexagonal: This is the most common shape for dome tents. While it supplies enough room next to your elbows for assorted items, it isn't exactly designed for the very tall.

Rectangular: Most A-frames and some domes have a rectangular shape. This limits floor space but allows the tall to stretch out without worry about hitting either end of the tent.

Square: This type of floor plan is most often found in three- or four-person tents where the hikers are stacked side by side.

Miscellaneous geometric shapes: There are trape-zoidal or otherwise unusually-shaped tents that feature odd corners for stowing gear.

Usage
Tents are now available in a number of different styles that allow you to choose a make and model specific to when you intend to do the majority of your camping:

Three-season: These tents feature screened canopies and full rainflies with enough ventilation for muggy summer nights and the option for enough cover in the spring and fall to ward off late and early winter chills. Most of these tents come with two to four poles and a vestibule and offer enough room for two hikers.

Summer/screen: These ultralight tents are mostly yards of mesh with a bare minimum for a rainfly. With only one or two poles, these tents seem to capture even the faintest breeze on even the hottest of nights but they are not made for even slightly cool weather.

Convertible: This hybrid is versatile because it comes with a number of pole, window, vestibule and/or rainfly options. In the summer, you can leave a pole or full vestibule at home to carry less weight and unzip the window panels for more ventilation. When it is cold out, carry along the extra pole for added stability and the full vestibule to allow for more storage space and then close the windows to increase the warmth inside the tent.

Mountaineering/high altitude: These tents feature full coverage rainflies and are made from heavy-duty materials. They are extremely stable as they have been designed to withstand the notoriously unpredictable weather of high mountains. Most of these tents have four or more poles along with a large vestibule. Because they are made for high altitudes, they tend to be heavier and more expensive than other tents and offer less ventilation.

Tent Materials

Most backpacking tents are made of a strong but lightweight nylon taffeta or ripstop nylon. The floor and fly are usually coated with urethane or another moisture-repellent substance to prevent moisture from passing through. Although the body of the tent is often left uncovered to increase the transfer of respiration and perspiration through the tent's walls, it is not unusual to wake up in a damp tent. We have found that moisture often gathers beneath our sleeping pads. The more water resistant and "breathable" the material (like Gore-Tex), the drier you'll be and the more expensive the tent will be.

Tent Poles

In the past few years, tent poles have evolved from unyielding aluminum to shock-corded fiberglass. Segments of the pole are threaded over elastic (shock) cord that allows the user to merely snap the poles into shape rather than piece them together. When dismantling the tent, the segments are pulled apart and folded compactly.

There is still some controversy as to whether fiberglass (available as tubular, which is more flexible, and solid) is superior to aluminum when it comes to designing tent poles. Fiberglass is less expensive and more flexible than aluminum. It does not require pre-bending or any special attachments. It also provides a better packing size when folded. Its major drawback is that it is affected by weather and can break. Unlike aluminum, which can be splinted when it breaks (although it is more likely to bend), fiberglass breaks into clean splinters and must be replaced. Durability is one of aluminum's main advantages along with the fact that it is easily replaced.

Today, some tentmakers offer high-strength aluminum poles and the more expensive but stronger carbon-fiber poles.

Workmanship

Although any tent may be adequate for your needs, you may want to consider how long you would like your tent to last. Good workmanship means a long-lasting relationship with your tent. A well-made tent should have lap-felled seams around the floor seam. Lap-felled seams (like the seams on the sides of your Levi's) provide extra strength because they are actually four layers of interlocking fabric joined by a double row of stitching. On uncoated nylon tents, check for taped seams. Because nylon tends to unravel, taping or hiding the end of the fabric behind the seam with another piece of fabric will stop or stall this process. Finally, make sure that all stress points are reinforced either with extra stitching or bar tacking. Tug at the material to make sure the load is equally distributed across the reinforcement. Unequal distribution can cause premature wear on your tent.

Waterproofing

Hikers agree that waterproofing is an important feature to consider. There is nothing more miserable than sleeping in a wet tent. The better the material (i.e., Gore-Tex), the more likely you are to sleep dry. But there are some days that it rains so hard that no matter how good your tent, you're going to get wet. It may rain for days on end or you may not have spare time to dry your tent. As long as your sleeping bag is dry, you can sleep warmly, if not entirely comfortably, in a damp tent.

Set-up

You will also want to consider how easily a tent can be set up and taken down—something particularly important when it comes to pitching a tent in the rain or wind. Practice setting up your tent before you begin a long hike. The time saved by knowing your tent could mean the difference between soggy and dry clothes.

Color

While color is a matter of personal preference, there are reasons why you may choose one over the other. Bright, neon-like colors are good only in search-and-rescue conditions because the blinding material will stand out against the snow or the green and brown of the woods or the sand in the desert. For the same reason, bright colors might be annoying to other backpackers, causing a visual disturbance in the wilderness.

If your tent is pale green or blue, the bright sunlight filtered through your tent will form a soft light inside. On rainy or overcast days, the light inside your tent could be slightly depressing. These colors are also a bit more inconspicuous in the backcountry.

Orange and yellow fabric are great in foul weather because they produce a brighter light inside your tent. Gray, light gray, white, and tan are popular colors now and are also pleasing to the eye inside and outside the tent. Blue and gold are also used in many tents.

Ground Cloths

One time we didn't take a ground cloth and the first night on the trail we regretted it: the dew and moist ground soaked through, getting everything wet. A plastic ground cloth, will not only help to keep your tent dry; it will help to prolong the life of your tent.

Keeping Your Tent Dry

To keep your tent as dry as possible, it is important to seal its seams. Although parts of the tent are coated, the needle holes in the seams will allow water to enter your tent. Buy some sealer (available at most outdoors stores) and follow the directions. Then seal the seams again. Depending on how much you use your tent, the sealer can last up to two years. If you use your tent a lot, seal the seams more often. On an extended backpacking trip (five months or more), it may be necessary to reseal your seams at least once, if not several times.

You can buy premade ground cloths, but it's a lot cheaper just to buy some plastic and cut it to fit the bottom of the tent. If the ground cloth is larger than your tent, you are likely to wake up in the middle of a rainy night sitting in the puddle that has formed beneath your tent. By cutting it to within an inch of your tent's width and length, you'll wake up much drier. Another possibility (rather than setting your tent on top of the ground cloth) is putting the ground cloth inside the tent. The bottom of your tent gets wet, but the equipment and people inside stay drier.

Digging a trench around your tent can help keep the rain from running under it, but this is hard on the environment; we recommend that you do not follow this outdated practice. We never met a hiker who had the time or the inclination for such a job. After a day of hiking, who wants to spend the time in the rain and mud digging a trench?

Caring for Your Tent

Never store your tent when it is damp. Make sure it is thoroughly dry if you are going to put it up for more than a day. Otherwise, the next time you pull it out of its stuff sack, you're bound to find it spotted with mold and mildew. It is important to make sure that even the seams are dry and that all the dirt has been cleaned from the stakes, the poles, and the bottom of the tent.

When packing your tent, stuff it rather than rolling or folding it. If the fabric is stressed at the same points every time, it will eventually crack and peel. Never store your tent in your car or its trunk. Cars can become as hot as a furnace, and those high temperatures can damage the coating on the tent's material.

To clean your tent, use a damp sponge and mild soap. Set it up before wiping it down and then let it air dry. If your tent is smeared with pitch or grease, use a bit of kerosene to remove it. Never machine wash your tent.

Never leave your tent set up in the sun for long periods of time. If you are camping in one spot for several days, cover your tent with its fly during the day to protect it from the sun's ultraviolet rays, which can damage the nylon material. A rainfly is less susceptible to the sun's damage and can be replaced at less expense than the tent.

Keep your tent poles clean to avoid corrosion of the metal. A silicone lubricant applied occasionally will help protect your poles and will keep them in good working order. Apply the silicone to your tent's zippers to keep them working smoothly when it's freezing outside. Also, to avoid damaging your tent, carry your poles and pegs in a separate stuff sack.

Repair kits for your tent are very helpful and are available from most outdoors stores. There are several kits, but the best, in my opinion, is made by Outdoor Research. This inexpensive kit contains adhesive-backed ripstop and adhesive-backed taffeta fabric to repair holes in tent and fly fabric; mosquito netting, needle, and thread to repair holes in no-see-um fabric; an aluminum splint and duct tape to repair broken tent poles; and braided Dacron utility cord in case you need to jerry-rig a guyline, tent-peg loop, et cetera. A small tent repair kit should take care of most of the mishaps that can occur to a tent on a backpacking trip (unless you set the tent ablaze with your cooking stove or campfire).

Tarps

If you are going out for short trips where you know the weather will cooperate, or you are willing endure an amount of discomfort in exchange for less weight and bulk, then you will want to consider the tarp. However, one of the drawbacks with a tarp is that it doesn't keep the bugs out. When the mosquitoes or black flies start to swarm, you will be at their mercy. Some hikers who rely on tarps for shelter from the rain also pack sleep screens to keep the bugs at bay. Escaping from bugs is no joke, and most hikers agree that a tent or sleep screen is indispensable when the mosquitoes, deerflies, and blackflies arrive to torture innocent hikers. When hiking out West (because of snow, grizzly bears, et cetera), you're probably better off in a tent. On the other hand, should you be hiking a beach trail in the summer, a sleep screen and tarp to protect you from bugs and rain would likely be more than adequate.

If you decide on a tarp, you have a number of options. Tarps are both inexpensive and lightweight, although some can end up weighing and costing as much as a tent.

One option tarpers have is to purchase a polyethylene sheet (one brand is Visqueen) that is a translucent white and comes in both 9- by 12-feet and 12- by 12-feet sizes. Unfortunately, these tarps do not come with grommets for you to attach your ropes so you will need to fashion some sort of clamp—be it a stone wrapped in the material and secured with a rope or the popular Visklamp that uses a rubber ball and a device to secure the ball and rope.

A number of tarps are available with metal grommets, including ripstop woven polyethylene and coated nylon. While the reinforced polyethylene is cheaper, it will decay faster in the sun than the nylon. The best tarp size is the 10- by 12-feet.

Once you have chosen your tarp, you will need the following to set it up: approximately fifty feet of one-quarter-inch braided nylon rope for the tarp's ridgeline; a hundred feet of one-eighth-inch braided nylon rope for guylines; six to eight tent pegs to secure the tarp should there be a lack of other objects (trees, roots, rocks, bushes); and of course, cloth tape or a tent repair kit.

Tent Tip

Before going on any backpacking trip, you should know your tent (and all your other equipment for that matter) backwards and forwards. Set it up in your backyard (or if that is impossible, your living room) over and over again until you can do it in your sleep. This will be invaluable once you're in the backcountry and setting up your tent in a downpour or in a raging wind.

Sleeping under the Stars

If you have a wonderfully comfortable sleeping bag, sleeping out under the stars is a viable option as long as you have a tent or tarp as backup. If you are hiking in the mountains, weather can change in an instant and you will need a backup plan.

Advantages to sleeping outdoors (other than not having to set up a tent or tarp) are falling asleep under the stars and waking up to a sunrise. With your head outdoors, you can fall asleep and wake up to the wonders of nature.

As long as you're in a relatively safe area, the weather is good, and your sleeping bag warm, there is no reason not to sleep under what Shakespeare called "this most excellent canopy . . . this brave o'er hanging firmament, this majestical roof fretted with golden fire."

But in some areas you may be putting your life in jeopardy. For example, in grizzly country you might find yourself nose-to-nose with a bear that is not too happy with a trespasser. As long as you use a little common sense, you should be able to reap the benefits of fresh-air camping.

WATER FILTERS

When backpacking, your water sources will vary from beaver ponds to cool, free-flowing springs. And you never know where you're going to run into one of those little nasties that can make a backpacking trip your ultimate nightmare. Fortunately, yet again, technology has produced more than its fair share of water filters to choose from. But how do you choose and what are you trying to get rid of? Well, I'll tell you . . .

The School of Water Treatment

There are two important factors to weigh before deciding on an appropriate filter—how easy and reliable is it to use and how effective it is at filtering.

The first one is easy. Just pick up the latest copy of *Backpacker* magazine's Gear Guide to find the most up-to-date information on what has been tested and what the testers personally think of each filter. These reviews focus on the mechanics of the filter—how easy it is to pump, how efficient it is, how durable it is.

The second category is tougher. There are, as yet, no independent tests done on water filters to determine how effective they measure up to the manufacturer's claims. Basically, you just gotta take their word for it. However, I can tell you what you need to look for in a filter.

Essentially there are two types of water treatments—filters and purifiers. Filters are the most common type used. They filter out protozoans and certain size bacteria (see "Pore Size" later in this chapter). Purifiers filter out everything a filter does as well as most viruses.

Whether you go for a filter or a purifier depends on how big a risk you are willing to take. Obviously, because they strain out viruses, the purifier is the safest option. On the other hand, they are more expensive than filters, take longer, and tend to clog more easily. One compromise is to purchase a filter that comes with an attachable iodine cartridge that will ward off some of the viruses, particularly if you're backpacking in some foreign countries. More and more filters are offering iodine as one of the filter components.

Types of Filters

There are three types to choose from:

Gravity feed filter: A great filter (if you're not in a hurry). Water is scooped into a reservoir and then the filter is hung from a tree or something along those lines. While you wait (or tend to chores) the water trickles through the filter element into a receptacle. Basically, a portable Brita.

The Hiker Filter by Pur is typical of most pump filters.

Pump filter: This filter uses a hand pump to suck the water through an intake hose before pushing it through the filter element and out through the outlet hose. Just stand over the stream (or pond or river, etc.) and pump away. These filters are faster and more efficient than gravity feed filters, and the better filters are fairly easy to pump. Because these filters require a lot of mechanical parts susceptible to breaking and clogging, always carry along a repair kit and extra parts.

Straw/squeeze bottle filter: These are water bottles with a filter element fitted within the lid or the straw that runs into the bottle. It works by dipping the bottle in the water source to fill it and then sucking or squeezing to filter. The filter in this type tends to remove only the larger organisms although some bottles offer an iodine back-up system.

Most of the filters on the market today use what is known as a depth filter. All this means is that the filter element has some depth to it that allows it time to capture the microorganisms that can make hikers feel like death warmed over. Depth filters can be cleaned by either scrubbing or backwashing (which is pumping the

water backwards through the filter to release the clogged sediment). Surface filters are also used but more rarely. These are essentially single-layer filters that catch as catch can.

Katadyn's Combi Water Filter is another typical pumpfilter.

The Heart Of The Filter
The following are the different types of active ingredients used in both styles of filter. All filters must be replaced occasionally.

Carbon: Carbon is often used with other filter materials to strain out organic chemicals like herbicides, pesticides, and chlorine. Carbon can also make bad-tasting water a little tastier.

Ceramic: This porous material has lots of little nooks and crannies (kind of like an English muffin) to capture microorganisms. Ceramic filters last a long time and can be cleaned over and over again before they have to be replaced. The major drawback is that ceramic is fragile and brittle and will often crack in cold weather.

Fiberglass or glass fiber: Long and slick, glass fibers can be molded into the intricate designs needed to catch microorganisms. While not as long-lasting as

ceramic, it is less fragile and doesn't crack in cold weather. Fiberglass cannot be scrubbed. Read the manufacturer's instructions on how to clean your filter.

Proprietary: Yes, it's that secret code word that manufacturers use to mean, "we ain't tellin' what our filter uses." So, how and why these work, we may never know. But, if you purchase a proprietary filter, the manufacturer will instruct you how to take care of it.

Pore Size

Another option to look at when purchasing a filter is the pore size. This is the size of the openings in the filter element and determines how big something has to be to get caught in the filter, which in turn determines the types of particles or microorganisms that are caught. To remove protozoans (Giardia, for example), the pore size must be no more than four microns. But, to remove bacteria, the pore size has to be no more than 0.2 microns in size (big difference in the world of microns). But if you want to hear something really scary, some viruses can be as small as 0.0004 microns in size. What does that mean? Well, the period at the end of this sentence is approximately 500 microns in size. Yikes! What does that mean? It means that no filter can effectively remove all types of viruses. On the other hand, the chance of happening on one of those micro-micro viruses is very slim.

When picking out a filter, check for the "absolute" pore size as opposed to the "nominal" size. The absolute will tell you that the filter will not pass anything larger than that size. The nominal, on the other hand, only lets you know that a filter will remove most, but not all, particles larger than that size.

OTHER EQUIPMENT

While being interviewed on CNN about hiking vacations, Frank and I were asked by a caller what we left at home in order to keep our packs light. The kitchen sink, I thought at the time. But upon later reflection I realized it wasn't such a silly question after all. What we leave behind to keep our packs light is different than what others leave behind.

I do not miss television when I am on a backpacking trip, so it's easy for me to leave mine behind. But there are those who can't live without it and there are now televisions small enough to fit in a pack or even on your wrist. Some people carry guitars while others can't live with out their tapes and portable tape player. And these days, don't be surprised to see someone ambling down the trail talking on their cell phone. Yes, I know, where is the sense in that? I thought we came to the wilderness to escape the hassles of everyday life! SIGH.

I usually carry a book and a journal while back-packing and I often try to find a book with some re-lation to the outdoors—perhaps something by Aldo Leopold, John Muir, or Ed Abbey; Frank carries camera equipment. Another of our concessions to luxury is spices. (Trail meals are unappetizing enough without the garlic, pepper, and Tabasco.)

While most of us agonize over what to take and what to leave behind, some people go to extremes to cut

The Bad Guys

OK. So what exactly are we looking to remove? Most water filters/puri-fiers are designed to remove some or all of the following:

➤ Bacteria. Smaller than protozoans, bacteria can range in size from 0.2 microns to 10 microns. They cause problems ranging from food poisoning to typhoid fever.

➤ Cryptosporidium. Crypto, for short, is one of those really tenacious little nasties. Unfortunately, no one knows for sure how prevalent this little bug is. It is found less frequently than giardia, but unlike giardia, even iodine cannot kill crypto. The only way to avoid them is to boil your water or use a filter with a pore size no larger than 2 microns.

➤ Organic chemicals. Blame this one on your fellow human beings, who created them. These contaminants are the result of industrial and agricultural pollution and include pesticides, herbicides, diesel fuel, fertilizers, and the run-off from strip mines—all of which are things you can come in contact with even in the deepest of wilderness. In general, watch out in areas that look like they have been farmed, logged, mined or used industrially. Gee, that pretty much covers at least the lower 48! And, if the water smells bad or is discolored, be extra wary.

➤ Protozoans. These hard-shelled, single-celled parasites or cysts are the largest of the water-borne microorganisms. They range in size from 2 to 15 microns and are the family to which the carrier of that infamous hiker disease, Beaver Fever, otherwise known as Giardia lamblia, belongs.

➤ Viruses. The smallest of the small, viruses range in size from 0.0004 to 0.1 microns. They are probably the most dangerous of the water-borne monsters because the types of diseases they carry—polio, hepatitis—are enough to make the strongest backpacker want to high tail it to the nearest Hyatt. Fortunately, in this day and age, very few people have not been inoculated against those diseases (and if you haven't been, you should be, just in case). And if you're still scared, buy the smallest micron-pore available.

down on everything in order to reduce the weight they are carrying. They even go so far as to cut the handles off their toothbrushes and the corners off their maps.

RELIEF VALVE

HOUSING

"OPPOSING ACTION" LEVER

"MARATHON" CERAMIC FILTER (inside)

INTAKE HOSE

ADAPTER BASE

CLEAN-SLIDE COVER

(PATENTED) INLET FLOAT

CERAMIC GAUGE

In addition to the basics—tent, pack, boots, sleeping bag, etc.—there are some other articles you will probably want to consider taking along on a hike, especially if you're out for a night or more. Carefully select the equipment you really need and leave at home things that are extra, or even ridiculous. You will be much more comfortable without the added weight.

Lighting

Very simply put, it is a good idea to bring along some source of light for evenings at camp and on the trail. From time to time, it will be a relief to have a light to help find things in a dark tent or shelter.

Lanterns

The big, heavy, white gas lanterns have a place in camping but not in backpacking. They are bright and efficient but are far too heavy and bulky to carry along on a backpacking trip. There are also heavy battery-powered lanterns that weigh even more and are made for family camping.

Candle lanterns (some of which can be equipped to use gas) are your best bet if you want to carry a lantern. We started out on our first backpacking trip with a candle lantern, and have continued to use ours, although we have also purchased a flashlight. They weigh as little as six ounces (sold by Limelight Productions, REI, and Early Winters and at some outdoors stores under the generic—Candle Lantern). One candle will give you as much as eight hours of illumination. The light produced by a candle lantern is not very bright, but it works better than a flashlight for cooking, cleaning, reading, writing, or making camp in the dark. Why? Because the light is more diffuse (it doesn't have to be directed), and candles are cheaper than batteries.

The candle lantern is safer and more economical than a candle alone. Housed in metal and glass, it is less likely to start a fire if it tips over, and because it is protected from the wind, it does not burn as quickly. You can purchase a candle lantern for ten to twenty dollars and refill candles for about fifty cents a piece.

Small oil and gas lanterns burn for up to twenty hours per fill-up and cost about twenty to twenty-five dollars. They weigh the same as candle lanterns, and some can take different grades of lamp oil, including citronella (the insect repellent). The main disadvantages are the need to carry extra oil as well as the possibility of spilling the oil.

All lanterns are equipped with a hanger and can often be rigged to hang from the apex of your tent by an attached nylon cord. Many tents have loops in the apex that will allow you to fasten a cord. If your tent does not have a loop at its apex, it may be possible to add a loop of Velcro or sew on a loop yourself. Some tents have loops in the corners designed to hold gear lofts from which you can rig a line to hold a candle lantern. Remember to keep the lantern a safe distance from the material of the tent so you won't burn holes in the tent or set it afire.

Flashlights

On our first backpacking trip, we didn't think we'd need a flashlight because we had a candle lantern. Whether or not you decide to carry a candle lantern, you will find a flashlight very handy.

First of all, it's not easy to wake up in the middle of the night and light a candle lantern just so you won't walk into briars (or worse!) when looking for a spot to relieve yourself. Second, if you intend to hike for any length of time, don't be surprised if you end up walking at night. Whether this happens intentionally or unintentionally, you'll need a flashlight. Candle lanterns produce good light but are hard to direct.

The flashlight you take backpacking needn't be really powerful. Most hikers use the smaller flashlights equipped with two AA batteries. They are small but adequate. Mini-mags are popular with hikers because they provide a lot of output for very little weight.

Some examples of candle-powered lanterns.

Flashlights that require two D-cell batteries, or more, are too heavy, and the illumination is overkill for what you'll need when hiking.

Remember, though, if you decide to depend solely on a flashlight for your light, you will need a steady supply of batteries. If you choose to use a flashlight rather than a candle lantern for your light, you may want to look into headlamps because they provide a light source that does not need to be handheld.

Headlamps

If you're seriously into night hiking, then you have another good reason to look into purchasing a headlamp. These illuminators are usually on a headband and light the way ahead of you for approximately 250 feet. They are safer than flashlights for night hiking because they leave your hands free.

But headlamps are good for more than just night hiking. They also leave your hands free for cooking, cleaning, and setting up your tent. But they, too, use batteries and have a few other drawbacks, as well.

Headlamps are designed two ways—either with the lamp and batteries attached to the headband or with the lamp attached to the headband and the battery unit (sometimes including yet another light) attached to a belt and connected to the headband by wire. The problem with the all-in-one unit is that it tends to be heavy and to induce headaches if you use it for long periods of time. The problem with the latter is that the wires can get caught by branches, arms, etc. The more loose parts you have, the more likely you are to have a short in the wire. Advantages to the two-part system: it does eliminate headaches and the batteries stay warm when kept on your person (cold weather can render batteries useless).

One important factor to keep in mind when purchasing a headlamp is that battery switches tend to come on while sitting in your pack. The Petzl has a screw-type off/on switch that eliminates this problem. Otherwise, you will probably need a piece of duct tape to make sure your headlamp remains in the off position while packed away.

Depending on your needs, there are a number of functional headlamps available. For three-season back-packing, the Hartford Easter Seals HL-4AA (also sold as the REI Combi and the Black Diamond Forty Below), REI Cordless, Panasonic Headlamp, and Petzl EO3 Micro are your best bets. Except for the Petzl, which uses only two AA batteries and requires more "fill-ups," the others have decent battery burn times (approximately eighteen hours at seventy degrees).

Major manufacturers of headlamps include Hartford Easter Seals, Hitachi, Panasonic, Petzl, REI and Streamlight.

Toiletries
Depending on the length of your hiking trip, you may want to consider bringing along items such as towel, shampoo/soap, deodorant, razors/shaving cream, toothbrush/toothpaste, eyecare items and toilet paper.

Towel
Most hikers do not carry a towel, per se. We usually carry bandannas and one handcloth for the purpose of washing and/or drying. In warm weather, we let the sun

Two styles of head lamps by Petzl.

do the job of drying our skin. In cold weather, we use the cloth to hand bathe ourselves with heated water and then we dry off with a bandanna.

For those who need a towel, the super absorbent Pack Towl that the manufacturers boast can absorb up to ten times its weight and then dries quickly (which is important because who wants to carry around a soggy, one-pound towel). Most outdoors stores offer this towel and other variations on the Pack Towl.

Shampoo/Soap

Never, ever, wash yourself or your hair in a stream, a pond, or another body of water. And never use anything but biodegradable soap. Would you want to drink water that someone had rinsed soap off into? A lot of the water sources along trails provide drinking water for hikers as well as for animals.

Biodegradable soap (at least the widely available Dr. Bronner's) does not work as a shampoo. While you can't beat it for washing your body, it leaves your hair lank and greasy. Before depending on a biodegradable soap as an all-round cleaner, I would suggest testing it on the various things you plan to use it for (i.e., your hair, your body, clothes, pots and pans). There are a number of biodegradable soaps available from outdoor stores, including Mountain Suds, Bio-suds and Sunshower Soap.

There is a soap product on the market called NO-Rinse that requires no water for a shampoo and only one quart of water to bathe. N/R Laboratories claims that you simply massage NO-Rinse in and towel dry it out.

If your soap doesn't work as a shampoo, most discount department stores (such as Wal-Mart and K-Mart) and drugstores offer trial or sample size products that are great for backpacking. Shampoos are commonly available in sample sizes as are toothpastes and lotions. I've used a variety of shampoos while backpacking, but if you can find a biodegradable shampoo you'll lessen your detrimental effect on the environment. As with soaps, though, never wash your hair with shampoo in or near a water source.

By the way, even the most hard-core hikers bathe occasionally.

Deodorant

While soap is a necessity, deodorant is considered optional. We use it only on visits to town. Otherwise, there's no one around to smell you but yourself (and other smelly hikers)! You may also want to consider that the less smelly you are, in terms of artificial odors such as perfumed deodorants, the less likely you'll be to scare wildlife away or to attract unwanted insects.

The most natural way to deodorize yourself is by using what is known as a deodorant rock. Composed of natural mineral salts, this crystal-like deodorant supposedly lasts a full year with normal use. My husband and I tried one at home and found that unless you thoroughly cleanse your underarms before each application, your underarm odor builds up very quickly. On the other hand, this makes it an ideal deodorant for backpacking because you would only use it occasionally, anyway. Deodorant rocks are available at health food stores and through some catalogs. Two of the more popular brands are NATURE'S Pure Crystal Deodorant and Le Crystal Naturel.

Another relatively natural way to deodorize yourself is to use a baking soda—based powder such as Shower to Shower. My father has used it successfully for years.

If you're not interested in these natural methods of stopping perspiration odor, you can always carry your favorite deodorant in its sample or regular size.

Do keep in mind, especially during the hot and humid days of summer, that you probably reek. The longer you're out on the trail, deodorantless, the more you become accustomed to your body's odor. This, believe it or not, isn't half as bad as the odor perspiration leaves in your clothes. The clothes you hike in ought to be washed every so often, as well.

People will be more willing to give needy hikers a hitch if they look presentable and smell as inoffensive as possible after spending days or weeks in the woods.

While staying with some friends during one backpacking trip we left a lasting impression on our hostess's olfactory nerves. She later told us that on our first night there she had prowled about the house, sniffing, unable to sleep or to determine the cause of the ungodly smell. Finally she stepped into the entranceway and found the odoriferous source of her nocturnal wanderings—our boots. She quickly banished them outdoors. Embarrassing? You betchum, Red Rider. When someone offers you hospitality while backpacking, the last thing you want to do is offend them. If someone invites you to stay, kindly leave your boots outside. Remember, you're used to their smell, but others will find it overwhelming. Most people will be too polite to mention it, so it's up to you to keep your odor under control, at least when you're off the trail.

Razors/Shaving Cream

Most men opt to grow a beard when hiking, although some do take the trouble to shave every day or now and then. The same goes for women—many prefer to let the hair under their arms and on their legs grow out while hiking. It's all a matter of preference. I shave at least once a week, using biodegradable soap and a disposable razor, when long-distance hiking because I am more comfortable that way. A battery-operated electric razor is another option.

Toothbrush/Toothpaste

Don't brush your teeth near a water source. Dig a small hole to spit into and then cover your spit.

As for toothcare products, there are a variety of options on the market, but a child's toothbrush works great because it is small and lightweight! Toothpaste can easily be purchased in sample sizes or you might want to try using baking soda that you can transfer to a small bottle for convenience.

Eyecare

I am continually amazed at the number of hikers who elect to wear contact lenses during their long-distance hikes. But as risky as it seems, I also wear contacts; although I carry a pair of glasses just in case. The new, disposable, daily and extended-wear lenses are easy to care for and the cleaning fluid does not add much weight to my pack. Personally, unless I am sitting still, my body heat raised by the exertion of hiking, fogs my glasses up so badly, they're useless. And, when I'm sweaty they tend to slide off my nose.

I remember one night counting three out of six of us wearing contact lenses. Two wore glasses and only Frank had 20/20 vision. Improvements for hikers extend beyond backpacking equipment!

And now, you don't even have to worry if you can't get your hands clean enough to remove your contacts. There are several products available now, such as Purell Instant Hand Sanitizer, that allow you to clean your hands by rubbing them with an antiseptic gel cleanser. Just make sure you wait a few seconds for the alcohol to dry before handling your lenses.

Toilet Paper

Of course you know you need to bring toilet paper. Even day hikers need it occasionally. A good way to pack it is to scrunch it flat and stick it in a resealable plastic bag. By removing the cardboard tube in the center and unraveling the paper from the inside, you will find that your toilet paper crushes down flatter in its plastic bag. Scott toilet tissue seems to have the most paper for the money.

And, while we're on the subject . . . one of the worst sights we saw while hiking through the Great Smoky Mountains were the wads of toilet paper scattered through the woods near shelters. Please take the time to dig a cat hole for your toilet paper and for your feces. A backpacker's trowel weighs a mere two ounces and costs next to nothing. That's well worth the "trouble" when you consider how much it will lessen your environmental impact.

Never relieve yourself near a water source. Always find a site at least fifty yards downhill or to the side of a water source. This is for the protection of wildlife as well as other hikers. According to the Centers for Disease Control, beavers living downstream from national parks and forests contract giardiasis (caused by humans) more often than humans pick up the infamous stomach ailment.

A note to women: Urination for male backpackers is as easy, if not easier because there is no seat to lift, as it is in the "real" world. And although some trails offer the occasional outhouse, the chances of your stumbling upon one at the appropriate moment are about nil. Even then, you're likely to find a note requesting you to relieve yourself in the woods because some outhouses are reserved for defecation only.

If you're strong enough and have a good aim, it is possible to pee with your pack on—release the hipbelt, drop your drawers to your knees, bend your knees a bit, lean forward with your hands on your knees for support, relax and go.

Another option is take off your pack and find what Kathleen Meyer, author of *How to Shit in the Woods*, calls the perfect pose. Find two rocks, a rock and a log, two logs, or if necessary, a steep slope and a log or rock. Sitting on one, you balance your feet on the other and avoid the splashed boots that are so common when women try to pee outdoors.

A third option is a funnel, but make sure you purchase one with a long hose. The funnels are designed to slip easily into your pants and transport your urine outside. I never even got up the nerve to try mine, feeling certain that no matter what I did I'd end up with soggy britches.

Menstruation is another problem women face in the wilderness. On most trips, it's going to be "pack it in, pack it out"; so make sure you bring along enough resealable bags to hold your used tampons or napkins. Burning is another option, but the fire must be very hot to completely burn a tampon or napkin. Never burn plastic applicators because they release poisons into the air.

Your best choice is going to be an applicatorless tampon such as OB. They are compact and produce the least amount of waste all the way around. Once used, wrap them in a bit of toilet paper and seal in a plastic bag until you reach a suitable dumping station. You should never drop your tampons or napkins into a latrine nor should you bury them because it will take them years to disintegrate, if animals don't dig them up first.

First aid Kit

Keeping in mind the fact that it is next to impossible to create a perfect first aid kit, the following is a list of what makes up a close-to-perfect kit:

➤ A Ziploc or other brand zipper-lock plastic bag to hold the items in your first aid kit.

➤ Approximately six one-inch by three-inch Band-Aids. These can be used to cover most scratches, cuts and scrapes.

➤ Two four-inch by four-inch sterile gauze pads that can be cut down or doubled up depending on the size of the wound.

➤ A roll of athletic tape one inch wide by ten yards in length. This has a variety of uses from holding on the sterile gauze to wrapping ankles.

➤ Tincture of benzoin. Not only does this liquid toughen feet but it helps tape stick better when rubbed on the skin.

➤ A couple of butterfly Band-Aids for closing small, gaping wounds.

➤ An individually wrapped sanitary napkin, which is great for stanching heavily bleeding wounds.

➤ Povidone-iodine ointment. This has a number of uses: it disinfects wounds (straight from the tube); it dissolves in water for a wash for larger scrapes; and it can even be used as a lubricant or to treat water in an emergency.

➤ Moleskin to treat hot spots and blisters.

➤ Your favorite painkiller for aches, pains, fever, et cetera.

➤ A six-inch-wide elastic wrap (such as made by Ace). These can be used to wrap strains and sprains as well as to hold bandages in place, constrict snake bites, compress heavy bleeding or splint a broken bone.

➤ A few safety pins always come in handy. They can be used to hold the Ace bandage, drain blisters, repair clothing, et cetera.

➤ A few antihistamine tablets such as Benadryl to combat insect bites and poison oak or ivy.

➤ Pepto-Bismol or some similar tablets for upset stomachs.

➤ Scissors and tweezers. (You may be able to find a pocket knife with these items. My Victorinox has both and they have come in handy many times.)

Other items to consider, depending on the time of year and the location of your hike, are meat tenderizer or Sting-eze for insect bites, sunscreen, alcohol to help remove ticks (and toughen feet), lip balm, lotion, prescription drugs if you need them, a bee sting kit if you are allergic to insect stings, and DEET repellent for mosquitoes and other insects (see the information on insects in the On the Trail section of this book). Remember that a first aid kit is a very personal thing. For example, if you have trouble with constipation at home, by all means carry a laxative while hiking.

I use lip balm (Chap Stick works best for me) constantly both at home and while hiking. I can't abide the feeling of chapped lips and I always carry several tubes of Chap Stick with me where ever I go. Other good lip balms are Blistex, Carmex, and Labiosin. You can find many options both at drugstores and outdoors stores.

Some people have problems with hemorrhoids while hiking and always include Preparation H or Tucks Pads in their kits. Some women may find it necessary to carry birth control pills.

Hiking in the summer, desert, or snow might make it necessary for you to carry a sunscreen with a sun protection factor (SPF) in line with your skin's sensitivity to the sun. The higher the SPF number, the less likely you are to be burned. As with lip balms, you can find a wide range of sunscreens to choose from at your local drug, discount, and outdoors stores.

Lotion is another product you may wish to add to your kit if you intend to be hiking in hot, dry weather. Some sunscreens combine lotion with the screen or you may wish to carry a sample size of your favorite brand.

Remember, though, that baby oil acts as a suntan lotion as well as a skin softener and could be potentially dangerous if you intend to use it as a lotion. If you will be doing some desert hiking you may want to carry along a lotion with aloe vera that will help soothe any sunburn you might get. If your skin is very sensitive to the sun, a sunburn therapy such as Solarcaine or Ahhh might be worth the extra weight in your first aid kit.

But, unless you have a special need or problem, do not carry too many specific items in your first aid kit. The kit and its contents should be as versatile as possible. It won't matter that you have to cover a two-inch wide wound with a four-inch wide bandage, for example.

Also, remember to repack your first aid kit seasonally or yearly. Medicines expire and may need to be replaced so always check the expiration dates before heading out on any trip. And there is no use carrying insect repellent on a winter trip when there are no bugs around. Your first-aid kit should reflect your personal needs as well as the season and geographic area through which you're hiking.

Most importantly, do not carry anything in your kit that you do not know how to use. For example, a suture kit will be useless to you unless you have been trained in suturing wounds. Don't carry prescription medicines unless you are fully aware of their side-effects and how to use them.

Depending on how safety-conscious you are, there are all sorts of items available to ease your mind while hiking. Everything from dental emergency kits to accident report forms can be purchased for your first aid kit.

Although I've never known any one to use one, some people feel safer if they carry along a snake-bite kit. There are several kits on the market ranging from five to fifteen dollars. The simplest kit contains two big suction cups plus a smaller suction cup for bites on small surfaces such as fingers. The kit also includes a lymph constrictor, scalpel, antiseptic vial, and instructions. The ten-dollar Extractor is a double-chamber vacuum pump with four cup sizes, antiseptic, Band-Aids, a safety razor, instructions, and a carrying case. The Extractor is the only recommended first aid for snake bites these days and it is said that even it does little to help.

Outdoors stores offer a variety of first aid kits ranging in price from eight to eighty dollars. Outdoor Research, Adventure Medical Kits, and REI are some of the major manufacturers of first aid kits.

Items for Emergencies

When it comes to emergencies, some people like to carry along a mirror, flares, and a whistle. I carry a mirror, anyway, because I need it to insert my contact lenses, but you may want to consider carrying a mirror should you need it to signal someone below or above you. If your watch has a reflective surface you can discard the mirror and use it instead. Some compasses have sighting mirrors that can be used for signaling or you can use foil, your stove's windscreen (if it reflects) or even your sunglasses. Signal mirrors, on the other hand, are usually too heavy to be carried by a backpacker.

I've never carried one, but some backpackers feel safer if they carry along a flare or smoke bomb for emergencies. The bombs emit clouds of orange or red smoke that can be seen from both the ground and the air. Flares can be shot up into the air and usually burn for an average of seven seconds. I have seen both smoke bombs and flares available through catalogs—eight dollars for the bomb, sixteen dollars for three flares—and most outdoors stores keep them in stock as well.

For use in both an emergency and as a warning to bears, you can also carry a whistle in your "emergency kit." Just make sure you use the whistle only in emergency situations, because in addition to crying "wolf," you'll also be disturbing the other people out there who are seeking peace and quiet. If you purchase a whistle, make sure the balls inside are made of metal or plastic. Cork, if it gets wet, will ruin your whistle. Survival whistles can be purchased for under three dollars.

There is a gadget on the market called the Survivo II that includes an accurate compass, waterproof matchcase, whistle, striking flint and signal mirror. It is packed in a 4.5-inch by 1.25-inch case and weighs a mere ounce.

Sunglasses

There are so many options when it comes to sunglasses that I cannot begin to recommend any one particular brand. If you do carry sunglasses, and I recommend that you do, make sure that the lenses are designed to filter out the sun's harmful rays—both ultraviolet and infrared. Sunglasses are especially essential for desert and snow hiking where the sun reflects off the ground and into your eyes.

Sunglasses can be purchased from for as little or as much as you want to spend. Straps to hold your sunglasses around your neck—Chums, Croakies, and others—are worth the extra money because they keep you from losing your sunglasses. This is especially beneficial if you just paid a lot of money for your shades.

There are also a number of other "gadgets" that can be purchased for sunglasses (and glasses, if you wear them) including defoggers and lens cleaners, cases, windguards, and clip-on sunshades for eyeglass wearers.

Sunglasses are now manufactured for children, including glasses that filter out ultraviolet and infrared rays.

Sunscreen

Walking in shorts and a T-shirt leaves a hiker exposed to the sun's rays for several hours a day. To prevent burning, wear a sunscreen or sunblock. If you have fair or sensitive skin, you will need a sunscreen with a sun protection factor (SPF) of at least 15.

Water Bottles

There are two essential choices when it comes to carrying water these days—whether to go in for the hydration system or whether stick to the time-tested water bottle.

Hydration system: The hydration system is basically a water bladder that either comes as part of your pack or fits inside your pack or that you wear almost like a backpack (harder to do if you're already wearing a pack). They seem to hold, fairly standardly, about

seventy ounces of water. You get at the water by sucking on a tube that stays constantly at the ready over
your shoulder and near your mouth.

Water bottles: The Nalgene is still one of the most
popular water bottles with its easy-to-fill widemouth
design. Also popular is the sports-type bottle with its
screw-off cap and pull-out drinking spout.

The style of water bottle you choose is a matter of preference, and not being real familiar with the hydration
system, I cannot recommend one over the other.

Binoculars

Carrying binoculars is a matter of preference but modern technology has made them both lightweight and
tough so the heavy, bulky binoculars of yore are no
longer an excuse not to bother.

When purchasing binoculars, there are two things
to keep in mind besides weight and durability. First of
all, binoculars are identified by two numbers: the magnification and the lens size (for example, 10 x 25). It
will be these two numbers that determine the quality of
your binoculars.

Magnification: The larger the number, the greater the magnifying power. Numbers greater than ten though, mean you will have a hard time keeping your hand steady enough to focus on whatever object you've sighted.

Lens size: The second number identifies the diameter, in millimeters, of the objective lens. The objective lens is the lens farthest away from your eye. The larger the objective lens, the more light that reaches your eye and the brighter the image you see.

Obviously, the higher the magnification number and the larger the objective lens, the more expensive your binoculars will be.

There are a number of binocular manufacturers including Brunton, Leica, Nikon, Minolta, Swarovski, Pentax, Steiner, and Bushnell.

Batteries
When it comes to backpacking, there are only two types of batteries that are worth considering—alkaline and lithium.

Alkaline: These batteries are far more efficient and longer-lasting than standard and heavy duty batteries. They offer as much as double the life yet weigh and cost just a bit more. Unlike carbon-zinc cells, the alkaline battery dies suddenly rather than fades out—a minor disadvantage. Alkaline batteries do recharge themselves a bit and will last for another twenty minutes or so if left to recharge for half-a-day unlike standard batteries that recharge only enough to put out a dim light for another five minutes. Alkalines cost about two-fifty for two AA batteries, three dollars for two C batteries, and three dollars for two D batteries.

Lithium: Extremely light and efficient, lithium batteries are also expensive (though in ratio to their effectiveness and weight not inordinately so). Unlike alkaline batteries, lithium will work in cold temperatures. Lithium batteries also have a much longer shelf life than alkaline batteries.

As for drawbacks, they are still not widely available. Alkaline batteries can be purchased in almost every supermarket, drugstore, convenience store, and discount store in the United States. Lithiums are much harder to find but are usually stocked by good outdoors stores. They also require special bulbs and there are restrictions about carrying them on aircraft. It is said that under certain conditions (intense heat or prolonged shorting) lithium cells may explode, although it is more likely that they will release a small bit of sulfur-dioxide gas than explode. Lithiums range in price from eight dollars for AA to fifteen dollars for a C to twenty dollars for a D cell.

Rope

A length of rope, at least ten-feet long and approximately three-sixteenths of an inch in diameter, is absolutely necessary for hiking. As a matter of fact, it would be wise to carry several lengths of rope ranging from a few feet to twenty-feet in length. Rope will definitely prove its usefulness on a hike down any trail.

For instance, many trails are in bear country. Whether protected or hunted, bears love human food. Some national parks provide bear-proof shelters or poles on which you can hang your food. In other areas, rope can be used to suspend a bag containing your food and other "smellables" from a tree to keep them out of reach of bears.

Rope can also be used to hang sleeping bags to air or clothes to dry, to rig tents and tarps, to lower or pull up a pack, to hang a pack from a tree, to replace a belt or frayed straps on gaiters or laces on boots, or to dip a water bottle into water.

Keep in mind that if you intend to use a tarp on your backpacking trips you will probably need at least fifty feet of rope because you never know how far apart the trees, rocks, or shrubs will be that you will use to set it up. (Remember that you can tie two lengths of rope together, if necessary. If you do, the tail of each knot should be at least a couple of inches to insure that the knot won't slip.

Most outdoors stores offer several types of rope, but the best for general backpacking is heavy-duty twisted or braided nylon rope ranging in width from one-eighth of an inch to one-quarter of an inch (or three to eight mm). Before using nylon rope, always burn the ends into hard knobs so that the rope does not unravel.

Knots: There are dozens of knots that can be learned, but fortunately only a few you'll need to know. These will come in handy while backpacking.

Double fisherman's knot: This is the most common backpacking and climbing knot because it can be used to tie two pieces of rope together. It is the safest and easiest to tie.

1. Wrap the end of the first rope (white) around the second rope (dashed), moving away from the end of the second rope.
2. This time moving toward the end of the second rope, wrap the end of the first rope around the second rope again. Keep the loops loose.
3. Following the path of the second rope, pass the end of the first rope through the loops you have just created.
4. Repeat steps 1 through 3 for the second rope, then tighten both knots and pull together.

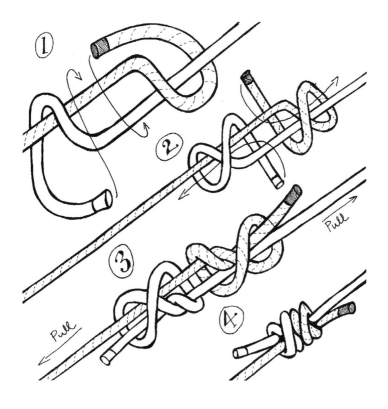

Sheet-bend: This is the simplest way to tie two unequal sizes of rope together and is very strong but the double fisherman is still recommended for climbing ropes.

1. Create a bight in the larger of the two ropes to be joined. Pass the free end of the second rope through the middle of the bight.
2. Wrap the free end around the back of the bight, then pass it over the bight and under the second rope's standing part. Cinch the knot tight.

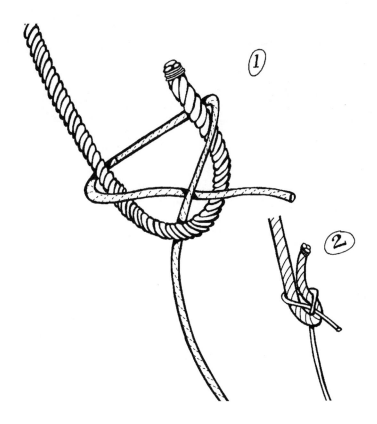

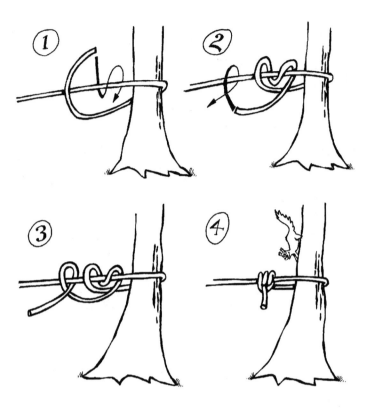

Tautline hitch: This knot can be used for securing lines from a grommet to a stake or tree.

1. Create a bight by passing the free end of the rope through a grommet or around a pole you are tying the rope to. Loop the rope end twice under the standing part of the rope, moving toward the grommet or pole.
2. Make another loop around the standing part with the free end, by wrapping over, then under the standing part and pulling it through the loop.
3. Pull the hitch taut.
4. It can now be worked up and down the standing part as needed and will hold tight under pressure.

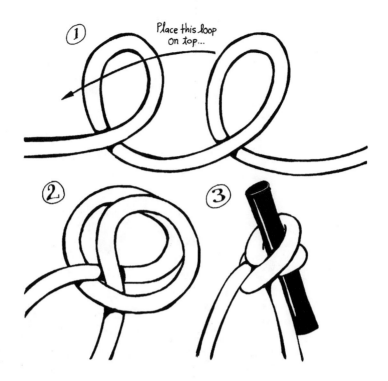

Clove hitch: You might use this knot when hanging your food for the night or securing your tarp to a tree.

1. Holding the standing part of the rope, in your left hand form a loop so that the line in your right hand comes from beneath the loop. Make a second loop the same way.
2. Place the right hand loop over the left hand loop.
3. Drop the loops over the top of the post. Cinch the knot tight.

There are a number of additional items that you may choose to carry on your hike, including books, journals, radios, maps, and a compass.

On the Trail

PART TWO

Hiking Technique

You have arrived. The car is locked and slowly ticking as it cools. The hum of tires on the asphalt will soon be replaced by the rustling trees and the electronic call of the vireo as you hike farther and farther from the roadway. Now it's time for all your planning to come to life. You are ready. But having food and the right kind of equipment will not ensure an enjoyable and safe trip. This chapter, and those that follow, will guide you step-by-step on your trip.

FIRST THINGS FIRST: PUTTING YOUR PACK ON

Unless you know how to live off the land, you are going to have to carry everything you need to survive. Getting your pack on your back is surprisingly difficult at first, but it gets easier with practice. There are three basic ways to get it on your back:

➤ Method 1: Settle your pack on your right knee if you're right-handed, left if you're left-handed.

➤ Insert your arm through the pack strap and swing the pack around your back. Finally, insert the other arm in the arm strap, tighten your hip belt and sternum strap, and you're on your way.

➤ Method 2: Sit down with your back against your pack, insert your arms through the straps. Roll on to your knees and stand up. This may sound easier, but it's actually a bit more difficult.

➤ Method 3: If you are particularly strong, you can flip over your back. First, set it on the ground with the straps facing away from you. Reach down through the straps, grasping the middle of the pack (if it is an external frame, grab the frame). Lift the pack over your head and slide it down onto your back, pushing your arms through the straps.

➤ Once you get your pack on your back, it's time to hike. The next question is . . .

HOW FAR AND HOW FAST?

In fiction, the heroes always seem to be able to sling on a pack, hike fifty miles at a four-mile-an-hour pace, and never rest. Knowing better, I smirk and wonder if I should enlighten the author. I'm not saying it's impossible to hike fifty miles nor am I saying that a four-mile-an-hour pace is impossible. But add a thirty-five- to fifty-pound pack to the natural ruggedness of trail and try to keep up that kind of pace for twelve-plus hours. As the old hiker joke goes, "How long is two hours?" The answer, "About five miles."

The best advice when it comes to backpacking: don't bite off more than you can chew. It is very easy to run yourself into the ground, and it takes a lot longer to hike ten rugged miles than you would think. That is why I suggested earlier that you start with short trips, ones where you can learn to gauge your limits—how much weight you can carry and how far you can go with that weight.

Knowing how far and how fast you can hike comes with experience. How far you can hike is a function of how fast you can hike as well as how many hours are in the day. A lot of people assume that a four-mile-an-hour pace is standard. Well, it is if you're walking around a track or on a level stretch of road. But even the most seasoned hiker finds it next to impossible to keep up that pace on tough terrain. A two- to three-mile-an-hour pace is more likely for a typical hiker in peak condition, and even this can flag depending on weather conditions and your own state of energy. When you first start hiking, don't count on more than a one-mile-per-hour pace. Your actual walking pace will probably be faster, but your body will crave frequent breaks. It won't take long before you can easily walk two miles per hour.

Once you know how fast you can hike, you are ready to determine how far you can go. When starting out, plan on hiking ten miles or less in one day. A five-mile day hike is a good, conservative choice—it will allow you plenty of time to enjoy the scenery without overextending yourself. For an overnight hike, plan a route that covers a total of twenty miles or less, or conservatively, ten miles or less. After several smaller hikes, you may decide that you can extend your backpacking trips without ruining the fun. You don't have to be in great shape to backpack. But if you're not in good shape, you should allow yourself time to adjust.

A good rule of thumb for planning your trip is to allow an hour for every two miles of trail plus one hour for each one thousand feet of elevation to be gained.

BACKPACKING TIP

For a rough estimate of how long you have until sunset, hold your hand out at arm's length and line your fingers up with the horizon. Each finger that you can fit between the horizon and the bottom of the sun represents about fifteen minutes of daylight.

So, for a hike that will cover fourteen miles and have an elevation gain totaling three thousand feet, you should allow yourself ten hours.

Easy Does It

Phil Hall had a novel idea for training for his first hike: "I carried around a seventy-pound bag of birdseed on my shoulders for ten miles over a ten-day period," he said. "From this, I got a tired and sore neck but discovered a clever way of hitching rides easily."

Phil realized the folly of his plan, chucked the bag of birdseed, and took the direct approach. "I then decided that I would just start out slowly and do however many miles I could."

He had the right idea. The only way to adjust to backpacking is to backpack. Unfortunately, there is no other way to prepare yourself. Being in good cardiovascular condition helps, but it takes the body time to accustom itself to the strain of even a light pack.

We trained for backpacking by taking up running and including an incredibly steep hill in our mile. We figured that when we could run a mile (including the hill) in eight minutes, we would be in good cardiovascular shape. But running up that hill was nothing compared to some of the climbs we faced with forty-pound packs on our backs. Unfortunately, in the long run, nothing prepares you for backpacking except backpacking.

TAKING BREAKS

It's unlikely that you will want to go the entire distance without a break, especially after a hill. When we first started hiking, we developed the following routine: We took what we called a pack-off break every two miles and a pack-on break after almost every hill. A pack-on or bend-over break is accomplished by leaning over and holding your knees so that your back supports all the pack's weight. Try it; it really helps when you first start hiking. If you are on an extended or long-distance hike, you may find out, like we did, that after five hundred miles, you can hike for hours without any breaks at all.

Always keep in mind that your body will tell you when to take breaks. But if you listen too much to the counsel of your aching muscles, you'll never make it to camp before dark. Of course, there are some things you can do to help out.

Whittle down your pack weight, carrying only what you really need. Plan on hikes that are short enough to be easily done in a day. When you do take a rest stop, alternate between pack-on and pack-off breaks. Try to reserve pack-off rest stops for after you have topped out a tough climb, so that you do not lose all the momentum you have built up. When you stop, always take a sip or two of water to keep yourself well hydrated.

UPHILL AND DOWNHILL TECHNIQUES

Taking breaks does slow down your overall pace. One way to avoid frequent stops is to use the rest step when ascending mountains. This is accomplished by resting on the back leg with its knee locked and then taking the next step by leaning forward and bending the forward knee. As the weight transfers to the forward leg, straighten that knee and step forward with the other leg. Now pause for a moment with all your weight centered on the downhill leg, then continue the process, once more leaning forward onto the front leg, shifting the weight to that leg and straightening it. Vary the length of the pause as needed. This step will not only get you up a steep slope faster but will get you up a mountain with less effort. The idea is to use this step on extremely tough sections of a hike by pausing slightly with each step—continual movement instead of vigorous hiking separated by a number of breaks.

Hiking downhill is as tough on your body as an uphill climb. Whereas an ascent places cardiovascular stress on your body, a descent takes its toll on your feet and knees. To lessen the impact, try pausing with your weight on one foot between each step; this will relieve some of the strain. Also, spring forward with each step, flexing your legs as you put weight on them. This is the fastest and safest way to get downhill.

HIKING IN THE RAIN

Let's be honest here, hiking in the rain can be the pits. First you have to get wet in drop-by-cold-drop increments as water splashes off your neck and works its way down into your clothes. You counter the wet with rain gear and soon heat up under the rain jacket and pants. The sweat makes you wonder if the rain wasn't so bad after all. Either way, if it rains long enough and hard enough, you will get wet.

The flip side to all of this is the joy of hiking in the rain. There is the soft spring rain that brings a special stillness to the forest. Then there's the urgent downpours that soak you so quickly and completely that you soon realize you may as well enjoy it. That's when you find yourself splashing in puddles you haven't jumped into since sometime this side of sixth grade. The best course of action is to make peace with the rain, follow these suggestions, and hike on in relative comfort:

The author with her daughter hiking in the rain.

➤ If it is warm out, you can forgo the rain gear altogether. Slip on a pack cover to keep your gear dry and keep hiking. If you start to get cold, don't wait

it out. Stop and don your rain gear before you get too deeply chilled to readily warm up.

➤ In a cold rain, avoid cotton clothing. It is better to wear only underwear on with rain gear than to wear a layer of warmth-sapping cotton.

➤ Wear gaiters to keep water from dripping down into your boots. Even ankle length gaiters will keep out most of the rainwater.

➤ Pay close attention to your feet. If you feel hot spots, stop and put on some moleskin. Even with well-worn boots, blisters form more readily on softened, soggy skin.

➤ If the rain keeps up for two or more days, put your wet clothes back on. Unless you are already chilled and at risk for hypothermia, you will stay warm enough and you can save your dry clothes for when the rain stops.

➤ Lastly, drink plenty of water, or stop and make a warm drink if you find shelter under an overhanging rock or stand of trees. Even while you are drenched, dehydration can sap your body of its ability to stay warm, increasing the threat of hypothermia.

Keeping your equipment dry can be challenging. On a late summer hike in New England, we were drenched by rain all day for three days running. On the third day, as we forded a stream, waves splashed repeatedly against our sleeping bags. That night, chilled from the hike, we opened our sleeping-bag stuff sacks with a little trepidation. The down and synthetic bags had only a patch or two of dampness on them. The remainder of the gear in our packs, once pulled out of the plastic bags, was bone dry. Careful packing had kept our equipment protected during even the wettest of hikes. When wet weather threatens to dampen your hike, try this:

➤ Fold your map until the section you need faces out, slide it into a plastic bag and seal.

➤ Stuff your sleeping bag into a trash bag inside your pack. For external frame packs, where the sleeping bag is on the outside, line the inside of your stuff sack with a trash bag.

➤ Pack toilet paper, books, a journal, and even your point-and-shoot camera in plastic bags, even when there is no threat of rain. That way when the thunderstorm moves in, you won't have to worry about the gear.

➤ Keep the gear you will need on the trail in a side pocket or at the top of the pack. This will keep the exposure to rain at a minimum when you have to slip off the pack cover to grab a snack, toilet paper, or something else in a hurry.

➤ When making camp after a wet day on the trail, wring out your socks and leave them with the soggy boots and rain gear under the tent's vestibule. If freezing temperatures are expected, stuff them in a trash bag and bring them in the tent.

➤ When, or if, the sun reappears, take a break from the trail and pull out your tent, sleeping bags, and clothes. Set them around on some rocks, or hang a line between two trees to dry the gear out. It will make for a lighter pack and a more pleasant hike.

STREAM CROSSINGS

In high-use areas you are likely to find a nice little bridge to help you cross a stream, but the farther you advance into the backcountry, the more likely it is you're going to have to cross a stream using your own initiative. I've crossed streams on logs and stepping stones, in ankle-deep and waist-deep water, and all very safely. I've also crossed streams during and just after rainstorms when they become very dangerous.

Following an amazing thunderstorm and torrential downpour, we came upon a stream in the throes of a flash flood. The stream was neither very wide (about six feet) nor very deep (thigh deep on a man, waist deep on me), but it was moving very rapidly and carrying all sorts of debris in its wake.

Although there was a log, which under normal circumstances might have made a nice bridge, it was too

slick at this point to cross over standing up. We walked
up and down the stream looking for another option.
There was none. The place we had intended to camp
was under several inches of water and we had just
passed a tree that had been struck and knocked over
by lightning. We were soaked and
our only thought was to get to higher ground and a road.

Always assist children
during a stream
crossing.

We tried crossing the log sitting
down but the current tried to pull our
dangling legs beneath the log. Our
only option was to cross the stream
using the downed tree as a brace. Frank made it across
successfully and I was within arm's reach of Frank when
I lost my footing and my right leg was pulled painfully
beneath the log.

BACKPACKING TIP

Clip several carabiners to the loops on the
outside of your pack, and use them to
hold your boots during a stream crossing
or to tie down exterior items.

With Frank grasping my arm, I was off balance and
unable to regain my footing. I was slowly slipping
beneath the log. He finally, reluctantly, let go. Using
both arms to hold on to the tree, I was able to pull my
leg loose and Frank quickly pulled me out of the water.

All of this happened within seconds. I neither had
the time to remove my pack nor harness myself with

rope, which I should have done earlier in this very dangerous situation. I was lucky. Many are not. Accidents at streams kill numerous hikers each year—along with falls and exposure.

If there is neither a dry log nor stepping stones, you must think carefully before crossing any stream. Take a good look at it. How fast is the current? How deep is it? If it is deeper than about eighteen inches, be especially careful. I've been knocked off my feet in knee-deep water. Using a rope will not prevent you from falling but it may help you in the rescue if you do fall. Never tie a rope to your body as this could create an even more dangerous situation. Keep these factors in mind when looking for a place to cross:

➤ The narrowest point in a stream may be the most tempting, but is probably the most dangerous point

Tools of the trade—these hiking poles can help keep your balance when hiking over difficult terrain.

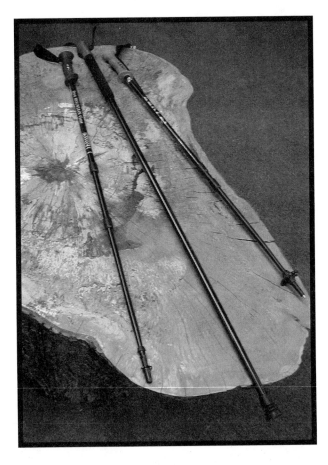

Using a Hiking Stick

A hiking stick can take some of the impact on the downhill and will keep you steady on rough sections of trail. If this was all they were good for, they would still be worth carrying. But hiking sticks also can be used to fend off stray dogs, keep your balance crossing narrow bridges or fording streams, flip small branches out of the path ahead of you, and more.

Some people simply pick up a different stick every time they hike, whereas others purchase a ski pole for the purpose. Some people swear by ski poles, noting that they are very strong and lightweight, and the basket at the tip prevents the pole from burying itself in mud or rocks. There are also several manufacturers of walking sticks; some of these sticks have a telescoping feature which enables the user to vary its length.

to cross because the current is more powerful there. The widest part is probably the safest. At any rate, going for the slow and deep is usually safer than shallow and fast.

➤ Always release your hip belt before crossing a stream in case you are knocked off your feet. This way you can easily rid yourself of the pack if you are washed downstream. This could save you from drowning, and it is better to lose your pack than your life.

➤ If you are trying to cross a snow-fed river near the end of the day, consider waiting until morning. Pitch camp and spend the night there. The stream's flow will be reduced during the cool evening and will be easier to cross before things heat up during the day. Had we waited a few hours, our flash-flooded stream would probably have eventually subsided. Hindsight being 20/20, the area suffered several more downpours that night, but that is rare.

➤ Long pants have more drag on you than shorts. Cross in shorts or even nude or in underwear. Once across, you can warm up by redonning your clothes.

➤ Some crossings are safe enough to do barefoot, but why take chances? Wear your boots or camp shoes, if you have them. A number of companies make water socks—scrunchable shoes with a rough sole made for gripping rocks and stream beds.

➤ When crossing rapids, face upstream and move sideways like a crab. Using a hiking stick or pole will help you maintain your balance.

HIKING IN SNOW

Hiking in the snow provides its own unique challenge. A path that would normally be a snap to follow is now buried under snow, and the trail blazes may or may not be visible.

Fortunately, there are a few things you can do to find your trail when it is buried beneath feet of snow:

➤ Always know exactly where you are heading. Study those maps, paying particular attention to topographical features and the layout of the land.

➤ Before heading out, note your location on the map as well as the time you are starting. Study the map's line of the trail and whether any switchbacks are indicated. A switchback can throw you off the trail quicker than anything, and if you are aware that the trail makes sudden turns, you will be more likely to spot them.

➤ As it is pretty reasonable to assume that the trail will not pass directly through a tree, you can guess that if you see a dense stand of trees before you, the trail does not go there. On the other hand, if you see a line or clear corridor proceeding through a stand of trees, then the trail is likely to be there. This works better in areas of dense trees.

➤ If there is not an obvious corridor, then try looking for sawed-off tree branches. These are not obvious when the trail is snow-free because you are not looking for them, but trail maintainers will often saw off branches that hang into the trail or ones that have cracked and broken.

➤ Occasionally, you might see the end of a sawed-off log. This could mean that a blowdown that was blocking the trail was sawed in half and pushed just off the trail. Of course, the blowdown might have been pushed well into the woods and you might be way off course, so keep an eye out for other clues as well.

➤ You might also look for evidence of the shovel cuts of trail builders. You will find these in steep terrain and around large trees. The snow melts quickly around the trunks of trees; in these moats, look down at the ground. If you spot bare ground rather than grass or plant material, you may be on or near the trail.

➤ If you are hiking in a northerly direction and there is sun-warmed south-facing slope ahead of you (perhaps way ahead of you), look for small patches of exposed trail on that slope. By keeping these distant patches of trail in sight, you might be able to keep to the trail.

➤ If you are hiking southbound and facing northbound slopes that receive less sun, keep an eye out for faint lines leading across the slopes. Straight lines leading across slopes are not natural and are indications of trail. Unfortunately, these are only apparent from a distance, so memorize where you see these lines start and end, if possible.

➤ Follow the trail up and over every snowbank even if it might seem easier to detour around it. You might expend more energy, but you won't risk losing the direction of the trail and maybe you'll get a good vantage point from the top of the snowbank.

➤ If you are following a snowbound trail through the forest, don't strike out cross-country unless you know exactly, and I mean exactly, where you are going. It is easier to spend your time searching for trail near or on the trail rather than attempting to find it at the end of a long day.

On some trails—the Pacific Crest and Continental Divide, for example—you will be confronted by snow even in the warmest months. It is during those warm months, June and July specifically, when you will have to be a little more wary about your path. Some of the snowpack you cross may have transition zones where the snow is rotten and collapses quite easily when stepped on.

Snowpacks melt in three different ways. On the surface, they simply evaporate from their solid state. Watch for the steaming snowfields on crisp mornings; they're worth seeing. Snowpacks also melt from the sun's heat as well as the sun-warmed air. You won't see puddles, though, because lower layers of snow will absorb the water. Finally, the heat put out by trees and other plants, rocks, and earth can melt the snow, creating pockets of fragile, transition snow. It is this type of melting that causes the most danger for the hiker. The snow around plants, trees, and rocks can be rotten and can unexpectedly collapse should you step on it, causing you and your pack to tumble. And transitional snow is not limited to the areas around such obstacles. If the overall snowpack is less than three feet, you can find yourself thigh deep in snow. You find rotten snow mostly at the lower elevations of a snowfield but it can easily be mixed in with snow that is still hardpack. Here are some clues to look for to keep from sinking:

➤ Keep an eye out for branches barely protruding from the snow and scan ahead for darker areas that might hint at buried branches and rotten snow.

➤ If people have been hiking in front of you, keep an eye on their tracks. Have they barely marred the surface? Follow them. Do they continually sink into the snow? Give them a wide berth.

➤ When you are hiking through meadows or areas that are open or gradually sloped, the transition zones can be hundreds of yards across. Pass through these areas in a line that keeps you farthest away from rocks and trees, and if possible, pass uphill of these things as well. You can recognize weakened snowpack in two ways—by the objects uphill from it and by the subtle sagging in the snow that runs downhill from such objects.

➤ Keep a lookout for moats. These occur around protruding and underlying rocks in all types of snow. The larger the rock, the wider its moat is going to be.

➤ When you are descending a snowfield and are nearing the lower end of it, watch for very subtle indications of a transition zone. Rotten snow is often a bit more crystalline in appearance and can also appear a little more yellow. If you notice this slight difference, you can avoid the posthole syndrome—sinking up to your knees or thighs in too-soft snow.

Keep in mind that no matter how alert you are to these "clues," you will still end up thigh-deep in snow at times. The best thing to do in these situations is to forget mileage goals and just progress forward as best as you can.

Snow season usually runs from early September through June at elevations above ten thousand feet (and sometimes lower or longer, depending on where you are). Unfortunately, it doesn't really matter whether the previous year's snowfall was particularly deep or not, the dangers remain about the same. If you hike often enough at higher elevations, you will eventually be faced with a section of rock-hard snow that covers several yards on a steep section of trail. These strips of snow are too long to circumvent by climbing (or descending) around them and they can be very dangerous.

That's not to say that there aren't those lucky few who will manage an entire long-distance hike without ever facing such a circumstance. I know a man whose trail name is Lucky, Lucky, Lucky because he managed an entire thru-hike of the AT without ever seeing a drop

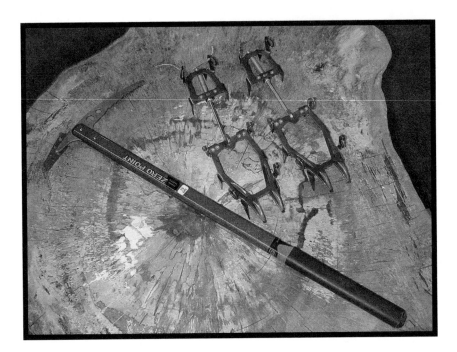

Ice-hiking essentials: an ice ax and crampons.

of rain. It happens. But can you guarantee it will happen to you?

A most important technique to learn before heading out for a trek in snow country is the ice-ax self-arrest. Though it is rarely needed (and the ice-ax is heavy and inconvenient to carry), the self-arrest technique is a lifesaver that you will not regret learning. If you can take a class in ice-ax technique before heading out, by all means do so. It is worth the cost and the time. If you cannot, try practicing the following technique in your backyard or the local park, if you don't have access to a backyard.

Ice ax Self-Arrest

This small tool is designed with a pointed end (the spike) and a head consisting of a spoon-shaped blade called the adze at one end and a long and narrow blade at the other end called the pick. Some hikers get double use out of the ice ax by using it as a hiking stick, too.

When learning the self-arrest technique without an actual instructor, keep in mind that the most dangerous thing is dropping down onto your "slope" and gouging yourself in the face with the ax. So, before you drop, concentrate fiercely on holding the adze away from your face. You don't want to be sitting in the emergency room saying, "Yeah, I was practicing how NOT to hurt myself . . ."

When performing the self-arrest technique only three things will come in contact with the ground—the pick of the ax, your left foot, and your right foot. Your body should be off the ground and your legs should be spread somewhat to form a triangle and provide you with some lateral stability.

Are you ready to try it? In your backyard (or wherever you are practicing):

➤ Lie down on the ground and fix your body in the self-arrest position. That is, spread your legs and brace your body off the ground using your toes and the adze (which is well away from your face, remember) for support.

➤ Memorize this position and recall it to mind, occasionally.

➤ Next, find an actual slope (with snow, if it's available) that you can practice on without hurting yourself. Don't get all gung ho and practice on a steep slope where you might end up in the hospital.

➤ Once again, when you fall, don't forget to keep a tight grip on the ax and to keep that adze AWAY from your face.

➤ Use your good arm, that is, your stronger arm, to hold the ice ax. Should you actually fall on an icy snow slope, you are not going to have time to THINK about what you need to do. The self-arrest will have to be a reflex action.

➤ When you practice falling, make sure you practice when you are climbing up the slope as well as when you are descending the slope.

➤ Never switch hands—always hold the ice ax with the same hand.

➤ If you slip and land on your back or bottom, roll over onto your stomach in the direction AWAY from the spike of your ax. This way, the spike won't catch in the snow as you roll over. If you are right-handed, for example, you would roll to the right.

Snowshoeing and Cross-country Ski Techniques

When it comes to choosing to snowshoe or cross-country ski in the winter, both sports have their advantages and disadvantages. It's up to you to weigh those and choose the sport that's right for you. Or, you may want to try both!

Snowshoes

Breaking Trail   Since you will be going where others have not, you will have to break trail, and this is difficult and exhausting in snowshoes, particularly if the snow is wet and heavy or more than a foot deep. With each step, you must raise your foot high enough to clear the surface in order to step forward. If you're going to be breaking trail, use larger snowshoes with as much flotation as possible. Trade off leaders every half hour or so to ensure that the trailbreaker doesn't become too exhausted or overheated.

Climbing Uphill   Snowshoes have crampons on the bottoms that are advantageous when it comes to climbing steep slopes, even on crusty or icy snow. However, the act of breaking snow, combined with the weight of a pack and the effects of high altitude, can make climbing extremely tiring.

Going Downhill   Unlike skiing, you don't need a lot of practice going downhill. Just aim and shoot; that is, just take huge steps downhill. This is the "runaway train" at its best. To plunge-step down a steep hill in snowshoes is loads of fun and it is much easier on the knees than doing the same thing on a hard-packed dirt trail.

Crossing a Slope   It is hard to traverse or switchback on snowshoes because your ankles tend to roll downhill. Not only is this painful, but the crampons on the bottom of snowshoes aren't really meant to grip the snow in that direction. A better option would be to exert the extra energy and kick your way directly uphill using the snowshoes' front crampon teeth. Head up until you find an area level enough to cross over on flat ground.

Navigating Blowdowns   Very simply put, it's much easier to hop over a blowdown in snowshoes than on skis. Simply climb over the branches or trunk as you would in snowless conditions, or walk around it.

Getting up from a Fall   With snowshoes, it's easy—just roll over, get the shoes under your body, and stand up. Of course, if your pack is weighing you down, you may have to release it first and put it back on once you're standing up.

Cross-country Skis
Breaking Trail   Trailbreaking on skis is easy, especially if the snow is light and airy—you can cut right through. It can be more difficult on crusty snow, depending on how deeply you sink. In either case, trade off leaders every half hour or so to ensure that the trailbreaker doesn't become too exhausted or overheated.

Climbing Uphill   On all but the most low-grade slopes you will need to you use skis with climbing skins, though even skins won't get you up really steep or icy slopes. In the case of steep and icy slopes, you will need to use the kick turn to switchback up the hills. To do a kick turn, plant your uphill pole behind you for stability and slide your uphill ski forward and up until the tip is pointing straight up and the tail is planted in the snow. Pivot that ski until it is resting on the snow and pointing in the direction you want to go. Stomp on the newly placed ski to set the skin. Then, swing your second ski around so it is parallel with the first ski.

Going Downhill   Cross-country skiing downhill can be fun if you are an experienced skier, and you will cover more ground in the same amount of time than with a snowshoe. If you can already link gracefully downhill using telemark turns, you're ready. Otherwise, you will probably wipe out a thousand times before you get it right. Ahh, but once you get it right . . .

Crossing a Slope   Cross-country skis were made for traverses. Just put pressure on the uphill edges of your skis and cut across the slope. If you are traveling uphill, let the edges of your skis and the skins do all the work and simply walk up at a gentle angle.

Navigating Blowdowns   The advantage to negotiating blowdowns clearly lies with snowshoes. Unless it is a small blowdown, you will probably have to take your skis off. If you're going to be "hiking" in an area with lots of trees, you may want to go for snowshoes.

Getting up from a Fall   If you fall in skis, try to look at the comic side of the situation—that is, if only someone could videotape how funny you look! OK. Really, here's what to do if you don't want to take off the skis and start all over again: If your skis are not downslope from you and facing across the hill (rather than uphill or downhill), swing around so that they are (yes, you will probably have to take off your pack). Then lay your poles in an X on the uphill slope, push on the center of the X, and try to let gravity do the rest.

Carrying a Pack   Well, of course you will be. This is a book about backpacking. The question is, how big a pack will it be? If you're out for an overnighter or a day trip, you can probably manage the skis if you're a novice. If you can handle a heavy backpack in hiking boots, then you can probably manage a heavy pack in snowshoes. Just make sure you are carrying trekking or ski poles to help maintain your equilibrium. If you are skiing, a pack combined with slippery ski bases, free-heeled bindings, and the ups and downs of hilly terrain is a great recipe for wipeouts. Balancing a pack on skis takes lots of practice not to mention confidence. Start out light (with a pack under twenty pounds), and eventually you might master the art of backpacking on cross-country skis.

DESERT HIKING

When it comes to hiking in the desert, there are a number of things you should keep in mind, particularly when it comes to the way you dress. I blistered the back of my neck on a hike in the mountains of New Mexico. That sunburn taught me a lesson about the intensity of the sun in that state that saved my hide on my first desert hike. By then I had figured out what Lawrence of Arabia had learned before me—covering yourself with light clothing from tip to tail is the best defense against the desert sun. When packing for a desert backpacking trip, be sure to include these essentials:

➤ A hat that shades your face and neck. There should be insulating space in the crown between the hat and the top of your head.
➤ Sunglasses that offer protection from both UVA and UVB rays.
➤ Long-sleeved shirts and long pants to protect you from the sun.
➤ Stick with cotton clothing in light colors. Cotton's penchant for holding moisture in makes it wrong for mountain hikes, but perfect for the desert. A

The author's daughter keeps hydrated while hiking in the desert.

light breeze will evaporate the sweat and cool you off.

➤ Sunscreen (and lip protection with sunscreen) with a sun protection factor (SPF) of at least 15 to protect areas not covered by clothes.

➤ A couple of bandannas. Dip them in water and tamp them on your face, neck, and wrists. Then, wrap them around your neck or hang them down from your hat along the back of your neck. The cool water will give you some immediate heat relief, and as the water evaporates, the bandannas will continue to cool you off.

➤ Bring warm clothes, such as a pile jacket and pants, for chilly desert nights, when temperatures can easily drop forty degrees from the daytime high.

Water

Probably the biggest concern when it comes to hiking in the desert is water. If you fall for the movie image of desert travel, you have conjured up images of bleached bones and water holes that turn out to be a mirage. Desert hiking isn't about survival, but about enjoying the scenery and the solitude of an arid world. Sure a desert is a harsh environment, but the stark landscape offers a rewarding backpacking experience worth a little extra effort.

Water will need to be one of your biggest concerns, but don't let it keep you out of the desert. Follow these tips and you will be ready for your first desert sojourn:

➤ Plan on at least one gallon of water per person per day. Keep up with your water intake by monitoring your urine flow. Dark yellow urine means you are getting dehydrated and need to drink more water to avoid heat-related illnesses.

➤ Also drink at least one canteen full of sports drink per day to replace needed electrolytes.

➤ Don't bet your water supply on one large water bag, as a leak could put you dangerously low on fluids. Carry water in several one- or two-liter canteens instead.

- Keep extra water in your car. A five-gallon jug of water stashed in the car will help if you get back to the trailhead low on fluids or if you have car trouble getting to and from the trailhead.
- When filtering water (which is a must for all water no matter how pristine it looks), take precautions to avoid clogging your filter on the silt-rich water found in desert streams. Ladle up water in a pot and let the sediment settle out. Filter from the top into a second container. This will keep the worst of the silt out of the filter. If you are in a hurry, strain the water through a bandanna and then use a water filter.
- Get the latest information on available water sources. Guidebooks written years before will be of little help. Call the local office of the land management agency that controls the land through which you plan to hike, and ask specifically about reliable water sources. Also ask hikers you meet on the trail where they got water.

Solar Water Still: You can also get water in an emergency by memorizing the following method of distilling water in the desert:

- Dig a hole two feet deep by three feet wide.
- Set a widemouth bottle or pot in the bottom of the hole.
- Fill the area around the bottle with any plant material you can find.
- Cover the hole with plastic (clear or translucent, if possible)
- Weigh down the edges of the plastic around hole so that it is "sealed."
- Place a lightweight, insulated rock in the center of the plastic so that a funnel shape is formed over the mouth of the bottle. Water will then drip from the "funnel" into the bottle. You can insulate the rock with a bandanna or piece of paper.

After three hours, the still will produce about a pint of water.

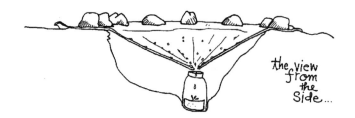

the view
from
the
side...

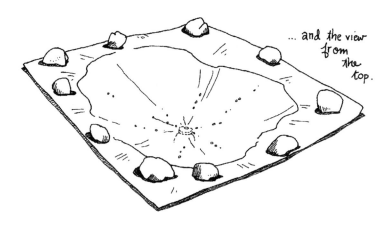

... and the view
from
the
top.

Keeping well hydrated will go a long way toward a safe and fun desert hike. Here are some other tips for arid trails:

➤ Winter is the best season for desert hikes. You will find more water, fewer tourists, and more people-friendly temperatures. If you can't swing a winter trip, avoid the summer and shoot for fall or tourist-heavy spring.

➤ Hike early every day. Then, when the temperature starts to rise, take a break in the shade of some rocks or a tarp to catch up on reading Edward Abbey or writing in a journal. You can hit the trail again in the evening for some cooler hiking.

➤ Never camp in dry streambeds or arroyos. A flash flood, even one miles up the bed, can send a torrent of water to sweep your camp away in the night and you with it. Severe thunderstorms are most common from June through August, which is another reason to avoid summer hikes.

- Camp well away from water sources to protect the wildlife. A campsite near the waterhole may scare away the other animals who rely on the water source for survival.
- Don't build campfires. You will rob the soil of the precious nutrients the slow rotting wood provides. Besides, scorpions like to hide under dead logs and fire-ring-size rocks.
- Check with the appropriate land management agency on how to handle human wastes. Don't be surprised if they asked you to pack it out. Decomposition is slow in the desert and the impact of the excrement of thousands of hikers could be devastating to the fragile environment.

THE HUMAN FACTOR

Problems with other humans while hiking are rare and following these few guidelines will help:

- Avoid camping near road crossings.
- Do not tell strangers exactly where you intend to camp for the night.
- Take any valuables (e.g., your wallet) with you; do not leave anything valuable in your car at the trailhead.
- If you get a bad feeling about someone you meet up with, move on to another campsite. (A valuable resource on the subject of protecting oneself is Gavin De Becker's book, *The Gift of Fear: Survival Signals that Protect Us from Violence*).
- Do not leave your pack alone in frequently traveled areas because there are people out there who will steal packs.

HIKING IN HUNTING SEASON

It's an uneasy feeling, to put it mildly, to find yourself in a hunter's sights. We once found ourselves at the business end of a hunting rifle during our Appalachian Trail thru-hike. It didn't take the hunter but a moment to realize we were larger than the turkey he was hoping to bag, but the disconcerting feeling it gave us is still with us years later.

213

Most hunters are skilled outdoorspeople who present no danger to hikers. However, there are trigger-happy neophyte hunters in the woods as well. We have all read, with frightening regularity, newspaper accounts of people mistaken for game and shot while hanging up laundry or sitting on their front porch.

Safely sharing the woods with people carrying firearms depends on two things: being unmistakably identifiable as Homo sapiens, and being choosy about when and where you go. As you plan a hunting season hiking trip, remember the following:

➤ Pick up a copy of the state hunting regulations. Once you know where and when hunting is in season, you can better plan your own hiking schedule.

➤ Wear a blaze orange hat, safety vest, or windbreaker. If you wear what the hunter's wear, you will be mistaken for another hunter instead of game.

➤ Tie strips of orange flagging tape to your pack, or use a blaze orange pack cover.

➤ Leave your dog at home. It will be nearly impossible to protect your pet from a careless hunter. If you must take your dog, keep it on a leash at all times and have the dog wear a blaze orange bandanna or something similar.

➤ Hike with companions and converse loudly.

➤ Attach stock bells to any pack animals. Don't rely on bear bells, because their delicate jangling simply doesn't carry far enough.

➤ Stick to established trails. Hunting season is not the time of year for bushwhacking.

➤ If the trailhead is crowded with trucks with empty gun racks, or is just plain crowded, consider hiking in another area, or at least be double cautious.

➤ Follow these guidelines even in national parks and other areas where hunting is not allowed. Remember, the many responsible hunters are not the problem, but sloppy hunters can't be trusted to stick to the letter of the law.

MAINTAINING THE TRAIL AS YOU HIKE

A well-maintained trail is fun to hike on. With a broad, well-marked path free of debris, hikers can concentrate more on their surroundings and less on the footpath. But even on the best cared for trails maintenance problems arise regularly. Wind, snow, and ice storms break off branches and fell large trees, creating blowdowns that must be climbed over or hiked around. Storm water runoff creates gullies in the trail. Briers and other weeds grow up to choke off little-hiked trails by late summer, while on well-worn paths, litter is a constant reminder that your backcountry hike isn't the wilderness experience you hoped for.

Trails would quickly become impassable if not for volunteers clearing trails of blowdowns.

Trail maintainers put in tens of thousands of volunteer hours each year on the Appalachian Trail alone. Keeping our footpaths open to hikers requires continual care, but there are ways hikers can easily make a difference. Here are several ways you can help maintain trails as you hike them:

➤ Don't create any new problems yourself. Hike in single file, stay on the established trail, and pack out all of your trash.

215

➤ Keep a trash bag at the ready and pick up trash.

➤ Remove downed limbs and branches from the trail. Even without a saw, you can clear much of the debris that litters the footpath.

➤ Clean out clogged water bars with your hiking stick or boot heel.

➤ Drag rocks or downed limbs across the makeshift paths that crop up as shortcuts to switchbacks or side trails around mud holes, fallen rocks, and downed trees.

➤ Move loose rocks to the side of the trail.

➤ Report bad trail conditions to the land management agency or trail club that takes care of the trail. This information is often in hiking guidebooks. The people responsible for maintaining the trail need to know about large downed trees, washed out bridges, and other significant problems.

Consider joining a local hiking club. You can get training and take on regular maintenance of a section of trail or you can opt for going on club-sponsored work trips to help build and maintain trails. It's a lot of fun and gives you a new, deeper appreciation for the trails you hike.

6

Finding Your Way

It often starts out the same way. A small group of hikers, having escaped into the woods for a couple of days, are late in returning home. Their car waits at the trailhead, empty. A search and rescue team is mounted, and the hikers are found—cold, wet, and hungry. Perhaps they were novices, unfamiliar with the area, or maybe they were experienced hikers who missed a crucial trail marker. Fortunately this ending was a happy one. No one plans on getting lost, but if you backpack long enough, chances are you will find yourself off course, wondering where you went wrong. If you know how to read a map and use a compass, you can reduce the chance of getting lost, and when you do get lost, you will be able to help get yourself back on track. The first step in prevention is to familiarize yourself with the area, and there is no better way to do this than with maps.

MAPS

In some cases, the only map you will need is the one found at the trailhead, especially if there is only one trail to follow. But not all trails have such a map. In most cases, you will have consulted a guidebook or the internet before heading out, and more than likely, a map will accompany the description. These maps are adequate as long as you don't wander beyond the trail area, and along with the trail descriptions, give you enough detail to make it along the trail. Good guide-books will also suggest other available maps, which frequently offer more detail. National parks, wilderness areas, and national forests often provide their own map; these are generally based upon the most detailed map of all, the USGS topographic or topo maps. If you venture into areas that aren't well marked, you would do well to carry topo maps to the area your are visiting. Since most maps are based upon the USGS maps, the rest of the discussion will refer to these.

In a topographic map, cartographers reduce the real world to color lines, shaded areas and symbols. The ability to interpret the lines, symbols, and colors will help you stay on the trail, or when the trail suddenly disappears, to find your way.

Map Colors

On USGS maps, colors are used consistently to make identifying map features a snap. Color on USGS maps is used as follows:

Green: Areas of vegetation, including forests, orchards, and fields

White: Areas with little or no vegetation

Brown: Contour lines, indicating the elevation at regular intervals

Blue: Water features, including streams, rivers, lakes, and marsh. Contour lines are given in blue for glaciers.

Black: Man-made features, including buildings, roads, dams, or even political boundaries.

Red: Highways and surveying lines

Yellow: Large cities

Purple: Indicates revisions made from aerial photos and not yet confirmed in the field.

Canadian topographic maps are often available in one-color editions as well as multi-colored maps. While the color maps are easier to use, you will want to opt for black and white maps if you want to make easy-to-read notations on the map, such as for trail design, or if you need to make a photocopy.

Map Symbols

To indicate geographic features, elevation, and man-made structures, cartographers use a variety of symbols. Fortunately, the symbols look like the object they represent, so the symbols found on USGS maps, guidebook maps, and foreign maps are often easily identified.

For example, on USGS maps a church is indicated with a square topped by a cross. The symbol for railroad tracks is a continuous line crossed by dashes at regular intervals, which resemble cross ties on a railroad track.

The symbols are centered over the location they represent, but are not to scale. A school may be indicated by a symbol much larger than the actual building, while the thin, blue line of a stream may appear smaller than it really is. The most commonly encountered symbols are:

Main Highway: ▬ ▬ ▬

Secondary Highway: ─────

Railroad: ┼─┼─┼─┼

Small Road: ═══

Dirt Road: ≈≈≈≈≈≈

Trail: ⌐⌐⌐⌐

Well or Spring :   °⁹

Stream: ⌒⌒

Large River: ～～

Marsh: ⋅⋅⋅

Building: ◢

School: ▮

Church: ⌖

State Boundary: — - -

County Boundary: — - —

City Boundary: - — -

Open Pit Mine: ✕

Understanding Contour Lines

The thin brown lines on a topographic map are the contour (or topographic) lines. The contour lines are meant to reflect the shape of the land, how it rises and falls. If you were to follow a contour line on the ground, it would take you neither uphill nor downhill, and would eventually lead back to where you started. On the other hand, if you were to leave the contour line, you would eventually encounter another one, gaining or losing elevation in the process. The height gained from contour to contour, called the contour interval, will differ from map to map. Most map legends will tell you the interval, but you can figure it out yourself. If you look closely, you will notice that every fifth contour line is thicker and darker than the others. This is called the index line. If you follow this line, you will find a number, which indicates the elevation of this particular line. Find an adjacent dark line and its elevation, subtract the lower number from the higher, divide by five, and you will find the contour interval.

As you examine a map, you will notice that some

Steep Slope:

Gentle Slope:

Ridgeline:

Valley:

Finger or ridge: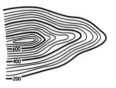

Draw, hollow, or valley: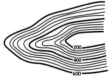

Depression:

lines are closer together than others. The closer the lines to each other, the steeper the terrain. Remember that as reliable as a map is, it can't tell everything. A twenty-foot cliff could lie between the forty-foot contour lines of the map, and won't be indicated in any way. Even the best of maps won't tell you all you may want to know about the terrain. A route climbing a ravine to the ridgetop may look ideal on the map, only to be an impassable tangle of downed trees left by a winter storm.

The following examples show how some commonly encountered terrain might look on a topographic map:

Map Legend

In the margins of a map, you will find the legend. Like the Rosetta Stone that opened up understanding to several ancient languages, the map legend will help you better understand the map itself. It contains the scale, a key to the map symbols, and other information essential to deciphering the map. Before using a map, scan this information.

On USGS maps, the legend will also contain:

➤ The map date: This is most important in determining the relative accuracy of man-made features. If the map hasn't been revised since 1968, the geographic features will be accurate, while information on roads and buildings must be assumed to be well out-of-date.

➤ The name of the map and adjoining maps: Even a short section of trail may be on two or even four quadrangles if it occurs where four maps join together. It is useful to locate all the maps for the area you are hiking in.

➤ Latitude: Horizontal, parallel lines running east and west. Lines of latitude are described as being north or south of the equator, which is at zero degrees latitude. The north and south poles are each at 90 degrees latitude. For example, the Great Smoky Mountains on the North Carolina–Tennessee state line can be referred to as being roughly 35 degrees north. Degrees in latitude are further divided into minutes.

➤ Longitude: Vertical lines running north and south on the globe. They start at each pole and widen out to there maximum width at the equator. The line at zero degrees longitude runs through England and is known as the Greenwich Meridian. Its opposite is the International Dateline at 180 degrees. Longitude is given as degrees east or west of the Greenwich Meridian. For example, the Great Smoky Mountains on the North Carolina-Tennessee State Line can be referred to as being roughly 83 degrees west. Longitude is further divided into minutes.

➤ Minutes are a unit of measure for longitude and latitude. There are 60 minutes dividing each degree. It is expressed as 45' for 45 minutes. Minutes are further divided into 60 seconds (marked as 30" for 30 seconds). An accurate position of longitude and latitude for a point might be described as N35° 36' 30", W83° 49' 35". This example refers to a point in Cades Cove in the Great Smoky Mountains National Park.

➤ The contour interval: The variation in elevation expressed by the contour lines on a topographic map. Typical contour intervals on USGS maps include 20- and 40-foot intervals. The closer the lines are together, the greater the gradient. In mountainous terrain, the contour interval will be greater than on gentle terrain. This is so that the contour lines do not crowd together making the map illegible.

➤ Declination diagram: Declination is the angle between magnetic north and true north for a given location. In North America, the line of no declination (or agonic line) extends roughly from Wisconsin down through Alabama and across the Florida panhandle. In Oregon, the declination is 20 degrees west so that 20 degrees must be subtracted for a true reading. In northern Maine, the declination is about 20 degrees east (subtract 20 degrees from the compass reading for a true reading). On nautical charts, the declination is referred to as variation.

➤ Scale: The degree of reduction used in creating a map. Scale is expressed as a ratio, such as 1:62,500. That means that the features on the map are shown at 1/62500th of their actual size, which translates to one inch equals approximately one mile. The scale for a 7.5 minute quadrangle is 1:24,000 or one inch equals 24,000 feet on.

Map Care

Many trail maps are now printed on water-resistant material. But USGS maps and some others you may encounter are still printed on ordinary paper. You may purchase a spray-on lacquer or acrylic to treat the map. The key is to spray several light coats on each side of the map, rather than one heavy coat. A resealable plastic bag works best for further protecting your map from water and abrasion.

Another important factor in caring for a map is proper folding. The following steps work best:

1. Lay the map flat, printed side up. Fold it in half vertically, with the face inside the first fold. Make the creases clean and sharp.

USGS Quadrangles

The United States Geologic Survey is the branch of the government that produces quadrangles and other topographic maps. They have created a library of more than 54,000 maps commonly called Quads that are available in 7.5-minute and 15-minute detail. The 7.5-minute maps are 7.5 minutes longitude by 7.5 minutes latitude covering about 70 square miles. The greater the number of minutes, the less detail shown on the map. The 7.5-minute maps are the most commonly used by hikers and are readily available. The maps may be purchased from a local outfitter or directly from the USGS. For maps east of the Mississippi River, write to U.S. Geologic Survey, Washington, D.C. 20242. For maps west of the Mississippi, write to U.S. Geologic Survey, Federal Center, Denver, CO 80225. Index maps for each state are available free of charge.

---

2. Fold one half in to the center, resulting in quarter-folds.
3. Fold the outside quarter-fold back to the edge, producing an eighth-fold. Use this one as a guide to fold the other quarter the same way. Don't worry, it's easier than it sounds.
4. Half the map should now have four accordion-style folds.
5. Repeat steps 2 and 3 on the map's other half so you end up with a full accordion of eight folds in a long, ruler-like shape.
6. Fold the map Z-like so it's in thirds. Now your map fits almost anywhere, so you can find out how lost you are without unfolding it entirely.

ORIENTEERING

Many trails you will encounter will be well marked, and require nothing more than the guidebook's directions and the provided map. Other trails, especially the Pacific Crest and Continental Divide trails, not only lack sufficient signposts, but, because they are still being developed, may actually have several possible trail routes; in these cases a certain amount of orienteering skill is required. Whether the trail is well-signed or not, if you do not pay close attention to trails and the signposts, you can quickly become lost. A compass is the key to finding your way.

Compass Basics

There are several different styles of compasses to choose from, but they all have several parts in common. The heart of the compass is the needle, which always points to magnetic north (more on this later); no matter which way you turn while holding the compass, the needle will always point to magnetic north (unless you are near metal or some other object that can act as a magnet itself). The needle is located in the compass housing, which on better compasses is filled with liquid. This liquid dampens the movement of the needle, giving you a more accurate reading than housings without liquid. You will also notice parallel lines and an

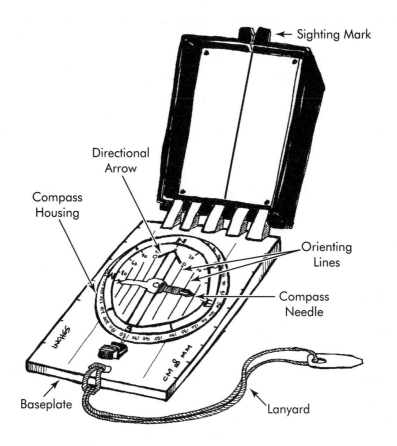

← Sighting Mark

Directional
Arrow

Compass
Housing

Orienting
Lines

Compass
Needle

Baseplate

Lanyard

arrow on the bottom of the housing as well as some letters and lots of marks on the housing ring. The parallel or orienting lines help orient the needle to north, and in conjunction with the baseplate, help you determine a bearing, or direction of travel. The marks, and the letters refer to the cardinal points of the compass.

Cardinal Points

The chief directions of a compass—north, south, east, and west—are indicated on a compass by the letters N, S, E, and W, respectively, and are called the Cardinal points. North is at 0 or 360 degrees, east is at 90 degrees, south is at 180 degrees, and west is at 270 degrees. The points between the cardinal points on a compass are known as intercardinal points—northeast (45 degrees), southeast (135 degrees), southwest (225

Global Positioning System (GPS)

A Global Positioning System (GPS) is a portable receiver linked to satellites which gives an exact fix on your location in latitude and longitude, as well as the elevation. A GPS unit can also be set to determine your average speed, distance to your destination, how far off course you are, and more. The 21 NavStar satellites, which a GPS unit can access at no cost, are part of a system created by the Department of Defense. The Department of Defense claims the commercial units to be accurate only to within 100 meters, but experienced users boast of more accurate readings. Though a handy tool in navigating in the backcountry, be sure you know how to use the unit before you go, and always have a compass as a backup should the GPS unit malfunction.

degrees), and northwest (315 degrees). The cardinal points and sometimes the intercardinal are marked on the housing ring; all other points are noted by numbers or degrees.

Taking a Bearing

Now that you know the parts of a compass, it's time to put it to use. For a compass to be useful in the backcountry, you will need to learn to take a bearing. A bearing is direction of travel from one point to another. If you walked on a bearing of 90 degrees, you would be walking directly east. If you walked on a bearing of 135 degrees, you would be walking southeast. To walk along a bearing of 148 degrees, align the 148-degree mark on the compass housing with the direction arrow on the base plate, then hold the compass before you, and rotate your body until the needle aligns itself with the orienting arrow. You are now facing 148 degrees.

You can also take a bearing on an object to see which direction it lies in relation to your location. Knowing an object's bearing can help locate your position on a map (see below). To do this, turn so that the direction arrow on the compass's base plate faces the object, then rotate the compass housing until the orienting arrow aligns with the needle. The number that aligns with the direction arrow is your bearing.

227

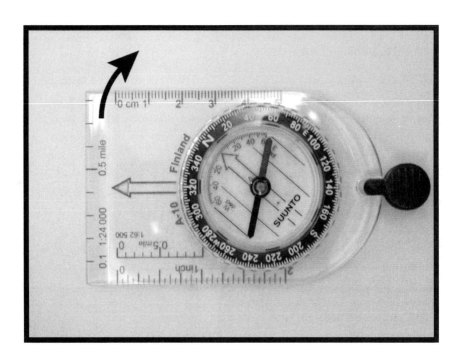

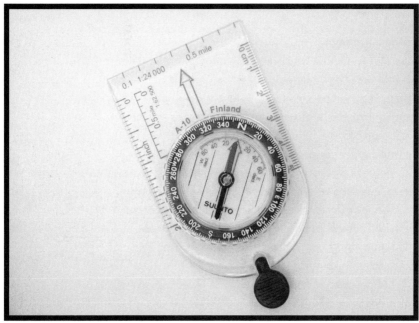

Taking a degree bearing. Determine the direction you need to go (in this case 320°), then turn you and the compass until the needle aligns with the directional arrow.

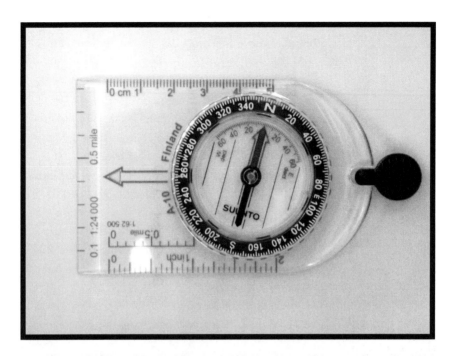

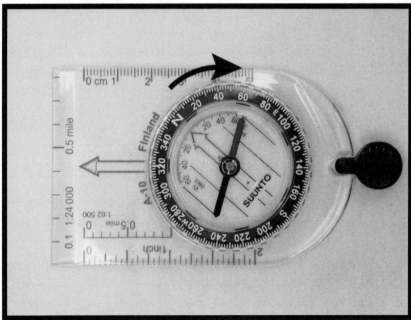

Taking a bearing on an object. Aim baseplate arrow toward object, then rotate compass housing until the arrow aligns with the directional arrow.

Following a Compass Bearing

Once you have a bearing, you are ready to start hiking. Following a compass bearing is made difficult by the obstacles that block walking along a straight line over rugged terrain. Marshes, ponds, boulders, trees, cliffs, and dense shrubs all bar hikers from following a true course. To account for this, always sight ahead on landmarks along your true compass bearing. If while following a bearing of 270 degrees, for example, you must detour around a bog, first note a tree, rock, or other easily identified point on the opposite side of the bog, which is located on your straight line compass bearing. Then after detouring around the bog, go to that landmark and continue following your previous course of 270 degrees.

If the obstacle blocking your path is very large, such as a deep ravine or a pond, a second technique will keep you on track. By using a series of right angle turns, you can return to your original course:

1. Turn 90 degrees from your course and begin the detour, counting the paces as you go.
2. After clearing the obstacle, turn 90 degrees back on to the previous course. Walk past the obstacle.
3. Turn 90 degrees back toward the original course and count off the number of steps from the first leg of the detours. This will return you to your original course.
4. Turn 90 degrees back to follow the original line of travel. The key to this technique is making sure that the out and back portions of the detour are equal in length. That is why keeping track of the number of paces is important.

Orienting the Map and You

It's about time to put the map and compass to work, but before you do this, you will need to orient the map so that the hills, valleys, roads and other features you see will match up correctly with what is on the map. As noted above, a compass points to magnetic north rather than true north. Because magnetic north is not a single point at the north pole but rather a large and non-uniform area, the direction a compass points differs from the true geographic north. This is why explorers to the north pole must use tools other than compasses to find their way. The difference between magnetic north and true north is known as declination.

Why is this important to know? Maps are created so that geographic north is at the top. If you did not adjust the map to take into account declination, you would start to go off course from the very first step. For example, if you did not orient a map that required an adjustment of one degree, for every mile you walked, you would be off by 275 feet. This difference can add up over several miles.

Before you can use a map, you must have it oriented properly to your surroundings. Using a compass makes it easy to orient the map. Follow these simple steps:

➤ Spread the map out and place the compass on top of it.

➤ Adjust for declination. Rotate the compass housing so that the orienting arrow is offset by the amount indicated by the map's declination diagram.

➤ Align the base plate along the bottom of the map and turn map and compass together until the needle lines up with the orienting arrow on the compass housing. The map is now pointing to true north, rather than magnetic north.

You can quickly orient the map without using a compass if you know where you are on the map and you can recognize a nearby landmark on the map.

➤ Locate a mountain peak or other landmark you recognize that is also on the map.

➤ Turn the map until the landmark on the map is the same direction as the actual peak.

This will only roughly orient the map, and can be used to identify other landmarks, such as the companion peaks in a mountain range. For wayfinding, you must orient the map with a compass.

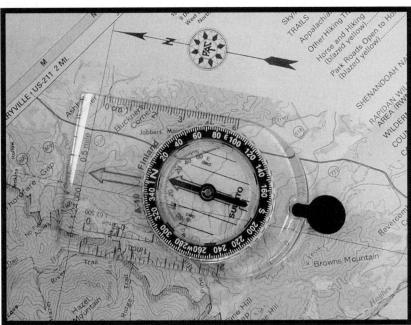

Orienting a map. Align directional arrow with base plate arrow, adjust for declination (in this case 9 degrees 15 minutes west of North), align base plate arrow with map's true north, then rotate compass and map until needle aligns with directional arrow.

Using the Map and Compass

Though you now know how to orient the map properly, it can only help you determine a course or locate other objects if you know your own position on the map. If you are at some spot that is easily recognizable on a map (a trailhead, a fire tower, a mountain peak), you are ready to go. However, in most cases, you will need to use triangulation to find your location.

To triangulate your position:

1. Orient the map.
2. Look for landmarks on the map you can identify in the field and find on the map.
3. Take a bearing on that landmark.
4. Place the compass on the map next to the landmark and draw a line on the map along the compass bearing, starting with the landmark and going back toward and beyond your approximate location.
5. Repeat steps 3 and 4 with a second landmark at least 45 degrees away from the first. Your location is where the two lines on the map intersect.
6. To further verify your location, select a third landmark between the first two and repeat steps 3 and 4. This third line should pass through the intersection of the first two lines to confirm your position. If not, recheck your work.

Once you have located your position on the map, you can identify other landmarks around you simply by taking a bearing on the landmark, placing the compass on the map, and drawing a line from your position to the landmark in question. Likewise, if you have a goal on the map you wish to reach but you cannot see it, you can draw a line between your position and the intended goal, place the compass's edge along the line, and adjust the revolving ring until the orienting arrow aligns with the north arrow. Pick up the compass and with the north arrow still aligned with the orienting arrow, follow the direction of travel line with your eyes. It is now pointing to the object you wish to find in the field.

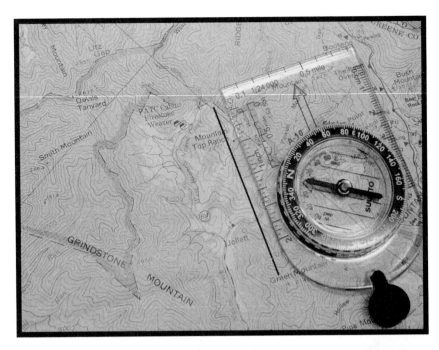

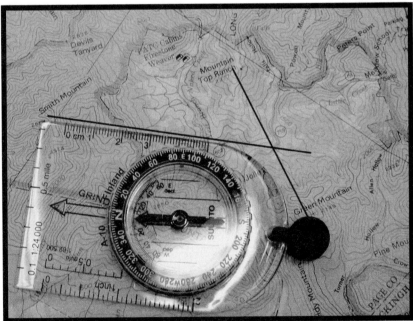

Finding yourself on the map.

Measuring Distance

If you want to find out how far you have come or how far you have to go, you can use one of two similar approaches to measure linear and non-linear distances on a map. For either one, you will need a piece of scratch paper and pencil or pen.

Linear Distance

➤ Lay the paper on the map so that the edge of the paper lines up with the two points you are trying to determine the distance between.

➤ Make a tick mark on the paper at each of these points.

➤ Lay the scratch paper alongside the map's bar scale and read the distance.

Non-Linear Distance

When measuring a trail route, or other non-linear distance on a map, try this:

➤ Make a tick mark for the first point as you did before.

➤ No, move the paper to follow the bends in the trail, making tick marks at significant turns until you reach the end point.

➤ Lay the paper along the bar scale and read the distance.

Some maps in guidebooks will have a scale, such as one inch equals one mile, indicated in the legend, but have no accompanying bar scale. Measure the distance on your scratch paper and multiply by the scale. This would mean that a distance of 3.75 inches on a map with a one-inch-equals-one-mile scale would represent 3.75 miles on the ground.

GETTING FOUND

Even skilled backpackers will occasionally get lost. If you find yourself clueless in the wilderness, here are a few things to keep in mind:

➤ Helping yourself get found starts before the trip. File a trip plan with a friend or a ranger before you leave. This can make the difference between life and death, as it gives search and rescue teams a general location to begin the search.

➤ Never, ever run when you get lost. Not only could you hurt yourself, but you can take yourself farther and farther away from your point of origin and become further disoriented.

➤ If you find yourself lost, retrace your steps until you are back on familiar ground. Yes, it might make your trip longer but it might also save your life.

➤ The only times you might want to leave your current position when lost is when the location is unsafe; severe weather is approaching; no one will know you are missing to search for you; a rescue signal is unlikely to be seen; or you do not have enough food or water to survive and extended wait.

7

Listening to and Caring for Your Body

STRETCHING

In the field of sports, backpacking stands alone as the only endurance sport in which the participants do not regularly perform a warm-up. Distance cyclers and marathon runners have long benefited from a good stretching routine before exercising. Stretching gradually increases heart rate, temperature, and circulation to your muscles. Basically, stretching is like warming up your car on a cold morning. After a night's rest, your muscles need warming. Stretching gets the body going and increases your flexibility.

The following warm-up routine incorporates 11 stretches designed to limber up the areas that hikers use most when backpacking—the legs, the back, and the shoulders. This fifteen-minute routine will help prepare your body for the day's hike by not only stretching your muscles but increasing blood flow to these areas.

How to Stretch

When beginning to stretch, pick a level spot free of stones and sticks. Your sleeping bag or pad makes a handy exercise mat. Each of the following stretches should be held for at least thirty seconds at the point of tension, during which time the tension should begin to decrease. Exhale as you lean into the stretch. During the stretch, relax and breathe steadily. Do not bounce during the stretch. Bouncing can tear at the muscles and tendons, creating damage that won't be able to heal as you hike. Also, do not overstretch. That is, don't push yourself too far. A small burning feeling is all right, pain is not.

These stretches also can be helpful during the cool-down period after a day of backpacking.

Calf Stretch

➤ Find a flat rock or stump that offers enough room for you to stand several inches off the ground.

➤ Stand on the rock with your heels hanging off the rock.

➤ Lower both heels until you feel the stretch in your calves.

➤ Raise both heels, then alternately lower your right then left heel, stretching each for thirty seconds.

➤ If you have a hiking partner, she can help you keep balanced.

Standing Leg Stretch

➤ You will need a tree, though a rock can work. If you use a rock, it needs to be at groin height.

➤ Facing the rock or tree, lift your right leg and rest the heel on the rock or rest the flat of your foot against the tree.

➤ Bend forward slowly from the waist and hold the stretch for about thirty seconds.

➤ Return to a standing position and repeat the stretch with your left leg.

➤ Return to a standing position and repeat the exercise, this time position your body so that your right side is toward the rock or tree when your right leg is up, and your left side is to the tree when your left leg is up. Bend sideways from the waist toward your raised leg.

Shoulder Stretch

➤ Standing, extend your arms over your head.

➤ Hold the elbow of your right arm with your left hand.

➤ Pull the elbow slowly behind your head but do not force it. Hold briefly.

➤ Extend your arms again and repeat the exercise with your left elbow.

Back Stretch

➤ Stand with your feet about shoulders' width apart.

➤ Slowly bend forward from the waist.

➤ Relax your arms, shoulders, and neck as you bend forward.

➤ Bend until you feel a slight stretch in the backs of your legs.

➤ Once you feel the stretch, hold your position for about thirty seconds.

➤ Return to a standing position by bending your knees to relieve the pressure on your lower back.

Side Stretch

➤ Stand with your feet about shoulders' width apart.

➤ Keeping your legs straight, place your right hand on your hip and extend your left arm over your head.

➤ Bend toward the right slowly, and hold.

➤ Return to a standing position and repeat the exercise with your left hand on your hip and your right arm extended. Slowly bend toward the left and hold.

The Squat

➤ Stand with feet flat and toes pointed outward about fifteen degrees.

> Squat and place your palms on the ground for balance.

> Return to a standing position, keeping your knees slightly bent, instead of locking them, to relieve pressure on the lower back.

Sitting Toe Touches

> Sit on the ground (or your sleeping bag if you need padding) and extend your legs in front of you, feet together.

> Lean forward, extend your arms, and reach for your toes.

> Complete the stretch by bringing your forehead as close to your knees as possible.

Hamstring Stretch

> Sit on the ground, legs extended in front of you.

> Pull the right leg in toward your body as you would to sit cross-legged.

> Reach for the toes of your left foot. Make sure to bend at the waist until you feel the stretch in the hamstring.

> Extend your right leg and repeat the exercise with your left leg bent.

Spinal Stretch

> Sit on the ground with your legs extended straight in front of you.

> Cross your left leg over your right leg, placing your left foot on the floor next to your right knee.

> Reach your right arm over your left leg so that the elbow is on the outside of your left leg.

> Twist your upper body to the left. Hold the stretch.

> Return to a sitting position with legs outstretched in front of you. Repeat the exercise crossing your right leg over the left and reaching with your left arm.

Groin Stretch

> Sit on the ground with your legs extended in front of you.

> Pull your feet toward you so that your knees are bent and the soles of your feet touch.

➤ Lower your knees toward the ground until you feel the stretch.

Butt Stretch
➤ Sit or lie down with your legs extended in front of you.
➤ Hold your right ankle and pull your leg toward your chest, bending the knee as you pull.
➤ Extend your right leg and repeat the exercise with your left leg.

MASSAGE
Stretching before exercise will help ease the strain on your muscles during the day, but the key to drug-free pain relief is a good massage after the day's hiking is through. Massage quickens the recovery during a cool-down period. Lactic acid and other waste products pool in the blood in your extremities after exercise. Those waste products, gathered in the muscles, contribute to sore and jittery feelings that come after a tough day on the trail. A good massage moves intercellular fluids through the body and allows the spaces created to be filled with oxygen-rich blood and nutrients.

The benefits of massage—increasing your oxygen supply and purging the body of toxins—can help before you hike as well.

When Not to Massage
There are some times when you should never massage. Hikers who have high blood pressure, have a fever, or have been injured during the day should not be massaged. You should also avoid directly massaging a sprained or bruised area. In these cases, an otherwise helpful massage will only worsen the situation. Treat the above problems using RICE—Rest, Ice, Compression, and Elevation. You should also avoid massaging persons who have varicose veins, tumors, rheumatoid arthritis, skin cancer, or an infectious disease; massage can aggravate these conditions.

Preparing for Massage

You need to properly prepare for massage for it to be most effective. Wear loose clothing if you wear clothing at all during the massage. The area to be massaged should be warm or else your muscles won't relax. It may seem picturesque to try a massage by the side of a mountain pond, but your tent offers a much better atmosphere. In the womb-like enclosure, the light is more subdued and you don't have to be self-conscious or worry about what other hikers might see or think. A sleeping pad and bag on the floor of the tent offers a good compromise between soft and firm that is ideal for massage.

Massage Tips

As you massage, be aware that the meatier areas on the body, such as thighs, can take more pressure than places, such as the spine, where the bones are closer to the surface. When working on the back, for example, you want to concentrate your efforts on the muscular areas that parallel the spine instead of the backbone itself.

All massage strokes should be done working from the extremities toward the heart. You are opening up the capillaries and pushing blood through the veins with the firm massage strokes, and you want to work with the natural flow of blood instead of against it.

If you are doing all of the massage techniques in the following list in a single session (which you should if time and energy permit), do them in the order shown. Work with the back and shoulders first, then the legs and feet. The only change for a whole body massage is that you will want to massage the back of the legs first, then the feet, and lastly, the front of the legs. Nonetheless, always remember that relaxing the muscles is the goal, not following a set pattern or hurrying on to some other activity. If your partner seems to need more work on one area than is suggested in these instructions, listen to his body, not our advice. If you allow enough time for a relaxing massage, the results will be more dramatic.

The Massages

The self-massages listed here use only a few massage techniques. More information and other techniques can be found in *The New Sensual Massage* by Gordon Inkeles, *Massage for Common Ailments* by Sara Thomas, and other books. You may also want to try a professional massage. To find a certified massage therapist in your area, look in the yellow pages, or contact the AMTA (American Massage Therapy Association) at (847) 864-0123.

Back and Shoulder Massage

The back and shoulders collect the stress and tension of the day, tensing up as you hike and staying tense, without massage, for hours or days. The back is an easy place to begin with massage, because it is very forgiving. Remember to take it easy on the spinal cord and work on the meatier portions of the back.

Your shoulders can move in more complex ways than any other joint. Consequently, they are more easily stressed than any other joint. Take your time on the shoulders and it will help the whole body relax.

Circulation for the Back   These long, rhythmic effleurage strokes will get the blood flowing and help your partner relax. Keep in contact with your partner's back and shoulders at all times with this stroke, completing it by circling back down the sides and starting again.

➤ With your partner lying on his or her stomach, straddle your partner's legs.

➤ If you are using oil, pour a little of it in one hand and rub your hands together, then apply the oil to the back and shoulders in light, even strokes. (The following back and shoulder strokes assume the back and shoulders are oiled if needed.)

➤ Place your hands on your partner's lower back (where it joins the buttocks).

➤ Pushing firmly with your entire hands, slide your hands up your partner's back with the delicate spine between your thumbs.

➤ Lean into the stroke as you push, conforming your fingers to the shape of your partner's back (and shoulders and sides).

➤ When you have reached the top of the back (or as far as you can reach), glide your hands out and back down along the sides, continuing to massage as you work back to the top of the buttocks.

➤ As you reach the side of the buttocks, bring your hands together and continue stroking in one smooth motion.

➤ Keep a smooth, even rhythm as you circle the back a half dozen times, pressing deep into the meaty flesh parallel to the spine.

Kneading the Shoulders   To relieve the tension in stiff and achy shoulders, try this kneading technique. Spend as much time as necessary on tight muscles to get them to loosen up.

➤ Lay both hands on one of your partner's shoulders.

➤ Push the flesh into your right hand using your left hand and pinch between your thumb and forefinger.

➤ Work your way around the shoulder, circling from the base of the shoulder blade up over the top of the shoulder and back around.

➤ Keep working around one shoulder until the muscles begin to relax, then work on the other shoulder.

Leg Massage   After a long day of hiking, your leg muscles can be filled with waste products that make your muscles ache. Remember that you should not massage varicose veins or near sprains.

Leg Circulation   Long, steady effleurage strokes on the legs get the blood flowing without exercise. Like all effleurage strokes, these strokes should be done toward the heart, not toward the feet. If you have limited time for massage, this is the one stroke to use on the legs. It will get the blood flowing and kickstart the natural self-healing process.

➤ Kneel beside your partner.

- If you are using oil, pour a little of it in one hand and rub your hands together, then apply the oil to the legs in light even strokes. (The following leg strokes assume the legs are oiled if needed.)
- Start at the ankle of one leg, cupping your hands.
- Push up the leg in slow, firm strokes working toward the upper thigh.
- Alternate hands as you complete a full-leg stroke with each hand.
- A dozen full strokes on the back and then front of each leg will get the blood flowing and get you ready for the other massages on the legs.

Leg Kneading   Kneading allows you to massage deeper into the muscles than the effleurage strokes do. Pinching the flesh between your fingers and thumbs will continue pushing toxins out of the leg muscles and replacing them with oxygen-rich blood. As with other strokes, a slow steady pace is most conducive to relaxing your partner.

- Grip the back of your partner's legs with both hands.
- Work your way up the legs from the ankle to the buttocks, squeezing the flesh in your hands and pinching it gently between your thumb and forefinger.
- As you work your way up the back of the legs, be sure to knead the sides as well as the top. The sides of the legs need attention too.
- Knead the back of each leg several times before moving on to another stroke (massaging either the feet or the front of the legs).
- Have your partner roll over and bend his or her legs at the knees so you can massage the calves and thighs from the front.
- Work your way up to the top of the thighs gently kneading as you go.

Kneading the Knees   Downhill stretches of trail give your knees a real workout. This complex joint is at the center of your powerful leg muscles, but requires more delicate treatment than the meatier flesh of the nearby thighs. Use your fingertips to knead this important area.

➤ Your partner should now be on his or her back, with knees bent.

➤ With small movements, rotate your fingertips and thumbs around the fleshy areas between the bones of one knee.

➤ Move your fingers down the sides of the knee, meeting under the joint as your thumbs stay on top of the leg. Knead the area just above the knee.

Foot Massage

Nowhere are the stresses of backpacking greater than on your feet. At the end of the day, a foot massage can help relieve the stress, and it can help you relax and get ready for a good night's sleep. The foot has hundreds of nerve endings packed into a small space. A few minutes with these massage techniques can take away hours of strain.

Rotating the Top of the Foot   The top of the foot won't rotate uniformly as you turn it. Work with the foot and don't force it.

➤ With your partner lying face down, bend one leg at the knee and grasp the ankle firmly in your left hand (use your right if you're left-handed).

➤ With your right hand, firmly grasp the top of the foot, clamping your hand over the toes.

➤ Pull up to the point of tension.

➤ Rotate the top of the foot in an uneven circle, continuing to pull gently.

➤ Do three full rotations in each direction and repeat on the other foot.

Knuckle Pressing the Arch   The foot is built to withstand a lot of pressure. You will have to be firm with this maneuver to get the desired effect.

➤ Continue kneeling alongside your partner after rotating the top of the foot, and cup your left hand under one foot.

➤ Make your right hand into a fist and push it into

the sole of the foot. Simultaneously, push back on the top of the foot with your left hand.

➤ Rotate the front of your fist back and forth as you continue to press it into the arch.

Repeat on the opposite foot.

Thumbing the Foot   Use heavy pressure with your thumbs to stimulate your partner's soles and ease muscle tension.

➤ With your partner still face down (and a leg bent at the knee so you can get at the foot), grasp one foot firmly in both hands so that your fingers fit around the top of the foot and your thumbs fall together in the arch.

➤ Push firmly with your thumbs into the sole of the foot.

➤ Keep your thumbs close together as you walk them all over your partner's arch while applying heavy pressure.

➤ Work from the heels to the toes and back again as you knead the bottom of the foot.

➤ Repeat on the opposite foot.

Just because you don't have a hiking partner (or don't have one that you want to massage you), that doesn't mean that your aching muscles have to fend for themselves after a day of hiking or backpacking. Don't pop those Ibuprofen tablets yet. There are a few techniques that you can use on yourself to get drug-free relief.

Compression   Use your fingers to compress the middle of a muscle against the underlying bone. This stroke spreads out the muscle fibers and gets the blood flowing. Press firmly and rotate the muscle several times in each direction. This technique works well on your calves and thighs. On the tops of the meatier thighs, you may want to use your elbow, instead of your hands, to compress the muscle.

Compression is well suited to a pre-exercise warm-up. Use it after stretching and before hiking to get your blood flowing before you hike (without raising your heart rate).

Wringing Grip one thigh firmly in both hands and work your hands back and forth from one side of your leg to the other. Work against the grain of the muscle as your hands move with the skin. This technique should cause a warm feeling deep under the skin. It works well on the meaty area just above the knee as well as on your upper thighs.

Massaging Your Own Feet After a day of pounding on the trail, feet cry out for attention. Luckily you don't have to have a partner to massage your soles and toes to relieve aching muscles and get oxygen-rich blood flowing.

➤ Sit up and cross one leg over the other just above the knee so that your ankle is resting on your thigh.

➤ Grasp the foot of that leg firmly in both hands so that your fingers fit around the top of the foot and your thumbs fall together in the arch.

➤ Push firmly with your thumbs into the sole of the foot.

➤ Keep your thumbs close together as you walk them all over your arch, continuing to use heavy pressure.

➤ Work from the heels to the toes and back again as you knead the bottom of your foot.

➤ Pull each toe apart from its nearest neighbors, gently separating the toes until the web of skin between them reaches the point of tension.

➤ Cupping the top of the foot in one hand, take the big toe in the other.

➤ Pull the toe out to the point of tension and rotate it three times in each direction.

➤ Repeat the process working through each of the four remaining toes on that foot individually.

➤ Repeat the entire process on your other foot.

KEEPING HYDRATED

The sun blazed brilliantly against the white sand as we stood in the shade of the ranger office and filled our gallon jugs with water from the fountain. We had been forewarned that water in Cumberland Island's back-country required treatment and we had decided to carry all we'd need for our two-day trip rather than boil or use iodine.

As we trudged down Grand Avenue with gallon jugs swinging heavily against our backs, I began to regret my decision to experience "real" backpacking. I longed for the half-mile walk to Seacamp and its raccoon boxes, cold-water showers, and pleasantly shaded campsites. About halfway to our destination, we were startled by a loud and sloshy crash. We whirled around to find one of the gallon jugs sitting forlornly in the middle of the road's sandy bed. Its sides were split and water formed the pattern of a starfish around it. Well, we weren't about to go back! With only a gallon of water and an "attack of the killer seed ticks," we cut our trip short by one day.

Several years and backpacking miles later, we returned to the backcountry of Cumberland. This time, we carried only enough water to get us to our first campsite—a couple of liters. We also carried a filter to treat the water we pumped from the "iffy" well. We had a wonderful time. But experience need not be your teacher. It is possible to learn from the experience (i.e., the mistakes) of others.

Dehydration

Your body does not always warn you that it needs water. As a matter of fact, your body's thirst indicators are usually overridden when you start to dehydrate. Whether you feel like it or not, do not pass up the opportunity to drink water. The worst that can happen to you is that you'll have to head into the bushes a few more times.

One of the first warning signs of dehydration is the color of your urine. If it is dark gold in color, you're heading into trouble. Drink now, not later. Coffee, tea, alcohol, and soft drinks (unless they're caffeine free) are a no-no because they are diuretics and will increase your fluid loss. Obviously, if you have nothing else, you'll have to drink them; but the best way to avoid this situation is not to carry these drinks at all. If you carry instant coffee rather than a thermos-full, you can have your cake and eat it too. Drinking three full cups of liquid at each meal will help reduce the need to drink in between meals.

On really hot, sweaty days, drinking an electrolyte solution such as Gatorade may help restock your body with more than just water. But many physiologists advise against using drinks like Gatorade because they cause water to leave tissue and flood the digestive system—leaving muscle tissue to fend for itself.

Four activities contribute to your body's loss of water:

1. Respiration: 1–2 liters per day average
                         6 liters per day in extreme cold/high altitude
2. Perspiration: 1–2 liters per day average
                         1–2 liters per hour when exerting oneself in hot, dry weather
3. Urination: 1–2 liters per day average
                         1–2+ with overhydration
                         1–2- with dehydration
4. Defecation: 0.1 liter per day average
                         As much as 25 liters a day with diarrhea

In most situations, without any water at all, a human can live for three to four days. Let's take a worst-case scenario—you're lost in the desert. Your best option is to find a shady spot and wait to be found. Why? Because if you have four liters of water, you could live as long as four days; ten liters, five days; and twenty liters, a week. But, get up and start walking (at night— during the day you wouldn't stand a chance) and you decrease your life span from a week to four days with twenty liters of water.

How Much Should You Carry
Like everything else, how much water you carry is up to you. We carry between two and three liters most of the time, which is usually adequate on most trails. I can think of only a couple of times when we had to eat cold

The Body and Water

Like the earth, the human body is 75 percent water. If you lose one and a half liters of water (through respiration, perspiration, etc.), you lose 25 percent of your body's efficiency. And, if you're expending energy in 110-degree, dry, desert heat, you could easily double the amount of water and efficiency lost. Fortunately, death from dehydration is unusual, except in the desert. Yet it is always wise to be conservative when it comes to keeping yourself hydrated. Drinking at least four liters of water a day will replace the minimum you expend.

How much water you'll need, even how much you carry, is always a matter of personal preference. We have cursed both carrying too much and too little. Though it may be uncomfortable at times, you will not die of thirst while hiking if you take precautions. First, always make sure you are hydrated before you begin to hike and before you go to sleep. If you do wind up thirsty and low or flat out of water, among the things you can do are chew gum or put a small pebble under your tongue and hold it there until you find something to drink.

meals for supper or go drinkless. Granted, there have been a few times when we spent more than half an hour waiting to fill our canteens as water dripped from an improvised funnel, but that type of situation is rare. Be prepared. Before planning a hike of any distance, find out the water situation in the area you plan to hike. You may have to carry more than is usually necessary.

You will want to take a serious look at how much liquid you take in on a normal non-hiking day. Do you drink a lot, even when you're not exerting yourself? You may need to carry more than the standard two liters of water. For example, on a cool day, I can easily get by with a cup or two of drink at breakfast and a half-liter at lunch and dinner. On hot days, I go through a liter or more at each meal. But I am an exception. Some people will want to sip on water constantly while hiking.

As a couple, Frank and I find we use approximately two liters of water at each meal: for oatmeal and hot chocolate or coffee at breakfast, for powdered drink mix at lunch, and for the meal and drink at supper time. We use the most water at supper because it is always our biggest meal and the hardest to clean up. Keep this in mind when planning your trip, especially when you intend to hike through water-scarce areas. Not only must you drink water to keep your body functioning properly and to avoid dehydration, but you must also use water to clean up after meals.

If you're a heavy drinker, so to speak, never pass up a good water source. Keep your canteens full of water. On hot days, Frank and I often slake our thirst at a cold spring before filling our canteens. When the temperature is high, it is best to drink cold, but not icy, water; cold water is absorbed by the body more quickly than warm or hot water, and thus speeds up your rehydration.

What to Carry It In
When we first started backpacking, we chose aluminum canteens to carry our water. We soon regretted that decision because the canteen's mouth was small, making it hard to fill and mix drink in. The canteens were also cumbersome and difficult to get at because they were a bit too big to fit in the side pocket on our packs. We stuffed them in anyway, and consequently, had to help each other work them back out.

We eventually ended up with the Nalgene bottle. Its wide mouth is easy to fill (and to mix drink in); it is also easy to drink out of and hold. We each carry a one-liter Nalgene bottle, but they are available in a variety of sizes. I have a holder for mine that attaches to my hip belt. Talk about easy access. Two bottles are easy to carry—one within easy reach and another packed away for later use. The screw-on tops are also recommended. (There are some that have a plug and screw-on top, but these seem prone to leaking.) The Nalgene type of bottle is used by most hikers.

Also good for this purpose are the new drink bottles used by athletes—the ones you squeeze to squirt the liquid into your mouth through a spout. There are even some bottles on the market that have a tube running from the spout so that you don't even have to remove your bottle to drink. A little more flimsy, but still a viable alternative, especially in a desperate situation, are empty plastic soda bottles. The one-liter size is used the most. They tend to leak a bit around the cap, but they are great when a heat wave hits and you need to carry extra water for a limited time. The same goes for plastic milk jugs with screw-on caps.

There are two new water containers on the market that can be fitted with a filter to treat your water. An adapter for this filter must be purchased from the manufacturer.

Something extra to carry (but worth it) is a collapsible water bag. They're wonderful at camp because they hold more than enough water for dinner, cleanup, and sometimes even a sponge bath. Water bags, however, are unwieldy to carry filled in your pack as your only water holder. Water bags also tend to stay damp and leak a bit. We carry ours in a plastic bag to prevent it from getting the others things in our pack wet. A cheaper alternative to purchasing a water bag through an outdoor store is to recycle the bladder found in the five-liter "boxes" of wine. They're strong, lightweight, and fold up easily when empty. They are susceptible to punctures, though, so use them with care.

Most distributors of water bags also sell shower attachments that connect to the spout. We bought one but have never used it. The weather always seems to be either too cold or hot enough to swim. My stepfather, on the other hand, uses his religiously.

Where to Find Water
For many trails, there are guidebooks that tell you where to find water. But don't depend on guidebooks. Springs can run dry and are often intermittent. The same goes for small streams. Local trail clubs and the National Forest and Park Services often post signs along the trail to let hikers know where the nearest water supply can be found.

While hiking, you will get your water everywhere—from a pump to a spring to a beaver pond. Along the dry desert stretch of the Pacific Crest Trail, many hikers pull their water (albeit illegally) from the Los Angeles Aqueduct. Hikers who have tried this have some very entertaining stories to tell. We know of a couple of hikers who lost several bottles while fishing for water in the aqueduct before finally getting a "bite."

Water sources vary from stagnant pools dribbling from their source half a mile or more away from the trail (and downhill to boot!), to clear, ice-cold springs gushing forth alongside the trail.

Although there are exceptions, the higher you are, the harder it will be to find water. Conversely, the lower you are, the more water there is, and the more likely it is that you'll have to treat that water.

Giardia

"During the past fifteen years giardiasis has been recognized as one of the most frequently-occurring waterborne diseases in the United States," said Dr. Dennis D. Juranek of the Centers for Disease Control in Atlanta. According to Juranek, Giardia isn't just a contaminant of beaver ponds or of burbling brooks that flow through cow pastures (and you'll get your water from both). Anywhere there are animals, including humans, there's a chance of Giardia. Believe it or not, 50 to 60 percent of all giardiasis comes from tap water.

One reason Giardia causes intestinal problems may be that the parasite interferes with chemicals the body needs to digest certain foods, including dairy products. For as long as the parasite remains in its host, the intolerance to certain foods remains.

"The disease is characterized by diarrhea that usually lasts one week or more," Juranek said, "and may be accompanied by one or more of the following: abdominal cramping, bloating, flatulence with foul-smelling gas, vomiting, fatigue, and weight loss."

Some people become infected but experience no symptoms at all (though they can still spread the disease), and the parasite vanishes in a couple of months. Others can have several of the symptoms but no diarrhea or they can have only sporadic episodes of diarrhea every three or four days. While most Giardia

A hiker filters water from Whiskey Spring in Pennsylvania.

infections persist only for one to two months, some people undergo a more chronic phase; the microbe hangs on, causing recurring attacks for many years.

"The problem may not be whether you're infected with the parasite or not," Juranek said, "but how harmoniously you both can live together, or how you can get rid of the parasite (either spontaneously or by treatment) when the harmony does not exist or is lost."

Juranek said that there are three drugs available in the United States to treat giardiasis: quinacrine or Atabrine, metronidazole or Flagyl, and furazolidone or Furoxone. All three are prescription drugs; they are listed in the order of their effectiveness, although Flagyl is the most often prescribed. You may want to ask your doctor about a prescription if you are worried about picking up Giardia, especially if you intend to be out hiking for a week or more. But we know of only one hiker who carries a prescription with him, and he has never needed it.

"Fortunately," Juranek said, "the Giardia parasites do not invade other parts of the body or cause permanent damage." Though rarely dangerous to adults, giar-diasis can prove life-threatening to both the very young and the very old because of the severe dehydration it can cause should the victim be afflicted with vomiting and diarrhea.

Treating Water

On a hot day, even a beaver pond can look good and it takes a lot of restraint not to dip your Sierra cup into the inviting liquid. I remember times I wanted water so badly that the sound of the last remaining drops of water sloshing inside my canteen almost drove me mad. But I saved that tiny bit of water just in case.

Don't succumb to the urge to drink water before you've purified it. It is easier to carry an extra pound or two of water than suffer the discomforts of Giardia and other stomach ailments that dehydrate you and cause you to lose your strength. Diarrhea and cramps are harder to handle while hiking because of the physical strain you're already placing on your body.

We know of only a few hikers who have picked up Giardia while hiking. If you are careful, the chances of contracting this parasitic disease while backpacking are few. But Giardia cases are increasing at an alarming rate—an estimated figure (because so many cases go unreported and/or misdiagnosed) is more than 120,000 nationwide.

"Water treatment steps range from doing nothing at all, to boiling water, to high-priced purifiers," said Bob Dowling, a long-distance hiker and victim of Giardia. "For the most part, I felt confident about the water sources I chose. Then I caught Giardia from an area I considered the most pristine—the wilderness stretch (of the Appalachian Trail) in Maine. This set me rethinking my practices on drinking water. A common question you hear is 'How is the water?'—the response usually being 'Fine.' How do they know? Did they test for giardiasis or other contaminants? Hell no! How can you be sure?

The answer is: you can't be sure. A hiker must treat all water as suspect. What to do? Use some common sense to decrease the chance of contaminated water."

Suspect water should always be treated, and, according to Juranek, portable devices with micro strainer filters are the only way to filter out Giardia. To be safest, Juranek says, the filters should have a pore size of one micron or less.

"Theoretically, a filter having an absolute pore size of less than six micrometers (microns) might be able to prevent Giardia cysts of eight to ten micrometers in diameter from passing into your drinking water, but for effective removal of bacterial and viral organisms, as well as Giardia, the less than one micrometer pore size is advisable."

Water filters are discussed in depth in the Equipment chapter of this book. The problems with filters are their bulkiness, weight, and cost. There are two other, lighter ways to get rid of Giardia, both with their own drawbacks.

Giardia can be killed by bringing your water to a boil. According to Dr. Dennis Addiss, also of the Centers for Disease Control in Atlanta, water need not be boiled to kill Giardia, only brought to the boiling point. Giardia is actually killed at a lower temperature; bringing your water to a boil is just insurance that you have killed the parasite. But, by boiling your water for a minute or more, you will also kill other viruses, bacteria, and parasites.

Obviously, the drawbacks to heating water are the time and fuel it takes to boil it as well as the time it takes to cool down. If you're boiling the water for a meal anyway, you can be assured the Giardia will be killed. You do not have to account for altitude when you're boiling water to kill Giardia.

Iodine and Halazone also can kill Giardia. One tablet in one liter of relatively clear, not-too-cold water for half an hour will effectively kill Giardia, says Addiss. The major drawback to this method is the taste. Iodine leaves a not-too-pleasant taste in your water, and, once again, you have to play the waiting game.

One way to combat the bad taste, according to
Addiss, is to leave your water container uncovered for a
while; this helps to dissipate the iodine.

Some hikers use two or three drops of chlorine
(usually in the form of bleach) to treat their water. But,

When to Treat Your Water

The truth is, most hikers take chances and don't treat their water, especially when the source is a spring or is at a high altitude. Pristine areas
(such as springs high in the Rockies) are as likely a source of Giardia as
your kitchen faucet. Because you can get Giardia from your tap water,
day care centers, swimming pools, food, pets, and sexual contact as well
as from streams, ponds, and springs, how can you possibly know if the
water is safe? You can't. But the following chart will give you some idea
of how safe your water might be.

Best to Worst Sources of Water	Confidence
Faucet or hose	High
Piped spring	High
Unprotected spring (Look for animal tracks around the spring.)	Moderate
Streams (Consider the source of the stream: Does it run by civilization or cow pastures or does it stay in protected wilderness? Also, how cold is it, how near is its source, and how fast is it running? It may need to be treated.)	Low
Ponds or Lakes (Assume the worst; treat the water. Take the time to be safe even if you feel lazy or tired.)	None

All hikers we've talked to agree with this analysis, and though many
rarely treat their water, almost all agree in retrospect that it's better to be
safe than sorry. As long-distance backpacker Nancy Hill put it, "Do as I
say not as I do."

It all comes down to a judgment call: when the source is question-
able, you're the one taking the risk. Many hikers agree that they are less
likely to treat their water when they are tired or depressed.

---

according to Addiss and Juranek, this is not a very good idea.

"There are too many variables that influence the efficiency of chlorine as a disinfectant," says Juranek. Among those variables are water pH, water temperature, organic content of the water, chlorine contact time, and the concentration of chlorine.

"There's just no way to be sure that you've accounted for all the variables," says Addiss.

Treating your water is important, but keep in mind that bacteria can also grow in your water bottle, especially if you use it to carry flavored drinks. Make sure you keep your water bottle clean. Pay particular attention to the threads on bottles with screw-on caps.

Alternatives to Treating Water

So, what if your filter is hopelessly clogged and you've used up all your iodine tablets (or you left your emergency supply at home)? And, for some reason you can't boil water . . . you're on the brink of dehydration, perhaps? Well, OK, there are some things you can do to make your untreated water a little safer to drink. But do this only in emergencies, please:

➤ If there is anything even remotely animal-like near the water source—beaver dam, animal scat, dead or decaying identifiable or unidentifiable Order Animalia, walk well upstream before drinking.

➤ If you are in snow country, then water dripping off a snow patch on a steep slope is probably a pretty safe bet. If it is cold out, warm it in your mouth before swallowing. No use risking hypothermia on top of dehydration.

➤ Springs are almost always (but not always) a good choice for clean water; definitely better than a big river that's caught who knows what on its trip to the sea. Look around the spring first, though. I was once disappointed to find one of my favorite freshwater springs contaminated by an UAC (unidentifiable animal corpse).

By the way, emergency situation or not, it is not a bad

idea to carry along a pre-filter; either one that attaches to your filter's intake hose or even a bandanna to remove the really large particles that are greedily looking forward to clogging up your filter element.

A Word of Caution

Don't risk clogging that precious filter (or purifier) by filtering your cooking water. You've got to bring it to a boil anyway—just boil it for three minutes no matter what (this can include cooking time) and you'll always be on the safe side. Not a single one of the little bad guys out there can survive a three-minute dip in a rolling boil. Just fill your cook pot with unfiltered water and set it on the stove.

When Hiking through Snow or on Cold Days . . .

➤ Never drink icy water in the winter or even on cool days. The cold water can cause your body temperature to drop. To avoid this, warm snow or water in your mouth before swallowing.

➤ Protect your water when temperatures drop below freezing by burying it deep in your pack. At night, stash it inside your tent or at the end of your sleeping bag. You can also turn your water bottles upside down so that ice won't block the spout.

➤ Keep your bottles full of water by topping off with snow after each drink.

➤ Use water to melt snow. An inch of water in your cook pot will melt snow more quickly. Add the crustiest, iciest, or wettest snow to your pot—it'll produce more water.

➤ It probably goes without saying to avoid yellow snow, but also steer clear of pink or "watermelon" snow. This snow gets its name from its color, taste, and scent, which are produced by microorganisms that can cause diarrhea.

➤ Burying your water in the snow will help insulate it. A lidded pot buried a foot or so under snow will not freeze. Remember to mark the spot carefully.

➤ Keep in mind that melting snow will take more fuel and more time. With a cold wind blowing, it can take an hour and a stove full of fuel to melt and boil a quart of water.

First Aid

Arising early one summer morning, Frank and I and several other backpacker friends hiked to a picnic area before fixing breakfast. The thought of enjoying our repast at a table (what luxury!) was worth breaking camp at dawn and hiking the couple of miles.

I so enjoyed my first cup of coffee that I asked Frank if there was enough water left for a second.

"Sure," he said, eyeing the pot still simmering on our Whisperlite. He picked up the pot lifter, but before he could pick up the pot, it tipped over, and spilled nearly boiling water right into my lap. Quick-thinking Phil Hall immediately doused my lap with cold water from his Nalgene and proceeded to use all the readily available water in the same manner. As soon as I was able, I hurried to the bathhouse and used water-soaked paper towels as compresses until the stinging sensation finally faded. I managed to survive the accident with only one small blister in the groin area. Phil's lightning fast reaction was the result of experience. He had once been burned by boiling water on a backpacking trip.

Whenever you head out into the wilderness, it is essential that you are prepared. We have found that preparation means planning. *Emergency Medical Procedures for the Outdoors* by Patient Medical Associates outlines what to do before you go:

➤ If you are hiking with one or more people, it is to your benefit to discuss any existing medical problems and knowledge of first aid.

➤ If any of your party suffers from a chronic illness, such as diabetes or epilepsy, or from serious allergies, list their names and illnesses. Also note types of medication, dosages, when the medication is given, and where it is kept.

➤ If there is no one in your hiking group that knows CPR, the Heimlich maneuver, artificial respiration, or basic first aid, it would be wise to have one of the group take a course that covers these important techniques. If one of your party is trained, he should review the procedures before heading out.

➤ If you don't have a first aid kit, prepare one.

➤ If children are hiking with you, explain to them how to get help in an emergency.

➤ Before you leave, inform a close friend or relative of your whereabouts, specifying when you intend to arrive and depart and your planned route.

Fortunately, in thousands of miles of backpacking, I have suffered only minor injuries that were easily handled by a basic first aid kit. And it is unlikely that you'll have to contend with anything more serious than a scratch or two. But even the best-prepared person cannot account for a seemingly stable rock that tips beneath the foot, twisted roots, or even slippery pine needles. No one intends to hurt themselves while hiking. I still bear the scar on my shin from a bad fall I took after slipping on a wet rock. I had walked over hundreds of rocks that day. Why did that one throw me?

Being prepared for backpacking is simply knowing what you're getting into and what to do when you or someone else is injured. Unfortunately, backpackers cannot carry everything they might need in case of an accident—they wouldn't be able to fit it all in their packs!

In their book, *Medicine for the Backcountry* (by ICS Books), Frank Hubbell and Buck Tilton claim that the first commandment of first aid kits is "Thou shalt find it impossible to put together the perfect first aid kit."

"Go ahead and try," they write, "but eventually, if you spend enough time in the backcountry, you will one day wish for something that is not there."

See the Equipment chapter for a list of what should be in a close-to-perfect kit. And carry that kit with you whenever you go hiking—even on day hikes.

Because it is impossible to carry everything you might need for an outdoor emergency, your next best bet is knowing how to improvise with what you do have. You can carry a first-aid instruction manual with you if you are really worried, but taking a first-aid course (Wilderness First Aid—the course and book offered by Outward Bound—is the best) is highly recommended for those who spend a lot of time in the outdoors. Taking a course in CPR is recommended for every soul on this planet.

Besides a first aid kit and knowledge of backcountry medicine, it is important to know what you're getting into. Backpacking is more than just a walk in the woods. If you are not prepared to deal with the discomforts that are inherent in carrying a thirty- to seventy-pound pack on your back as well as the inconveniences involved in a backpacking trip, you need to seriously reconsider getting into the sport. When backpacking, the out-

BACKPACKING TIP

Take a first aid course. The American Red Cross offers courses in CPR and first aid and Wilderness Medical Associates (888/945-3633) offer intensive courses on wilderness first aid.

doors is your home. You may have the shelter of a tent over your head at night, but other than that, the sky is your roof and everything beneath it shares its home with you, including poisonous plants (poison ivy and oak), nasty insects (bees, mosquitoes, and ticks), and rocks, roots, and mud, . . . all potential accidents waiting to happen.

I am not an expert and I am not going to try to be, but I think it is important to list the major categories of medical emergencies that occur in order to give you some idea of what's possible and how to prevent them. For the most part, I have listed them in alphabetical order because any other order would imply that one medical emergency is more significant than another. While that is generally not true—one medical problem in the outdoors is just as great as another—two medical emergencies are so important that they need to be mentioned first. If a person is not breathing they will die. If a person is bleeding profusely they may well die. If a person is breathing and they are not bleeding to death, however, you generally have time to react. So, here's the list . . .

POSSIBLE MEDICAL PROBLEMS

Breathing Problems

As I said above, if a person is not breathing they will die. If you do not know how to establish an airway and perform artificial respiration, you should take a CPR course before you head out into the wilderness. Artificial respiration is part of cardiopulmonary resuscitation and will be taught in a CPR course. There are many instances, particularly in drownings and heart attacks, where CPR has saved lives. Watch the television series Emergency 911 sometime—you're bound to see CPR used several times in every episode.

Bleeding

Unless you have a severe aversion to blood (that is, you get sick or faint at the sight of it), you should be able to handle minor injuries while hiking (see Wounds). But, what if you or a hiking partner slices an

265

arm or a leg while whittling and hits a vein or artery? Unfortunately, ignoring the problem won't make it go away. People can and do bleed to death. Knife wounds and other serious injuries resulting in heavy bleeding often demand an emergency trip to the hospital. I know of many hikers, a brother included, who have watched an emergency room doctor stitch their knife wounds together.

How do you stop the bleeding until you or the victim can reach help? If the usual methods don't work—direct pressure and elevation—you have a problem on your hands. A basic first aid course will teach you what to do should a situation like this arise. If you haven't taken a course in first aid, then what you do to stop the bleeding will have to be a judgment call on your part. Once again, a first aid course is highly recommended before heading out into the wilderness.

Altitude Sickness

A friend of ours was attempting an ascent of Mount McKinley when he began experiencing a headache and nausea, as well as unusual fatigue. Suspecting Acute Mountain Sickness (AMS), he retreated (with much regret) to a base camp that was at a much lower elevation. A pal descended with him, forfeiting his ascent to help out a friend in need.

Once back in camp, his symptoms faded, but it was too late to attempt another ascent. Fortunately, he was able to leave Denali on his own two feet. Many people are unfamiliar with high altitude environments, so when they do experience the first symptoms of AMS, they put it off to dehydration or a cold. These people often require emergency help because they let their symptoms go too far.

Although physiological changes (increased respiration) occur at 4,000 feet, complications from altitude sickness seldom occur below 10,000 feet. High altitude is usually considered 8,000 to 12,000 feet; very high, 12,000 to 18,000; and extremely high, over 18,000 feet.

Symptoms of altitude sickness usually begin eight

hours or more after a quick ascent. Your first symptom will be a headache followed by loss of appetite, nausea, lassitude, and unusual fatigue. You may even vomit and your skin could look bluish or purple.

AMS is severe when you no longer can walk a straight line heel-to-toe. Edema, or build-up of fluid in the lungs and brain, often kills victims of AMS. Those with edema of the lungs make a crackling noise when breathing that can be heard if you press your ear to their chest. Edema of the brain causes severe headaches, hallucinations, seizures, unconsciousness, coma, and then death.

The only way to cure AMS is to descend immediately; the best way to prevent AMS is to acclimatize yourself to new altitudes slowly. Never ascend from sea level to 8,000 feet in one day—always spend at least one night at 5,000 to 7,000 feet first. Once above 8,000 feet, you should spend each night at only 1,000 feet greater than the previous night, even if you climb higher during the day. And, you'll acclimatize better if you spend two nights and days at 8,000 to 10,000 feet before going any higher.

Blisters

Blisters heal slowly if you continue to hike and aggravate them. The best way to avoid this problem is to treat blisters before they occur.

When a part of your foot feels hot or tender, stop hiking. Take your shoes and socks off and inspect the tender area. Cut out a piece of moleskin that is larger than the "hot spot." Apply the moleskin to the hot spot, change your socks, and put your boots back on. Quick action at this stage may prevent blisters altogether.

If you do get a blister, try to leave the blister unbroken. If it is still small and relatively flat, cover the blister with moleskin and resume hiking. If the blister gets worse, wash the area with soap and water and make a small hole in the base of the blister with a sterilized needle (hold it in a flame until the tip turns red) so that the fluid drains. Once the blister is drained, apply a sterile bandage to prevent further irritation and infection.

If the blister is already broken, treat it like an open wound: cleanse and bandage it, and watch for signs of infection. If necessary, quit hiking for a day or two and let your blisters heal.

Bruises

Bruises occur while backpacking when your pack is improperly fitted or when you fall. It's easy to prevent bruising from your pack by making sure that your pack fits correctly (see fitting information in the Equipment chapter). It also helps to watch your step.

If a bruise is severe, it is not helped by elevation and cold compresses, and if it increases in both pain and size, it could indicate internal injuries or a fracture. Help should be sought.

Burns

Burns are easy to prevent because you need only use a modicum of caution. Sitting too close to a campfire, carelessly lighting your backpacking stove or igniting it in a tent, ignoring the sun and refusing to wear sunscreen, and improperly stabilizing your cook pot (on the stove or over a fire) are all sure ways to get burned. With a little extra care and caution you should be able to avoid hurting yourself. But, accidents do happen.

First-degree burns, including sunburn, appear bright red. Treat these minor burns by pouring cold water over the burned area and applying cold compresses for five to ten minutes. The skin should be allowed to air dry if possible. Sunburn can be prevented by the use of a sunscreen with a sun protection factor of fifteen or more. Continued exposure to sun can cause severe burning and, eventually, skin cancer. Antiseptic burn sprays may be used with first-degree burns, but should not be used with second- or third-degree burns.

Second-degree burns are characterized by bright red skin, blisters, and swelling. Do not break the blisters. Rather, immerse the burn in cold water or pour cold water over the burned area. Quick action will help reduce the burning effect of heat in the deeper layers of skin. Cover the burn with a sterile bandage.

Third-degree burns are highly unlikely on a hike. These burns are distinguished by charred flesh and must be treated in a hospital. If third-degree burns occur, do not remove clothing that may adhere to the burns. If you cannot get to a hospital within an hour, give the victim a weak solution of salt water to sip. The solution will help replace essential fluids that have been lost because of the burns. Unlike first- and second-degree burns, do not immerse the burn in cold water. Cover the area with a clean cloth and get the victim to a doctor immediately.

Stop, Drop, and Roll

A group of backpackers was sitting around a campfire in Michigan when several flaming limbs tumbled over the rocks of the fire ring. Most of the campers were able to jump back in time, but one unlucky hiker, Jack Lean, caught a flaming branch in his lap that ignited his pants.

Fortunately, he reacted quickly, dropping immediately to the ground and smothering the flame against the earth. His friends helped by dousing his thighs with cold water from their canteens. Then a couple of friends removed the burned clothing to assess the damage, and others high-tailed it to the nearest spring for more cold water. Jack's friends continued to douse his legs with cold water for ten minutes until they were sure that his skin and the tissue beneath it were no longer hot.

Due to his quick reaction and the help of his fellow backpackers, Jack suffered only second-degree burns. It is important that you remember—Stop, Drop, and Roll.

The natural tendency is to run, but this will only fuel the flames. By dropping immediately to the ground, you can smother the fire. By rolling back and forth or in complete circles (depending on the extent of the flames), you will completely douse the flames by denying them oxygen.

Fortunately, burns from campfires are rare. But keep in mind that many of today's synthetic fibers are prone to melting rather than igniting. This can make burns more dangerous because the material melts into your skin instead of turning to ash and flaking away.

Cold-Weather Medical Emergencies
Hypothermia and frostbite are the dangers you face when hiking in cold weather, on ice, or on snow.

Humid and windy conditions and wet clothes increase the effects of the cold. If you are fatigued, smoking, drinking alcoholic beverages, or under emotional stress, your body is even less resistant. You can prevent injuring yourself when hiking in cold temperatures by keeping these things in mind. If it is really cold, wet, and windy, your best bet may be to set up your tent and crawl into your sleeping bag. A little warmth and rest may be all you need to combat the cold.

Hypothermia

It was a rainy day in Georgia, about forty-five degrees, and Ken couldn't wait to get to his planned campsite and make himself some hot tea. A half hour later, soaked to the skin, he arrived at the spring that marked the camping area. Rather than pitch his tent, change into some warm clothes, and crawl into his sleeping bag, Ken decided to pull out his pack stove and make himself the tea he had been longing for.

With numb fingers and a slight case of the shivers, it took Ken several tries to get his stove lit. Cursing, he fumbled open the cap of his Nalgene and shakily poured water into his cook pot. Then, apathetically, he sat on the cold, wet ground and waited for his water to boil.

By the time little bubbles began to rise from the bottom of the pot, Ken was shivering so badly that he couldn't control his hand movements. Missing his cup entirely, he poured the hot water all over the soggy ground. Cursing and weeping, Ken stumbled over to the spring for more water. With much difficulty, he was able to get some water in his Nalgene; but when he returned to his stove, he was unable to light it, and frankly, he no longer cared to.

His shivering was stopping, he was feeling kind of sleepy, and he was enjoying the trees. They were dancing for him. The next morning, two hikers found Ken lying lifeless by his stove.

The first signs of hypothermia—shivering, numbness, drowsiness, and marked muscular weakness—are followed by mental confusion and impairment of judgment, slurred speech, failing eyesight, and eventually, unconsciousness. Be aware that the most serious warning sign that a hypothermia victim is going down fast is when the shivering stops. It means the victim is close to death. Death, if it occurs, is usually due to heart failure.

You are most likely to become hypothermic after you have stopped hiking, especially if you are tired. Movement keeps you warm. Your body's core temperature can drop once you stop.

Fortunately, hypothermia is easy to combat if caught early. If you experience any of the symptoms mentioned above, drop everything and make yourself warm. Strip yourself of your wet clothes and put on dry clothes if possible. Crawl into your sleeping bag and, if you're able, heat up something hot to drink—tea, soup, hot chocolate. Anything hot will help raise your internal temperature. Drinks with a high sugar content are best. You may want to carry along a pack of fruit gelatin. It tastes great when heated and contains a lot of sugar. But get your body warm first! Don't take the time to heat yourself something to drink until you've rid yourself of the wet clothes.

If you're with someone or you happen on someone showing signs of hypothermia, try sharing body heat. If you're not too shy, strip down to your underwear or nothing at all and crawl into a sleeping bag with the victim. Direct skin contact does wonders for transferring heat. Once the victim is in dry clothes, wrapped in a warm sleeping bag, and sipping on something warm to drink, you can try building a fire for added warmth.

Remember to take hypothermia seriously. Most hypothermia victims die in forty- to fifty-degree weather.

Frostbite

Frostbite occurs when crystals begin to form either superficially or in the fluids and soft tissues of the skin. Keep in mind that the effects of frostbite will be more severe if the affected area is thawed and then refrozen. Fortunately, the areas affected by frostbite are usually small. The nose, cheeks, ears, fingers, and toes are the most common areas.

A Note on Windchill

When the wind starts to blow, even temperatures in the fifties can be dangerous. The lower the temperature and the greater the wind, the more hazardous the conditions. As I sit here writing this, air temperatures in the teens have the feel of below-zero degrees because of ten- to twenty-mile-per-hour winds. The following chart will give you some idea of the temperature your body feels when the winds are blowing:

Windchill Chart

Wind	Actual temperature in degrees Fahrenheit						
(MPH)	40	30	20	10	0	-10	-20
	Windchill equivalent temperatures						
Calm	40	30	20	10	0	-10	-20
5	35	25	15	5	-5	-15	-25
10	30	15	5	-10	-20	-35	-45
15	25	10	-5	-20	-30	-45	-60
20	20	5	-10	-25	-35	-50	-65
25	15	0	-30	-45	-60	-75	-90
30	10	0	-20	-30	-50	-65	-80
35	10	-5	-20	-35	-50	-65	-80
40	10	-5	-20	-35	-35	-55	-70

Before frostbite occurs, the area will look flushed and then become white or grayish yellow. Pain is often felt early but usually subsides—if pain is felt at all.

If you suspect frostbite, the first thing to do is to cover the frozen part and provide the victim with extra clothing and blankets or double wrap him in sleeping bags. If possible, bring the victim indoors (a tent will do if nothing else is available) and provide him with a warm drink. Rewarm the frozen part quickly by immersing it in lukewarm water. Continue to keep the water warm. If water is not practical or available, wrap the affected part gently in warm blankets and clothes.

Handle the frostbitten area gently. Do not massage it. Once thawed, the area will swell severely and become flushed once more. At this point, discontinue warming it and have the victim exercise the part if possible.

Cleanse the frostbite with water and soap, and rinse it thoroughly before blotting it dry with clean towels or whatever you have handy that is clean and dry. If blisters have formed, do not break them.

If fingers or toes are involved, place gauze between them to keep them separated. Do not apply any other dressings unless you intend to transport the victim to medical aid. Also, elevate the frostbitten parts and protect them from contact with bedclothes. If toes are involved, the victim should not walk and additional heat should not be applied once the part is thawed. When you are alone and your feet and toes are frozen, do not attempt to thaw them out if you intend to walk to medical assistance.

If you decide to transport the victim, cover the affected areas with a clean cloth, apply temporary dressings, keep affected parts elevated, and continue to give the victim fluids.

Drowning

Knowing how to swim is essential for backcountry backpacking. You will often have to cross streams and on really hot days you will be tempted to immerse yourself in streams, ponds, and lakes even if you don't know how to swim. But even Olympic swimmers can have accidents. Between six thousand and eight thousand people die each year by drowning. And, drowning is a distinct possibility in the wilderness where caution is often thrown to the wind and certified lifeguards are nowhere to be found.

I have had two close calls while hiking—both times involved stream crossings after a storm. Once, as I previously described, I was nearly pulled beneath a log that I was using for support as I crossed. Another time I was actually flipped over before I could grab a large boulder and keep myself from being swept downstream. Both times I was wearing a backpack.

It is essential to unfasten your hipbelt when packing across a stream or river. Had I not been able to save myself at those moments, I would have been able to shrug my pack off my shoulders and increase my chances for survival. A pack will drag you under. People have died when they couldn't get their pack off their back.

Before heading into the wilderness, make sure that either you or someone else you are hiking with has recently taken a CPR course because once a drowning victim has been removed from the water (and sometimes even before) you may have to perform artificial respiration. If there is no pulse, you will need to use CPR. When dealing with a drowning, always send for help. Without proper care, lung infections and other problems can set in that might lead to death.

Foot and Leg Problems
Extreme pain, and often swelling, characterizes hiking-related problems in the knees, shins, ankles, and feet. Taking a day or two off will often relieve the problem, but if the pain continues (or the swelling increases), only a doctor can tell you if your problem requires medical treatment.

It is not unusual for a hiker to experience some sort of pain every day he is on the trail. As one back-packer put it, "If the pain moves around, you're probably all right; but if it remains in one place, then it is more than likely something serious." Don't wait to see a doctor if there is swelling and continual pain. Nothing is worth causing permanent damage to your body. The doctor probably will prescribe an anti-inflammatory and tell you to keep off your feet for a week or more.

Even if you're hiking long-distance, it's not the end of the world. Frank had shinsplints while hiking the Appalachian Trail and was forced to take a week off. We still managed to complete the trail in six months— five months of hiking and a month off for various reasons, including the shinsplints. But had he not seen a doctor, he could have caused permanent damage to his calves.

One of the most common complaints is knee pain. Fortunately, tenderness in the joints doesn't necessarily signal a problem. Aspirin or other pain relievers can help alleviate some of the pain. Wearing a knee brace can help prevent knee problems or aid in support once a problem develops. If you have a history of knee problems, it is a good idea to carry a brace just in case. But, if it is an emergency, try using a thick sock wrapped around your knee and bound with duct tape.

Also, keep in mind that if you have known problems with the lower extremities, you can look into having orthotics made especially for your hiking boots. These can prevent shinsplints, for example, in most cases.

Strains and Sprains

A strain is simply a pulled muscle (something weight lifters do on purpose to increase muscle bulk). A strained muscle should be treated with cold if the pain appears suddenly, with warmth if the pain sets in gradually. After a couple of days, heat should be used in most cases. The muscle can be used, but if it hurts, don't do it.

A sprain, on the other hand, is a more serious injury. A sprain occurs when a joint and the ligaments that hold it are damaged. Unless treated properly, a sprain can stay with you the rest of your life.

When I was a child, my brother, sister, and I would play Batman by jumping off my top bunk onto the trundle bed. One day, I missed the trundle and hit the floor; my foot rolled and there was searing pain. My father had a cloth full of ice on my ankle before I'd completed my first wail. (My brother wasn't so lucky—on a separate occasion, Batman missed the trundle and broke his collarbone.) My father's quick reaction saved me later pain. After my ankle had been thoroughly numbed, it was wrapped with an Ace bandage and I was forced (or should I say "bribed" with peppermint candy) to stay on the sofa with my foot elevated for a while.

A sprain can be as simple as overstretching the ligament or as complex as tearing the ligament. Unfortunately, sprains don't hurt as much as they should and are often not treated until the awful swelling is noticed many hours later (and too late).

Treating a sprain is relatively simple, even in the backcountry. Take all pressure off the sprained body part immediately. Let's assume it's your ankle because that is the most likely thing you'll sprain while backpacking. Lie down and elevate your leg (that means make sure it's higher than your heart). A cold compress can be made by soaking a bandanna or T-shirt in cold water—the evaporation will help cool the injury. Once numbed, let the injury rewarm for ten to fifteen minutes. An Ace bandage (there should be one in your first aid kit) is used to wrap the sprained ankle. After applying a gauze pad over the swelling on the sprained joint, use "figure of eight" winding to wrap the joint. Be careful not to wrap too tightly because you don't want to impair circulation.

Continue to use cold compresses on the injured joint for the next several days, and as soon as the swelling begins to recede, begin exercising the injured part. Never overdo it. If it starts to swell and ache again, retreat and begin the process over again. It is important that you exercise the sprain so that the muscles do not atrophy. And keep in mind that it will take a good two months before your joint is back to normal again.

Fractures

Fractures are serious injuries and will require evacuation from the backcountry. When you suspect someone has a fracture, your first move should be to look for swelling, discoloration, asymmetry, and severe pain. If you're not sure, assume it is a fracture.

Never try to set the fracture or straighten the injured part unless the limb is bent under the person and you are several hours from help. And in that case, move the limb very gently. Wet clothing should be cut away so that the victim may be kept warm.

If the fracture is of the collarbone, upper arm, elbow, forearm, wrist, finger, ankle, or foot, you may be able to splint it. Use heavy sticks or tent poles for splints and bandannas or clothing for padding. Splinting should immobilize the joint above and below the injury unless the break is isolated in a joint. If the victim is able to walk, get him to help as soon as possible.

If the fracture is not in one of the places listed

above, you should have the victim lie as quietly as possible. Protect and immobilize the injured area by surrounding it with sleeping bags, clothing, and other appropriate materials. Make sure the victim remains warm and go for help.

Hot-Weather Medical Emergencies

The three hot-weather ailments described below are serious problems. The best advice is to avoid them by taking a few precautions in hot weather.

First, when you are hiking in the heat, try to maintain a consistent intake of fluids. Dehydration can lead to these more serious hot-weather ailments. Second, if the heat starts to get to you, take a break. Sit down in the shade, drink some water, and give your body time to cool off.

Heat Cramps

Heat cramps are an early sign of heat exhaustion, especially if the victim is dehydrated. Cramps occur first in the muscles of the legs and abdomen. If you're experiencing heat cramps, make a potassium solution.

There are several methods for making a potassium solution:

Method 1: First, you will need two clean glasses. In one glass, mix 8 ounces of potassium-rich fruit juice (apple, orange, or grapefruit) and add 1 teaspoon of honey or corn syrup (or sugar if that is all you have available). Add a pinch of salt. In the other glass, pour 8 ounces of a soft drink (carbonated) plus $1/4$ teaspoon baking soda. Alternate sipping from each glass until your thirst is quenched or both glasses are empty.

Method 2: Mix together 1 quart of water, 2 tablespoons of sugar, and $1/2$ teaspoon salt. (You can also add the sugar and salt to a decaffeinated diet soda).

Method 3: To 1 quart of water, add 2 tablespoons sugar, $1/2$ teaspoon Morton's lite salt, and $1/8$ teaspoon table salt. You may flavor this concoction with diet Kool-Aid.

The key is to drink this solution slowly—sip, wait, sip, wait, sip, wait—you get the idea. Try to drink this over a period of an hour. If you are going to be doing a lot of hiking in hot weather, you might want to carry along some powdered Gatorade or other similar drink or some potassium pills, which you can find at most health food and drugstores. Massaging will help relieve the cramped muscles according to the American Red Cross book on first aid.

Heat Exhaustion

If the heat cramps are not treated, they can lead to heat exhaustion. You will find that the victim's skin becomes pale and feels cool and clammy. It is possible that the victim will faint, but lowering his head will help him to maintain or regain consciousness. Weakness, nausea, heavy sweating, severe headache, and dizziness are symptoms of heat exhaustion.

As with heat cramps, the victim needs to drink a diluted solution of potassium water. Lay the victim down, loosen his clothing, and raise his feet eight to twelve inches. Applying cool wet cloths will also help relieve heat exhaustion. If the victim vomits, stop the water intake. At this point, medical attention should be sought. If you experience heat exhaustion on a hike, it would be wise to take a day off or even cancel the remainder of the hike.

Heat Stroke

Treatment of heat stroke should be immediate. You will know when a hiker has heat stroke because his skin will be hot, red, and dry. His pulse will be rapid and strong, and he will probably lapse into unconsciousness.

Undress the hiker and bathe his skin with cool water. If possible, place him in a stream or some other cold body of water. Once his temperature lowers, dry him off. If cold water is not available, fan him with whatever you have on hand. If his temperature rises again, resume the cooling process. Never give a hiker with heat stroke stimulants such as tea.

In the case of heat stroke, the victim should receive medical attention as soon as possible. Heat stroke is a life-threatening situation.

Lightning

While playing Trivial Pursuit one night, our team was asked what natural disaster claims the most victims each year. We thought about it—floods, earthquakes, tornadoes, tsunamis. We finally decided on floods because of the number of people killed during monsoon season. We fell out of our seats when we learned it was lightning. We hadn't even considered it. Really? Lightning?

Sure enough. Lightning kills between one hundred and three hundred people each year, particularly between May and September. An encyclopedia informed us that lightning strikes a hundred times a second worldwide with as much as 200 million volts, 300,000 amps, and 8,000 degrees Centigrade. Ouch! Unfortunately, when you're outside during a lightning storm, it is usually just a matter of luck that you are not hit.

Lightning can strike three ways: within a cloud, cloud-to-cloud, and cloud-to-ground. Cloud-to-ground lightning can injure you in four different ways: by direct strike, when the bolt actually hits you; by splash or side flash, when lightning hits something else then flashes through the air to hit you as well; by ground current (this is the most common way humans are injured), when the lightning strikes a tree, for instance, and the current runs through the ground or water and into you; and by the blast effect, when you are thrown by the sudden expansion of air caused by a strike. Some people get lucky when the ground current charge passes over and around them without entering their body. This is called the flashover effect.

There are a number of types of injuries a lightning victim can receive—traumatic, respiratory, neurologic, and cardiac injuries, as well as burns and everything from loss of hearing to vomiting. Treatment depends on the type of injury the victim has sustained. A knowledge

279

of cardiopulmonary resuscitation will be invaluable to you if lightning stops the heart of someone you know; most victims can be revived by this method. Never assume that a lightning victim is all right. Always go for help.

Lightning can strike from a mile away. Once you see a flash, begin counting—one one-thousand, two one-thousand, etc. If you hear the thunder before you finish saying five one-thousand, you are within range of a strike. That's when you need to find a safe spot. Storms move quickly; it's doubtful you can outrun it.

So what's safe? Not much. Avoid bodies of water and low places that can collect water. Avoid high places, open places, tall objects, metal objects, wet caves, and ditches. Your best bet is a small stand of trees. Sit on a sleeping pad (unless it has metal in it) with your knees pulled up against your chest, head bowed, arms hugging knees. If you're in a group, spread out so that if lightening hits, not everyone will be hurt, but make sure you can all see at least one other person in case anyone gets hit.

Rashes

While camping in the Los Padres National Forest in California, my family had one of its worst experiences. As we sat eating dinner at our picnic table, we watched another family gather wood for their campfire. After a while, their roaring fire began sending streamers of smoke our way. Coughing and waving our hands, we were eventually forced to flee our dinner table.

While gathering wood for our own fire, my father made a disconcerting discovery—the other family was burning poison oak. Unlike poison ivy, poison oak is hard to recognize (even though it has leaves of three). We had been playing in the poison oak all day.

By the next day, we were absolutely miserable and covered from head to foot in a light rash (fortunately, it was an early rash for me—poison oak, ivy, and sumac get worse each time you get it). Our throats ached and itched from the smoke we had inhaled.

The best thing to do once you realize you've had contact with one of the poisons—ivy, oak, or sumac—is to take a cool or cold bath and completely cleanse yourself with soap. After that, use Calamine or some other poison ivy- or oak-specific lotion. Cortisone creams help some (I've had poison ivy so bad I've needed cortisone shots). Antihistamines such as Benadryl also offer some relief. Prophylactics are available, although how well they prevent you from getting rashes from poison plants is debatable.

Your best defense against poison ivy, sumac, and oak is to be able to identify and steer clear of them. As the saying goes—leaves of three, let them be.

Poison ivy isn't the only rash you're likely to get while hiking. Rashes caused by friction, heat, and humidity are also common, especially in the crotch area. One way to deal with this problem is to apply Vaseline to the areas that rub against one another. If heat is the problem, try to keep the area as cool as possible. Shorts with built-in liners will keep you drier than shorts and underwear because they are made to allow moisture to escape. If the rash gets to be a real problem, try sleeping nude at night to allow the area to dry as thoroughly as possible. Powder will also help keep the problem area dry. If the rash begins to look fungal, there are a number of over-the-counter products, such as Desenex, that will clear it up.

Hip belt rashes—when the hip belt is too loose and rubs the hiker's hips raw—are common. This happened to me in the heat of the summer, and the combination of the hip belt rubbing through my cotton shorts and the sweat soon caused a mean wound across my lower back in the shape of the hip belt. It bled and scabbed and bled and scabbed and left me nearly frantic with pain. Changing to a pair of nylon shorts solved the problem—the material was slick enough to keep the hip belt gliding rather than rubbing against my hips. I already had the smallest hip belt available for the pack so changing that wasn't an option.

The opposite also happens; many hikers develop swollen and bruised hips from the pressure of a heavy load on the hip belt. Other than lightening your pack, there is really no way to avoid this. Fortunately, every day you're on the trail the pack gets lighter until you resupply again. The welts on our hips usually reappeared a day or two after we settled an especially heavy load on our backs.

Wounds

It is not unusual to experience minor and sometimes major wounds—abrasions, incisions, lacerations, and punctures—while hiking. Avulsions, though rare, are also possible.

I still bear the scars of some of my falls, most of which involved slipping on leaves, roots, or rocks. Sometimes it doesn't matter how careful you are, you're just going to fall. Any backpacker can relate a major fall story. Our favorite is a fall that I wish had been captured on video. Hiking on what was really a very minor slope, somehow I slipped (on a rock or slick leaves) and my feet went flying out from under me. Soon I was rolling down the hill. Although Frank laughed at me, he soon found himself in the same predicament. It wasn't long before we were entangled and rolling down the slope together. It must have been a comic sight. Fortunately, neither of us suffered more than a few bruises. We picked ourselves up, dusted off, and headed up the trail.

When someone is injured to such a degree that there is a flow of blood from the wound, you need to do three things: (1) stop the bleeding, (2) prevent infection, and (3) promote healing.

Here are two methods, described in order of preference, that should be used to stop bleeding:

Method 1: With a dressing or a cloth, apply direct pressure over the wound. In most instances this will stop the bleeding; the thick pad of cloth will absorb blood and allow it to clot. Once the blood clots, leave it alone. If blood should soak the pad before clotting, do not remove the pad but add another layer to the already soaked cloth and increase your pressure on the wound. If you need both your hands to help the victim, apply a pressure bandage with a strip of cloth. Place it over the pad on the wound, wrap it around the body part, and then tie a knot directly over the pad.

Method 2:   Elevate the wounded part, unless there is evidence of a fracture, above the victim's heart. This will also help reduce blood-flow. Wounds of the hand, neck, arm, or leg should be elevated and direct pressure should be continued.

These methods will stop most bleeding, but taking a course in first aid will teach you other options (methods too technical and risky to discuss here) to use if the bleeding doesn't stop with direct pressure and elevation.

Preventing infection goes hand-in-hand with proper cleansing of the wound. Your first step is to wash your hands and to avoid contaminating the wound further. That is, don't breathe on it, cough or sneeze on it, drool on it, throw dirt on it, etc. Cleaning means cleansing around and sometimes in the wound. You can make an antiseptic wash by using the povidone-iodine in your first aid kit or by using soap and water or just plain water if that is all you have.

Cleanse around the wound with a sterile gauze pad and in the wound only if there is foreign material in it. Always rinse everything, even the antiseptic wash, from the wound before you dress it. You can irrigate the wound with water from a plastic bag that has a pinhole (to direct the stream of water).

If foreign matter remains in the wound after irrigation, you may try using sterilized tweezers (sterilize by holding them to a flame until red hot or by boiling them in water—make sure they cool down a bit before you apply them to the wound). If you can remove all foreign objects and have stopped the bleeding, allow the wound to air dry a while before dressing it. If you can't remove the foreign objects or the wound is big, keep it moist until you can get to a doctor. If it is a gaping wound, apply a butterfly bandage after bringing the folds of skin together. Some first aid books do not advocate the use of butterfly bandages because it is felt that the bandages promote infection. In the backcountry, you need to judge whether the risk of infection is worse with our without such closure. Do as your conscience sees fit.

When dressing a wound, do not touch the sterile dressing except at the edges where it will not come in contact with the wound. If possible, the dressing should extend at least one inch past the edges of the wound.

The dressing should be bandaged snugly but not too tight. Remember to check it often and never apply tape on the wound. Also, if you use tincture of benzoin on the healthy skin, the tape will stick better; but don't get the benzoin in the wound because it will hurt it and encourage infection.

Abrasions

Most of the wounds you'll suffer when hiking will be abrasions, which occur when the outer layers of the protective skin are damaged, usually when the skin is scraped against a hard surface.

Although bleeding is usually limited, danger of contamination and infection still exists. Simply cleanse the wound, apply an antiseptic, and keep it clean until it heals. This will help avoid serious problems.

Incisions

An incision occurs when body tissue is cut with a sharp object. When hiking, most incisions are the product of poor knife handling. People can never seem to remember that they are supposed to cut away from their body. I've seen a number of hikers who had to head off for emergency help because they sliced their hands while whittling.

An incised wound often bleeds heavily and rapidly, and if it is deep, there can be damage to muscles, tendons, and nerves. Incisions need immediate attention, even if small, because they can easily become infected. Whether a deep or shallow cut, the bleeding should be stopped immediately. If the wound is large, you should also treat for shock.

Punctures

The most likely puncture wound you will receive while backpacking is a splinter. But if you walk around barefoot, you're asking for all manner of foot wounds. Keep shoes of some sort on at all times.

When several layers of skin are pierced by a sharp object, you have a puncture wound. Although bleeding is usually limited, internal damage can result if tissues and muscle are pierced. Infection is likelier because there is no flushing action from blood. Cleanse the wound as best you can, and if there is a foreign object (such as a splinter) that can be easily removed, do so with a pair of sterilized tweezers or needle. Objects imbedded deeply in the tissue should be removed only by a doctor.

Amputation

If tissue is forcibly separated or torn from the victim's body, seek help as soon as possible. Bleeding will usually be quite heavy and should be stopped before transporting the victim, if possible. Send the detached body part along with the victim to the hospital. It can often be reattached.

GETTING HELP

While talking to a couple of rangers on a mountain trail in Washington, a friend of ours took a step backwards while saying farewell and stepped off a cliff. The rangers quickly sent for help, but it took a major evacuation effort before she could be reached and her injuries assessed. Even two rangers, with a knowledge of wilderness first aid, were forced to make a judgment call on how to handle this outdoor emergency.

I can't tell you how to evacuate a person who has just fallen off a cliff, but if I had to make that decision, there are a number of questions I would have to consider. How far is help? Is the person already dead? Is there someone around more qualified to deal with the situation? Can the victim be reached? Is the temperature detrimental (too hot or too cold) to the victim? Is the victim breathing or bleeding? And so on.

In emergency situations that require evacuation you will be faced with many choices. But unless you're trained in wilderness rescue, you are probably best advised to go for help rather than trying to evacuate the victim yourself. I can't put it more simply: Let professionals handle it. If you try to evacuate the victim yourself, you may injure him further. And unfortunately, that means you can be sued. The world is in a sad state when good Samaritans are sued for trying to rescue someone, but it happens all the time. Fortunately, because of this, all the states have developed Good Samaritan Laws. Most such Good Samaritan Laws require that the person giving aid does not deliberately cause harm to the victim. The person giving aid must also provide the level and type of care expected of a responsible person with the same amount of training and similar circumstances. Finally, before one can give first aid, one must get permission from the injured party UNLESS that person is unconscious.

If something has happened and someone needs to be evacuated, send for help as soon as possible. In the meantime, there are a number of things you can do to make the injured person more comfortable. According to *Emergency Medical Procedures for the Outdoors,* you can:

➤ Set up a shelter and protect the victim from direct contact with the ground.

➤ Cover the victim with a shirt, jacket, sweater, or blanket to retain body heat.

➤ Provide food and water.

➤ Make sure the victim is comfortable.

If it is an extreme emergency and time is of essence, you may want to try using distress signals:

➤ Standard ground-to-air signals: One rectangular shape means "require doctor—serious injuries," and two rectangular shapes, side by side, mean "require medical supplies." Build these symbols as large as possible by digging in sand or snow or earth. You can also use tree limbs, rocks, clothing, or whatever else you might have on hand to represent the image. The most important thing is to make sure the image is clearly visible from above and that it contrasts with the ground color as much as possible.

➤ Universal distress signals: A series of three sights or sounds. These can include shouts, whistle blasts, high-frequency beeps, gunshots, and flashes of light.

➤ SOS Morse Code distress signal: A series of three dots, three dashes, three dots (...- - -...) means SOS or Help! The signal can be made by blows on a whistle, high-frequency beeps, or flashes of light.

➤ Other possibilities: A large flag or some other tall object-the brighter the better-can be placed at the top of a tree. A mirror or some other shiny object can be flashed across the sky several times a day to attract planes. Flares can be used.

If you must leave the victim, alone or with others, it is important to mark your trail (unless it is already clearly blazed). You can do this with branches, cairns (rock mounds), arrows carved in the dirt or snow, grass tied in bunches, sticks dug into the ground at the side of the trail, torn pieces of cloth tied to branches, or whatever you can think of to ensure that help can find its way to the victim.

It's a dangerous world out there and the Boy Scouts had the right idea when they chose as their motto the succinct, "Be prepared." It's easily done! Courses in CPR, first aid, and self-defense are offered in nearly every county, parish, and township in the United States. So, before you head out into the backcountry, be prepared. Or hike with someone who is.

Problem Animals

The sun had set and Laurie and Dean Turner were dozing off in their tent when they were startled out of imminent sleep by the gentle snuffling of a large animal. Camping in Yosemite National Park, they had expected bears to invade their camp and had carefully strung their food bags more than ten feet off the ground between two trees. What they hadn't expected was what they were soon to term "Kamikaze Bears." Cringing inside their sleeping bags, they listened to the bear claw its way up a tree. Peeking out of their tents, they were treated to a most unusual sight.

Launching itself from the tree, the bear was attempting to dive bomb the food bag. It worked! The rope snapped and the food bag and the bear tumbled to the ground. Our friends watched, dumbfounded, as the bear opened up the bag and began to munch its way through their week's supply of food.

Bears, raccoons, and other animals are ingenious when it comes to parting backpackers from their food. When recommended methods to protect your goods don't work, you're left with no other option than to hike backward or forward to restock your supplies. Fortunately (or maybe unfortunately), you rarely find these street-smart animals outside of state or national parks. This chapter will introduce you to the types of animals you might meet while backpacking and how to deal with these creatures.

BEARS

Black Bears

The black bear has a commanding presence and can summon an ominous "woof" to warn backpackers to stay away; but a face-to-face encounter will probably end with the bear ambling, if not scurrying, away. Bears are hunted in national forests and so they are usually wary of humans; but in national parks, bears can be conniving and aggressive in their search for food. Bears are also notoriously unpredictable and can be very vicious.

The National Park Service offers some tips for how to handle black bear encounters as well as how to prevent them from getting into your food and pack. The following list is based on those recommendations:

➤ If you stop to take a break, keep your pack nearby. If a bear approaches, throw your pack on, pick up whatever you have out, and leave the area. Bears have been known to bluff hikers into leaving food behind. Don't fall for this ploy, but on the other hand, don't take your time getting out, either. Avoid trouble at all costs. Bears seldom attack, but when they do they can cause plenty of damage.

➤ If the bear continues to approach, loosen your hip belt in case you have to drop your pack. Keep your face turned toward the bear and slowly back away from it.

➤ If a bear charges, don't run. Like many animals, bears have an instinctive prey drive; a running person is seen as "food" trying to escape. They also can outrun you.

➤ Don't bother trying to climb a tree, either; bears are adept at climbing trees, and can probably do so faster and better than you can.

➤ If the bear is a lone black bear, you can try and fight back by screaming, yelling, and kicking at it. That is often enough to scare it away. You may also want to try dropping your pack to distract it. If these ploys don't work, react as you would with a grizzly or a mother with cubs.

➤ If you are charged by a grizzly or a mother with cubs, your best bet is to lie on the ground in the fetal position, arms drawn up to protect your face and neck. Most bears will leave you alone if you do this or will content themselves with a scratch or two.

➤ Never, ever look a bear (or any animal) in the eye. Direct eye contact is perceived as aggressive.

➤ If, while backing away, you lose sight of the bear, move downwind of the bear and continue on your way. Keep an eye out for the bear until you are positive the bear has not followed you.

➤ Never, under any circumstances, try to feed a bear or leave food to attract one. Once a bear has tasted human food, he will continue to search for it, which means trouble for the bear as well as for humans.

Grizzly Bears

Edward Abbey once said, "If people persist in trespassing upon the grizzlies' territory, we must accept the fact that the grizzlies, from time to time, will harvest a few trespassers." But what if you're not willing to sacrifice your life to the Great Griz? Fortunately, when hiking in griz country, there are some precautions you can take to avoid meeting up with one of these legendary creatures.

When hiking, stop and listen every five minutes or so, especially if it is windy. Grizzly bears are loud, particularly when they are not yet aware that their territory has been invaded.

Keep your head up. It is very likely that you can spot a grizzly before it spots you and thus avoid a potentially dangerous situation. If you've got your headphones on and are just hopping it to your next campsite, chances are you won't make it there. If you're hiking in griz country your life may depend on your alertness.

I once left a sign on the trail that spelled out in rocks, "Get water here." I used sticks to make arrows to point at a spring. We had found out the hard way that once we'd made camp (at an established site) that it was a good quarter-mile trek back to the spring for water. Only one out of eight hikers saw the sign! But that was nothing compared to the time that a fellow hiker was oblivious to a 16-foot by 20-foot painting of the Pope that was propped against a trailside tree. I still don't know how he missed it! If you can't spot a garish painting of the Pope, you'd better reconsider any trip into grizzly country.

Whether or not to walk into or with the wind depends on who you're asking. Grizzly expert Doug Peacock says that he walks into the wind for the most part, confident in his ability to spot grizzlies before they spot him. Peacock does say he does this only when he's heading toward potential bedding sites that he cannot otherwise get around. The government says you ought to walk with the wind so that grizzlies smell you before you spot them and so they disappear before you arrive.

While hiking in grizzly territory, you do not have to be unnecessarily loud to scare off the bears. A normal, conversational tone interspersed with some singing and a yell or two will suffice to alert bears of your impend-

Critter Proofing Your Food

In most places when making camp for the night, stash your food in a bag (a heavy-duty garbage bag may mask the smell of your food) and make sure it is securely tied off the ground and between two trees. The bag should be at least twelve feet off the ground and ten feet from the nearest tree. In areas where there are a lot of bears, bearproof means of storage are often provided for hikers. For example, in the Great Smoky Mountains, chain-link fences keep bears from getting into shelters (although bears have been known to keep humans from getting into the shelters when the door in the fence has been left open). In other places, the park service provides bear poles—tall, metal poles with four prongs at the top from which food bags can be suspended. A gaff is provided to lift the food to the top of the pole. In places where there are Kamikaze bears, particularly in many western national parks, you should carry a bear canister, a container specially designed to protect your food from bears. These can be purchased or rented at many parks and outdoor stores.

ing presence. If you feel as if you must make lots of noise (banging pans or clanging bells) just to feel safe, forget it and hike somewhere that is safe.

Be on the look out for cached carcasses (if you're downwind of it, you'll smell it) because it probably means there is a grizzly nearby. If you see a carcass, freeze and look around to see if you spot any grizzlies. Then retreat slowly without turning around.

Avoid bedding areas whenever possible (grizzlies like to sleep in cool places such as thickets, under deadfalls, and next to trees). If you spot such an area walk around it or, at least, make a little noise.

Always, always, always sleep in a tent in grizzly country and keep a knife (for cutting an escape hatch in the tent), flashlight, and firestarter handy. Although often illegal, camp away from established areas and any area where a bear is likely to travel (like people, bears prefer the ease of paths). If you bushwhack into the brush a hundred yards or so off a trail (check for bear beds, food, and trails), you'll probably be safe.

Don't bother bringing a gun, it'll only make the bear mad. And never drop your pack. Grizzlies are intelligent animals and we don't need to teach them that they can find food in backpacks. Bear repellents are iffy at best and are better left at home. Never travel at night. If possible, travel in groups because bears rarely attack a group of four or more.

If you actually come in contact with a grizzly, don't panic. Young (not baby) grizzlies can probably be scared off—stand your ground, act a bit aggressive, and you'll probably send the young adult scurrying. On the other hand, if you run into cubs, there is probably a mother griz nearby. If you're within a hundred feet to a hundred yards of her precious babies, you are probably within the mother bear's critical distance, that is the distance in which she will violently defend her young'uns, and you will need to get out of there. Back slowly away, keeping an eye out for the grizzly.

The first thing to do when you encounter any adult griz is to speak quietly, hold your arms out at your sides and avert your head. I'd like to reiterate this—never, ever run from any bear. As I said before, they run faster than you and will probably chase you if you flee. Avoid direct eye contact but do keep an eye on the bear to continue to gauge its mood. Unless the bear flattens its ears back and looks directly at you, begin to retreat—slowly. If it does flatten its ears, freeze and wait and then slowly begin to retreat.

Never make sudden movements or loud noises. Don't try to climb a tree—it takes too long and grizzlies can knock down some trees or possibly shake you out of your perch.

If you should be attacked, play possum but—in this case—don't expose your vitals. Draw up into a fetal position. Use your pack and hands to protect your neck and skull and as painful as it might be, try to stay still. It might be your only chance to save your life.

Finally, don't worry too much about sex or menstruation. Bears are not drawn irresistibly to those human odors. Keep yourself as clean as possible. You don't have to avoid backpacking trips into grizzly country just because you might be menstruating, but if it would make you feel a bit safer, delay your trip by a day or two. The same goes for sex. While a griz may not notice the sounds and scents of your coitus outdoorsus, do you really want to take that risk?

SNAKES

In the wild, snakes lie in wait along a path for small rodents or other prey. Coiled along the edge of a trail waiting for food to pass by, the patient reptiles test the air with their flicking tongues for signs of game.

This image of the snake lying in wait just off the trail is a cause of concern among some hikers; but what about the snake's view of things? The snake is aware of its place in the food chain; it must watch for predators as well as prey. A hiker making a moderate amount of noise will usually be perceived as a predator and the snake will back off or lie still until the "danger" passes.

To avoid confrontations with snakes, make a little extra noise when you are walking through brush, deep grass, or piles of dead leaves that block your view of the footpath. This will warn snakes of your approach. By kicking at the brush or leaves slightly, you will make enough noise to cause a snake to slither off or lie still.

Many species of poisonous snakes prefer areas near rocky outcrops and can often be found among the boulders that border rocky streams as well. Generally, coral snakes appear in the south and southwest, water moccasins in the wetlands of the south, copperheads throughout the east, and rattlesnakes throughout the United States. Poisonous snakes do not occur in the far north where the temperatures remain cool or downright cold most of the year. When in doubt, avoid all snakes. And though it may not be comforting if you have just stirred up a nest of yellow jackets, keep in mind that more people die each year from insect bites than they do from snakebites.

Rattlesnakes

Rattlesnakes are heavy-bodied and can be from three to five feet long, although large rattlesnakes are increasingly rare. They have large blotches and crossbands that run the length of their body. Depending on their color phase (they have two—a yellowish and a dark yellowish phase and an almost black phase)—their overall color may be dark enough to obscure the telltale pattern.

The real giveaway is the prominent rattle or enlarged "button" at the end of the snake's tail. Rattlesnakes usually warn predators with a distinctive rattle; but this can't be relied on because they may also lie still as hikers go by.

Rattlesnakes are frequently seen on trails both in the West and in the East, although their presence has been greatly reduced by development encroaching on their terrain. Although found throughout the United States, cases of rattlesnake bites are almost unheard of, and when quick action is taken, they will almost never prove fatal, except among the very young or old. Even so, rattlesnake bites are extremely dangerous and are more potent than the copperhead and water moccasin.

Copperheads

Copperheads are typically two to three feet in length. They are moderately stout-bodied with brown or chestnut hourglass-shaped crossbands. The background color is lighter than the crossbands, anything from reddish-brown to chestnut to gray-brown. The margins of the crossbands have a darker outline. This pattern certainly helps the copperhead blend in among dead leaves. Other, nonpoisonous snakes (e.g., the corn snake) have similar patterns, but the hourglass shape is not so prominent.

Copperheads prefer companionship; if you see one copperhead, there are probably others in the area. In the spring and fall they can be seen in groups, particularly in rocky areas. Their nests have the strong and distinctive odor of cucumbers. Copperheads avoid trouble by lying still and will quickly retreat as a last resort.

The bite of the copperhead is almost never fatal. Rarely has someone weighing more than forty pounds died of a copperhead bite. While not fatal, the bite is dangerous and medical attention should be sought immediately.

Copperheads can be found from Massachusetts south to North Florida and westward to Illinois, Oklahoma, and Texas.

Water Moccasins or Cottonmouths
One of the largest poisonous snakes in America, the cottonmouth's head is diamond-shaped and very distinct from the neck. Also known as water moccasins, these snakes are dull olive to brownish in color and a bit paler on their sides. Their sides also sport indistinct, wide, blackish bands. The body is very stout in proportion to length—they can be as long as five feet. With an abruptly tapering tail and eye shields, the cottonmouth is a very sinister-looking snake. It is also the most aggressive poisonous snake in the United States.

As the name "water moccasin" implies, these snakes can be found in swamps and along streams, ponds, lakes and rivers from Southern Virginia (sometimes) south to Florida and westward into Eastern Texas. They range as far north as Illinois and Indiana.

Coral Snakes
Also called the Harlequin snake, the brightly banded coral snake rarely reaches a yard long. When it comes to recognizing the coral snake, just remember, "red on yellow will kill a fellow." Broad bands of red and blue-black are separated by narrow yellow bands. Other snakes imitate the coral snake's colors but not its pattern.

Although small and rarely known to bite, the coral snake is the most venomous of the poisonous snakes inhabiting the United States. An antivenin is needed to counteract the poison of a coral snake, which unlike the venom of the three pit vipers above, is a neurotoxin. Most coral snakebites occur when the snake is being handled because it has small fangs and needs direct contact.

The coral snake can be found from northern North Carolina to the Gulf of Mexico and westward through Texas. A smaller, less venomous species, occupies parts of Arizona.

Treating Poisonous Snakebites

The reaction to the bite of a poisonous snake will be swift. Discoloration and swelling of the bite area are the most visible signs. Weakness and rapid pulse are other symptoms. Nausea, vomiting, fading vision, and shock also are possible signs of a poisonous bite and may develop in the first hour or so after being bitten.

It is important to know that tourniquets can cause more damage to the victim than a snakebite. If improperly applied, a tourniquet can cause the death of the infected limb and the need for amputation. The cutting and suction methods called for in snakebite kits also are not recommended.

The best treatment is to reduce the amount of circulation in the area where the bite occurred and seek medical attention immediately. Circulation can be reduced by keeping the victim immobile (which isn't easy if the bite occurs five miles from the nearest road), by applying a cold, wet cloth to the area, or by using a constricting band. A constricting band is not a tourniquet and should be tight enough only to stop surface flow of blood and decrease the flow of lymph from the wound. The constricting band should not stop blood flow to the limb.

The Extractor is state-of-the-art, so to speak, in snakebite kits because it uses mechanical suction (rather than mouth suction) and it does not involve cutting the bite with a razor or knife. It is also said to remove approximately 30 percent of the venom if used within five minutes of being bitten.

Treating Nonpoisonous Snakebites

The bite of a nonpoisonous snake can be dangerous. If not properly cleaned, the wound can become infected. Ideally, the victim should be treated with a tetanus shot to prevent serious infection, although all backpackers should have a current booster before heading out into the wilderness. Nonpoisonous snakebites will cause a moderate amount of swelling. If large amounts of swelling take place, the bite should be treated as if it were caused by a poisonous snake.

POISONOUS LIZARDS

There are only two poisonous lizards on God's green earth and both of them can be found in the United States, though not in the woods and forests. The Gila Monster and the Mexican Beaded Lizard occupy the deserts of the Southwest and will bite if picked up or stepped on. Prevention is pretty easy—leave them alone. To get poisoned, you must come in direct contact with these critters (i.e., stick you fingers near their mouth); their jaws must clamp down on you so they can drool venom into the wound they make with their primitive teeth. Should you be bright enough to get bitten by one of these critters, you may have to heat the underside of their jaws with a flame before they'll let go. The bite should be treated as you would treat a snake bite.

COUGAR

While wildcats, in general, are rarely seen, hikers are occasionally confronted by cougar. They range from central Canada to Patagonia from sea level to swamp, jungle, desert, forest, and even high alpine regions. Depending on where you are hiking, you might find the cougar referred to as the mountain lion, puma, or panther.

Like most animals, the cougar will fiercely protect her young. Never, ever approach that adorable little kitten because no doubt its mama is nearby. And, like most animals, it really doesn't want to confront you but it is perfectly capable of doing so, if necessary.

If, indeed, you are approached by a cougar, back away slowly. Running nearly always triggers that, "I gotta chase my prey" instinct that most mammals possess. If the cougar continues to follow you, defend yourself by throwing sticks and rocks at it. This tactic seems to frighten most cougar away. Don't run towards the cat when throwing, though. Just continue to back up as you throw. Chances are the cougar will beat feet in the opposite direction.

BOARS, MOOSE, ELK, AND OTHER BEASTS

Boars, which are not indigenous to the United States (they were brought here from Europe for hunting purposes), can be found in the southern Appalachians and throughout the deep South. They are rarely seen, and like most animals, will disappear if they hear you coming. If you happen upon a boar, try to avoid direct confrontation; just continue hiking.

Male moose and elk should be avoided during rutting season because they may mistake you for a rival and attempt to chase you out of their territory.

Females of any and all species should be avoided when they have their young with them. The instinct to protect their young is strong and you cannot predict what a mother will do if she feels her children are threatened.

Birds are especially vicious. You may not see the grouse and her babies, but she'll spot you and let you know that she is not pleased with your presence.

Only the very lucky will catch glimpses of other wild animals—wild cats such as the lynx and bobcat, wolf, coyotes, bighorn sheep. Chances of confrontation are slim.

SMALL PESTS

Backpackers often attract rodents and other small mammals. These creatures are searching for food and can do much damage, especially if you do not take care to protect your belongings. It is never wise to leave your pack, and particularly your food, out on the ground for the night. Food, and sometimes whole packs, should be hung where these animals cannot reach them.

Porcupines

These nocturnal creatures love to gnaw on anything salty. Outhouses, shelters, and particularly hiking boots and backpack shoulder straps are all fair game to the porcupine. That may sound strange, but they are after the salt from your sweat. So hang your packs and boots when you're hiking in porcupine country, and take particular care in areas that are known to be frequented by porcupines.

Direct contact is necessary to receive the brunt of the porcupine's quills. Although it is unlikely for a hiker to be lashed by a porcupine's tail, it is not unusual for a dog to provoke a porcupine into defending itself. Porcupine quills become embedded in the flesh of the attacker, causing extreme pain. If the quills are not removed immediately, they can cause death because they work themselves deeper and deeper into the flesh. The ends of the quills have barbs that are the first defense for holding the quill in the wounded party. The scales on the tips of the barbs are the second defense. These scales spread open to make the quills harder to remove.

Skunks

During the night at Ice Water Springs Shelter north of Newfound Gap in the Smokies, a brazen skunk wove around our legs as we warmed ourselves in front of the campfire. It was very pleasant, scrounging for scraps of food on the shelter's dirt floor and along the wire bunks. The skunk occasionally stood on its hind legs and made a begging motion, which had no doubt been perfected on earlier hikers. We didn't give in to the skunk's pleas for food, and it eventually crawled back up under the bunks as we sighed in relief.

We heard of another skunk encounter in the same shelter, perhaps with the same skunk, a year earlier. Two British hikers, who were unfamiliar with the animal, tried to chase the skunk away by throwing a boot. They were given a quick course in skunk etiquette!

Skunks can be found nationwide but are usually only a problem in high-use areas. Generally if you leave them alone, they'll reciprocate. Dogs, on the other hand, can provoke skunk attacks just about anywhere. Although we've only seen a few skunks, we've been aware of their presence (that telltale odor!) on many a trip.

Mice

Mice are the most common pests to be found in the outdoors. If you leave your pack sitting on the ground

Hantavirus

This virus was first identified during the Korean War and it was named for the Hantaan River there. The mostly deadly strain of the virus has developed in the United States where it has, because of where it is found, affected backpackers.

The hantavirus is a respiratory disease that is carried in wild rodents such as deer mice. People become infected after breathing airborne particles of urine or saliva. Most cases have been associated with (1) occupying rodent-infested areas while hiking or camping; (2) cleaning barns or other out-buildings; (3) disturbing rodent-infested areas while hiking; (4) or harvesting fields; or (5) living in or visiting areas which have experienced an increase in rodents.

Because of an abundant crop of pinon nuts in the Southwest in 1993, that area of the country was the first to experience the widespread hantavirus. The virus produces flu-like symptoms and takes one to five weeks to incubate. It is 60 percent fatal. Among the strains of hantavirus to be found in the United States are Sin Nombre Virus (SNV) or 4-Corner Virus, NY-1 Virus, Black Creek Canal Virus, and Bayou Virus.

beside your tent, don't be surprised the next morning if mice have gnawed their way into your pack (if you neglect to hang it) and have helped themselves to a mouse-sized portion of your food or clothes. While we were hiking in Virginia, I decided to change into a warmer shirt, and was shocked to find that mice had gnawed several holes in the shirt's collar. On another trip, I discovered holes in my socks. Mice use the fibers they gnaw from clothes in their nests.

A few hikers carry along mousetraps, but this is a little controversial. Some hikers feel that the mice have a place in the "trail ecosystem."

Raccoons

Raccoons are also a widespread nuisance. They, too, will invade your pack searching for food. Camping along Ontario's Bruce Trail, Doug Hall was awakened one dawn by a rustling sound outside his tent. Quietly unzipping his tent fly, the beam of his flashlight soon found the culprit. Atop his pack sat a portly raccoon contentedly munching on a piece of pemmican. Several pine cones had to be lofted at the raccoon before it decided it was time to leave its comfortable perch.

Dogs

Some dogs encountered on the trail are hiking companions and others are strays or the property of people who live along the trail's route. If they are strays, they can be very friendly as well as hard to get rid of. They can also be aggressive, especially if they are hungry or

Rabies

While hiking in Kathmandu we were horrified to read of a sudden outbreak of rabies in the capital's surrounding villages. After our experience with the stray dog, we were even more determined to steer clear of the animals when we heard this awful news.

For those of us who enjoy backpacking, it is wise to keep in mind that ninety-six percent of the carriers of rabies in the United States are wild animals. Skunks are the chief carrier followed by raccoons, bats, cattle, cats and dogs. Wolves, bobcats, coyotes, groundhogs, muskrats, weasels, woodchucks, foxes, horses, and humans can also host the disease.

Transferred through saliva, death from rabies is very rare in the United States because treatment is available. Symptoms appear anywhere from three weeks to a year after being bit and include headache and fever, cough and sore throat, loss of appetite and fatigue, abdominal pain, nausea, vomiting and diarrhea.

If you have been bitten by a mammal that you suspect may have rabies, get to a doctor immediately. Once symptoms appear, it is too late for treatment. The rabies vaccine (a series of five shots in the arm—no longer the painful abdominal shots) may be recommended and has so far always been successful.

When bitten by any mammal, it is best to thoroughly cleanse the wound and see a doctor. You may need nothing more than a tetanus or antibiotic shot.

Please don't take the risk and for go seeing a doctor. Rabies is an incredibly painful and unpleasant disease, and past a certain stage—fatal.

if they feel they are defending their territory or their masters.

Fortunately, most of the dogs you'll meet while backpacking are friendly, but we have had the occasional bad experience with dogs. In Kathmandu, we were befriended by a friendly mutt while hiking in the hills north of Swyambunath. As we passed through a small village, we were soon surrounded by a circle of vicious dogs, all eager to get their teeth into the stray, who suddenly chose to use us as its bodyguards. With hiking sticks we were able to chase all the dogs (including the stray) away and were careful not to befriend any more dogs while visiting that country.

If you are confronted by an angry dog, as with bears and most other animals, don't run. Don't look directly into a dog's eyes. If it is necessary to defend yourself, use your hiking stick or small stones. Sometimes just picking up a stone and holding it as if you're going to throw it is enough to dissuade a dog. Throw the rock only if it's absolutely necessary.

INSECTS

You can't escape them. They're everywhere. Even in the coldest reaches of the Arctic and Antarctic, it is not surprising to stumble upon a bug. Mosquitoes, bees, hornets, wasps, fire ants, scorpions, ticks, chiggers, blackflies, deer and horse flies, gnats and no-see-ums are among the millions of insects out there that torment the human soul . . . and skin.

They invade our lives both indoors and out, and to be perfectly honest, I find insects much easier to deal with in the out-of-doors than inside my home or car. They may be demons outside, but they are Satan incarnate when trapped somewhere they do not want to be. So, because you can't live with them and you can't live without them, how do you handle insects, especially those that like to feast on human blood?

No-see-ums

These are the smallest of our tormentors and perhaps those most likely to drive us insane—the tiny midges and gnats that tend to swarm otherwise happy campers. But there are ways to avoid that which you cannot see. First of all, camp away from running water and make sure the no-see-um netting on your tent is a very fine mesh, otherwise they will torment you all night long. If hiking through a swarm, use DEET (more on this repellent later) and wear a long-sleeved shirt buttoned up to your throat and closed at the cuffs. For those of you who are really irritated by no-see-ums, you can purchase headnets made out of no-see-um netting. The covering fits over your head and is secured by a cord around your neck. Be careful not to pull it too tight.

If you are bitten, grin and bear it because there's not much you can do to stop the fortunately brief pain. On second thought, don't grin because no-see-ums are not averse to flying in your mouth.

Bees, Hornets, and Wasps

I've only been stung once by a yellow jacket in thousands of miles of hiking. Mostly, these insects will try to avoid you but they are attracted to food, beverages, perfume, scented soaps and lotions (including deodorant), and bright-colored clothing. Also, they nest anywhere that provides cover—in logs, trees, even underground.

Yellow jackets are the most obnoxious of the bunch, often stinging more than once and without provocation. By keeping your camp clean and your food and drink under cover, you should avoid these stinging pests.

If stung by one of these insects, wash the area with soap and water to keep the sting from becoming infected. Apply a cool cloth for about twenty minutes to reduce swelling and carry an oral antihistamine to reduce swelling as well.

Check your damp clothing and towels before using to make sure one of these stingers has not alighted on it. And remember, bees, hornets, and wasps kill more people each year than snakes.

Numerous stings can induce anaphylactic shock, which can be fatal.

Anaphylactic Shock

Bees, wasps, yellow jackets, hornets, ants, and blackflies can all cause an extreme allergic reaction in some people that is referred to as anaphylactic shock. If you know that you are susceptible to anaphylaxis, then it would be wise to carry an Anakit whenever you go backpacking. The kit contains a couple of injections of epinephrine and antihistamine tablets. Your doctor should be able to prescribe one for you. If you must use the injection, always get to a hospital as soon as possible in case the anaphylactic state returns.

Anaphylactic shock occurs when the body produces too much histamine in reaction to a bite or sting. The reaction turns your skin red, itchy hives appear, and your airways begin to close down and will eventually shut completely, causing asphyxiation.

If you are presented with a first-time case of anaphylaxis, give the victim antihistamine tablets if they can swallow. You should be carrying Benadryl or some similar antihistamine in your first aid kit. Seek help immediately.

For those not allergic to bites and stings, Sting-eze is supposed to be a superior product when it comes to relieving the pain and itching caused by most insects. It is said to combat infection from poison oak, cuts, burns, and abrasions, as well.

Blackflies, Deerflies, and Horseflies
Most abundant during late spring and summer, these flies produce a painful bite and leave a nasty mark on your skin. They sponge up the blood produced by their bite, which is why the wound is often so big. Deerflies, in particular, seem to prefer to dine on your head. When swarmed by the monsters, I have covered my head, Arab-style, to avoid their nasty bites. If bitten, wash with soap and water and use an oral antihistamine to reduce swelling and itching.

Fire Ants
So far these nasty little creatures are found only in the South. But both Frank and I have experienced firsthand their tenacity and painful bite. Frank found one little ant clinging stubbornly to his foot hours after he stepped in

a fire ant bed. These ants are very aggressive, consider your passing a provocation, and will sting you repeatedly. They build distinctive foot-high mounds but you don't necessarily have to kick one to be the brunt of their anger. Water-borne fire ants will attack you as viciously as those defending their territory, which often appears to be the entire universe. Treat a fire ant bite as you would a bee sting.

Scorpions

Scorpions hide under rocks, logs and other cover during the day; and although they pack a powerful wallop when they sting, only one species is potentially fatal. You'll rarely encounter scorpions in the woods, but keep a look out for them in the desert where they may crawl into your boots, clothing, or sleeping bag during the night. Make sure you inspect your boots and clothing before putting them on and shake out your sleeping bag before crawling into it. Once again, wear shoes around camp, and if you are building a fire ring, be careful. My brother, Tom, was stung a few times while gathering rocks for a fireplace in central Georgia.

If stung by a scorpion, treat the wound as you would a wasp sting. If the scorpion that stings you is about one-half to three inches long and yellow or greenish-yellow and you are in Texas, Arizona, New Mexico, southern California, or northern Mexico, seek help immediately. It may be the one exception to the rule, the potentially deadly Ceturoides sculptuates. If unsure and if it's possible, kill the scorpion that stung you and show it to the doctor.

Chiggers or Red Bugs

Although reputed to burrow beneath your skin and to retreat only when full or suffocated, chiggers actually cause that red, itchy irritation on your skin when secretions are released during feeding. Treat chigger bites as you would bee stings.

Mosquitoes

As monsoon season approached in Kathmandu our room was suddenly invaded with all manner of insects, but the most annoying were the mosquitoes. They would buzz around our heads nearly driving us insane. Likewise, when camping, there is nothing worse than a mosquito caught in your tent with you. They always seem to vanish, mysteriously, when you turn your flashlight on. Only the females bite, but there always seem to be plenty of them around.

Most of the time it is impossible to avoid mosquitoes, but if you camp in open, breezy areas away from still water, there's a good chance your sleep will be mosquito-free. Go for light-colored clothing that is too thick for mosquitoes to penetrate. If they are really bad, wear long-sleeved shirts and pants and use DEET.

Wash mosquito bites and use an oral antihistamine to reduce swelling. A paste of baking soda and water also often helps reduce the itching of mosquito bites.

Ticks

A relative of spiders (another insect that leaves nasty bites), the tick has become a serious health threat. It is the carrier of both Rocky Mountain Spotted Fever and Lyme disease. Rocky Mountain Spotted Fever is carried by the wood ticks (in the West), lone star ticks (in the Southwest), and dog ticks (in the East and South). Lyme disease is carried by the deer tick, which is about the size of a pinhead.

Whenever you are hiking in tick country—tall grass and underbrush—make sure you check yourself afterwards for ticks. Wearing a hat, a long-sleeved shirt, and pants with cuffs tucked into socks will also discourage ticks. This can be very uncomfortable in hot weather. Using a repellent containing permethrin will also help, as will keeping to the center of the trail.

Like mosquitoes, ticks are attracted to heat, often hanging around for months at a time waiting for a hot body to pass by. Wearing light-colored clothing will allow you to see ticks. After a hike on Cumberland Island, my husband arrived back at camp with his sock literally covered in tiny seed ticks. We quickly removed the sock and proceeded to send the ticks on to their next life. If a tick attaches itself to your body, the best way to remove it is by grasping the skin directly below where the tick is attached and removing the tick along with a small piece of skin. Once removed, carefully wash the bite with soap and water.

It takes a while for a tick to become imbedded. If you check yourself thoroughly after each hike—every mole and speck of dirt as well—you are more likely to catch the tick before it catches you. Tick season lasts from April through October and peak season is from May through July. But in warmer climates, tick season may last year 'round if there has been a warmer than average winter.

Lyme Disease
More than 21,000 cases of Lyme disease have been reported in 45 states since it was first identified in 1982. The cases are rapidly on the rise, with 4,574 reported in 1988; and 7,400 in 1989, and 13,000 in 1995.

Among the symptoms of Lyme disease are fever, headache, pain and stiffness in joints and muscles. If left untreated, Lyme disease can produce lifelong impairment of muscular and nervous systems, chronic arthritis, brain injury, and in ten percent, crippling arthritis.

Lyme disease proceeds in three stages (although all three do not necessarily occur):

The first stage may consist of flu-like symptoms (fatigue, headache, muscle and joint pain, swollen glands) and a skin rash with a bright red border. Antibiotic treatment wipes out the infection at this stage.

The second stage may include paralysis of the facial muscles, heart palpitations, light-headedness and shortness of breath, severe headaches, encephalitis and meningitis. Other symptoms include irritability, a stiff neck, and difficulty concentrating. The pain may move around from joint to joint.

The third stage may take several years to occur and consists of chronic arthritis with numbness, tingling and burning pain, and may include inflammation of the brain itself. The disease can also lead to serious heart complications and attack the liver, eyes, kidney, spleen, and lungs. Memory loss and lack of concentration are also present.

Although antibiotics are used for treatment in each stage, early detection and diagnosis are critical. If you suspect you have Lyme disease, see a doctor immediately.

Fortunately, there is now a three-shot regimen called Lymerix, which is a vaccine against Lyme disease. The shot was developed by SmithKline Beecham and more information can be found at their Web site at www.lymerix.com or by calling (888) 596-3749, ext. 200.

Repellents

DEET is the hands-down winner when it comes to repelling insects. Short for N, N-diethyl-meta-toluamide, DEET is found in some percentage in most repellents—lotions, creams, sticks, pump sprays, and aerosols.

This colorless, oily, slightly smelly ingredient is good against mosquitoes, no-see-ums, fleas, ticks, gnats, and flies. Although it can range in percentage from 5 percent to 95 percent, the longest lasting formula contains approximately 35 percent of DEET.

Repellents containing DEET in the 35 percent range are (in ascending order): Deep Woods Off! lotion, Deep Woods Off! Towelettes, Cutter's Stick, Cutter's Cream, Cutter's Cream Evergreen Scent, Cutter's Cream Single Use Packets (35 percent), Muskol Ultra Maximum Strength, Repel and Kampers Lotion (which is 47.5 percent DEET and includes suntan lotion).

Avon's Skin-So-Soft is a highly recommended deterrent against no-see-ums and some bigger bugs such as sand fleas and blackflies. It appears to work differently on each person. I have better luck with it than my husband, for example.

During a trip to the low country of South Carolina, I was glad I packed the Skin-So-Soft. My daughter, Griffin, was bitten only on the head (where she was still greatly lacking in hair)—the only place I couldn't slather her with the stuff. I received only one bite, my husband quite a few more.

Day's End

PART THREE

Setting Up Camp

FINDING YOUR CAMPSITE

Finding a site is best done before you ever hit the trail, as I once found out during a hike on the Appalachian Trail in North Carolina. It was about an hour before sunset when my husband and I began our search for a campsite. With more than a dozen miles behind us during the shorter daylight hours of an early spring hike, we were ready for supper. The ridge we were on wasn't steep, but there was also nothing like a level campsite on its slopes. We topped off our canteens at a spring and decided to make supper and clean up nearby. Then we could press on until dark if we had to in search of somewhat level ground. We quickly fired up the stove and heated some Ramen noodles. With darkness coming, we ate in haste and were soon packed up and hiking.

Sunset found us a mile and a half farther down the trail with the elusive just-right site having escaped us. Finally, by the dim light of our mini-flashlights we scoped out a spot just big enough for our tent. The site was not flat, as we prefer, and it was among a clump of rhododendron far closer to a stream than I would ever admit now. We hastily put up the tent and got ready for bed. Through the night, we slowly slithered in our sleeping bags to the downhill side of the tent. Scooching to the uphill side, we would just start to drift off before we began the process anew. We fought gravity for sleep all night long. Before dawn, we packed up and started hiking. Sunrise found us breaking our fast in the most pleasant of campsites about a half mile farther up the trail. If we had planned our campsites ahead of time, we could have actually slept some the night before.

BACKPACKING TIP

When camping in desert canyon country, always camp above the high water mark, which is marked by a line of debris on canyon walls. This way you will avoid being washed away by a flash flood.

On many trails, the site will have been selected for you. Check maps and guidebooks for designated sites as you plan your hike. When established sites are available, you need to use them to concentrate the human impact and preserve the surrounding environment. Failing that, look on the map for areas with wide spaces between the topographic lines, meaning a flat place or gentle slope. Setting an area like this as your day's goal will prevent you from spending a sleep-free night bivouacked on some mountain slope. If you cannot plan ahead, or find that you were able to go a lot farther than (or not quite as far as) you wished, you should start searching for a site several hours before sunset, just in case. Remember to make allowance for the time it takes you to set up camp, cook dinner, and clean up so that you can be finished before dark.

When no sites have been established along the

trail, you can find a good spot by following a few guidelines. Look for a site that is:

➤ At least two hundred feet from the trail, water sources, and game trails.

➤ Out of sight of trails, water sources, and preferably other campers.

➤ Relatively flat and level, with good drainage.

➤ Durable, with soil that resists impact.

➤ Near or under trees that provide shelter from the elements (without having any widowmakers—branches, or the tree itself, that seem prone to falling).

➤ On high enough ground to catch a breeze (when it is hot out) because this will discourage bugs.

➤ Away from cliffs harboring loose rocks.

Sounds ideal, doesn't it? Perhaps a little too perfect. Well, that's why I recommended, first, that you use an established site. But, following these guidelines to find the right site is not as daunting as it may seem.

Two further pieces of advice for safety's sake:

➤ In a lightning storm, you will want to be camped out in a dense stand of trees all about the same height in a relatively low area away from water.

➤ In the West, stay out of dry creek beds, or arroyos, since flash floods can take out your entire camp.

During hot and cold weather extremes, you will also want to make some adjustments to fit the conditions.

CAMPING IN THE HOT AND COLD

The best site for a winter hike will not usually be the ideal spot for a summer backpack. In each season, you will want to work with nature to heat (or cool) your site as much as possible. In the summer, keep this in mind:

➤ Wind blows down mountain slopes at night, cooling off valleys and canyons. This natural air conditioning also keeps the bugs at bay on a summer hike.

➤ Be wary in summer of flat grassy areas near streams and ponds. They get boggy after a rain and often attract bugs in warm weather.

The cool mountain breeze that attracted you to a mountain slope on a summer's hike will add to your frustration level in winter, especially if you are already questioning the sanity of the person who set your sleeping bag's comfort rating. In the winter, you should:

➤ Choose a site higher on the mountainside, sheltered by trees or rocks.

➤ Look hard at the trees as snow and wind could send dead branches or trees crashing down in the night. Set up your tent well away from these widowmakers.

➤ If practical, point the door of your tent to the east or southeast to maximize the early morning sun your tent catches.

ORGANIZING THE CAMP

So, you've found a place to camp. How should you lay out your campsite so that it's comfortable and it also discourages roving animals? At home, you would probably never bathe in your living room. Just as your house has areas set aside for specific purposes, so should your home in the woods. With a properly laid out campsite, you will discourage animal pests, minimize your impact on the environment, and have an enjoyable stay in the backcountry. You will have six main areas within your campsite:

1. Tent site. The hub that the other spokes of the campsite radiate from, this will be selected for several reasons as discussed previously.

2. Water source. If there is one, it should be at least two hundred feet from all of the other areas of your campsite so you don't contaminate the water supply. A large, collapsible water bag will make it easy to limit trips to the water source.

3. Cooking area. You should cook twenty-five feet from your tent in most areas and one hundred feet away in Grizzly country. In either case, the cooking area is best located downwind of your tent site.

4. Cleaning area. Dishes should be cleaned at least two hundred feet from the tent so wastewater

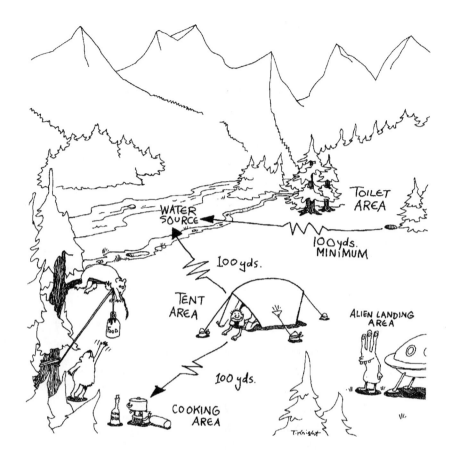

smells won't attract animals to the tent area. If the soil isn't porous, dig a cat hole to pour your wastewater into and bury it. Use a small strainer to strain the food particles from the wastewater and pack the particles in with your garbage.

5. Bathroom. Locate any cat holes out of sight of the rest of the camp and two hundred feet from your water source.

6. Tree to hang bear bag. This should be located at least one hundred feet from your tent but it can be near your cooking area for convenience.

YOUR HOME AWAY FROM HOME

Before going on any backpacking trip, you should know your tent (and all your other equipment for that matter)

317

backwards and forwards. Set it up in your backyard (or if that is impossible, your living room) over and over again until you can do it in your sleep. This will be invaluable should you ever have to set up your tent in a downpour or in a raging wind. If there is a knock-you-off-your-feet storm blowing, go over the steps for setting up your tent before you start. If you get panicky it will take twice as long. Pitching your tent in the rain is merely a matter of speed. It all comes down to how quickly you wish to get out of the rain. The faster you set up your tent, the quicker you can get dry. Getting the rainproof fly on as quickly as possible is also very important

The first step, before setting up your tent is to find a place to lay it out. It should be as level as possible and you should remove any sticks, stones, pinecones, or anything that may cause you discomfort. Before unrolling your tent, get the poles, pegs, or whatever you need to set it up, ready. As you slowly unroll your tent, stake it to the ground if it is not a freestanding tent. If it is freestanding, place heavy objects on the tent to keep it from blowing away.

Once pegged or weighted to the ground, insert poles windward side first. This sounds easier than it is, but with a little determination and imagination your tent will soon be up. If it is a freestanding tent, throw your pack inside to weigh the tent down until you get in. If it is a pegged tent, make sure none of the stakes threaten to pull loose.

If you plan a backpacking trip in the snow, make sure that you have pegs that will hold in both soft and hard snow. Most outdoor stores offer special anchors and pegs for snow camping. You may want to purchase a full-time replacement for the spindly pegs that come with your tent. Some of the heavy-duty options available are T-stakes, I-beams, half-moons, and corkscrews. The salesman at your outdoors store will be able to tell you which stake best suits your purpose. It is particularly important to make sure your tent is securely pegged when you set it up on snow. Before you can set up your tent, you must first stamp down the snow, including an area for you to walk around while pitching your tent, a broad area for the entrance, and troughs for the guylines, if you need them.

To keep your tent as dry as possible, make sure that you rid yourself of as much snow as possible before climbing in. A large garbage bag outside the entrance to your tent can work as a waterproof doormat.

If you intend to camp in extreme snow conditions, you will need either a snow shovel or something that can be used as a shovel, such as a snowshoe. If snow keeps falling for more than a day, your tent will likely become buried in the snow, which risks a collapsed tent and even suffocation. If caught in a prolonged snowstorm, take down your tent and rebuild your platform by shoveling snow onto the stamped down area and restamping. Finally, repitch your tent.

Setting up a Tarp

There are many ways to set up a tarp, but the most common is the shed roof. This is the easiest method of rigging a tarp and requires only two trees reasonably close to each other. The high side of the tarp is suspended six to eight feet off the ground (facing away from the wind) with one corner attached by rope to each tree. The low side faces into the wind with two to four tent stakes pegged flush to the ground.

The A-frame is another common tarp set-up. The tarp is set up between two trees at least ten feet apart. Your fifty feet of rope is used as a ridgeline for the tarp and attaches to each tree six to eight feet off the ground. Make sure the ridgeline is pulled tight so that the tarp does not sag in the middle. Depending on the weather, guylines are then tied to grommets or clamps on both sides of the tarp and then nailed to the ground with tent pegs in bad weather or settled several inches off the ground in good weather for more room and ventilation.

Should the area you are hiking afford no trees or boulders large enough to rig your tarp, another possibility is rigging the A-frame with four makeshift poles—

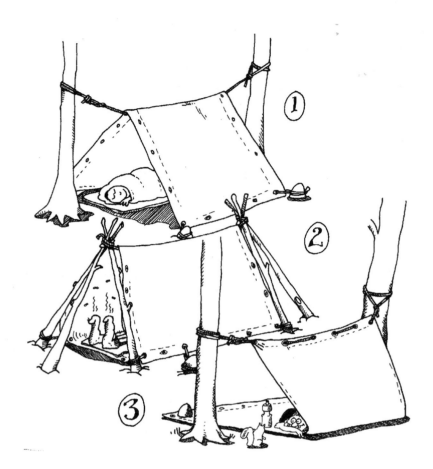

sound branches, driftwood, or whatever is handy—at
least a few feet long. One end of the ridgeline is
pegged into the ground. Making a teepee shape with
the first two poles, wrap the ridgeline rope twice vertically and horizontally around the top of the A-frame
where the poles cross. With enough space left to lay
your tarp over it, lash the other end of the ridgeline
rope in the same way to the second set of poles. Make
sure the ridgeline is tight, then lash the end of the line
to a peg and then stamp it into the ground. Throw your
tarp over the ridgeline and lash the edges to the
ground as needed.

PROTECTING YOUR FOOD

My first experience with animals getting into food came
during a camping trip to Yosemite in California. The

ranger patiently explained to my father how the bear bag had to be hung to keep it away from marauding bears or "there'd be trouble a 'bruin.'" OK, so the ranger was a punny guy. He added a few more "bearly" acceptable puns before stressing once again that the bears would dearly love to turn our weekend provisions into a midnight snack. My father then hung the bag of food from a carefully selected limb, just as we had been told. When we went to bed that night, we were all confident that no bear would get our food.

It was well past midnight when we were awakened by an unusual sound. It was a heavy, padded whumpf followed by snuffling noises. Later, we heard it again. Third time is lucky, they say, and it was for the bear. We heard shouts, and the clatter of banging pots filled the air. The folks at the neighboring campsite were chasing a bear away. We climbed out of our tent to survey the damage. Our bag still hung safe and sound, gently swaying from the limb of the tree. But our neighbors had lost most of their food, not to mention the bag it was hanging in. Why was their bag chosen for the attack and not ours? Perhaps it hadn't been far enough off the ground or maybe the smells emanating from it were more enticing. Only the bear knows.

Some areas provide wooden boxes or metal canisters you can use to protect food from the small and large critters, but in most cases you are on your own in establishing a secure place for your food. The following method of bear bagging can help protect your food from anything from mice and raccoons to bears (unless, of course, they're Kamikaze bears, in which case, this will only delay them):

1. When you first set up camp, select a tree at least one hundred feet from your tent that has a stout limb at least twenty feet off the ground.
2. Weight your rope and toss it over the branch at least ten feet out from the trunk of the tree. A stuff

BACKPACKING TIP

Your flashlight can occasionally do double duty as a lantern. Place a Nalgene brand or other translucent bottle over the end of the flashight to disperse light. Stand the bottle up on the open end and you have a serviceable lantern.

sack filled with rocks is great for this and can act as the counterbalance bag later on. The branch should be sturdy enough to hold your sack, but not sturdy enough to hold a bear, nor should any branch nearby. It should also be somewhat flexible, so a bear can't snap it off the tree. The rope should be long enough to reach from the ground to the branch and back.

3. Tie the other end of the rope to the tree's trunk.

4. When you are ready to turn in for the night, pack food and other items whose smell might attract animals into an empty stuff sack. This should include soap, toothpaste, pot scrubber, garbage (which should be double-bagged before going into the stuff sack) and anything else you might have that smells.

5. Untie the rope from the tree and pull the counterbalance bag up to the tree limb. (Often, this counterbalance might be another bag that needs to be tied up, or it might just be a bag with rocks.)

6. Fold the end of the bag over the stick and, using the free end of the rope, tie a knot around the bag beneath the stick, cinching together the bag and the folded section. This keeps the bag from slipping out of the knot during the night.

7. Also tie a loop of rope that hangs below the bag and can later be used to retrieve your bag. (You may also want to tie a retrieval loop to the counterbalanced bag as well.)

8. Find a stick roughly two inches thick and long enough to push the bag twelve feet off the ground.

9. Push the counterbalance up until both bags are at least twelve feet off the ground and five feet below the branch.

10. Be prepared to bang pots and pans and throw rocks to chase away any animals you hear going after the bag during the night.

Alternately, rather than suspending your bag from a branch, you might want to suspend it between two trees. Use two trees 20 to 30 feet apart and hang the bag 12 to 15 feet off the ground. You can do this by lassoing and tying off the first tree and then lassoing the second. While the line is slack, tie on the food bag. Then yank on the line to suspend the bag and tie the rope off.

BACKPACKING TIP

You can buy a small pulley or use a couple of carabiners to make hoisting your food bags a lot easier.

THE LATRINE

When you are a backpacker, it seems the whole outdoors is your bathroom. But for neophytes, weaning themselves from porcelain can be a tough adjustment. We had forgotten that when we took our church youth group on an early winter camping trip. The privy didn't even smell bad; with the temperature hovering in the upper twenties, it wasn't even close to that thick, fly-infested smell of a pit latrine in summer. But it wouldn't do for Margie. Of the dozen teens on the outing, Margie was the one who had to put on make-up before getting out of her sleeping bag. And Margie, who also dreams of thru-hiking the Appalachian Trail, waited it out. She preferred to stubbornly hold on until she could relax on the plastic and porcelain comfort of a toilet in a climate-controlled fast food restaurant on the way home. We hated to clue her in to the fact that she would be hard pressed to hold out for American Standard during a five- to six-month

BACKPACKING TIP

When hiking in fragile or heavily used areas, consider a "poop tube" (a 4-inch diameter piece of PVC pipe capped at one end and threaded for a screw-on lid on the other end) to pack out all solid waste.

hike of the AT. When nature calls in the backcountry, even a pit latrine is a luxury; usually there's no latrine in sight.

Here is what to do when a privy isn't available:

➤ Always carry a lightweight, plastic backpacker's trowel when you hike.

➤ Go at least two hundred feet from any water source including springs and streams, and go out of sight of both the campsite and trail.

➤ If it makes you more comfortable, seek out a tree or rock to hug when squatting.

➤ When you need to defecate, dig a cat hole about four inches deep.

➤ Always cover the cat hole with soil when you are finished and place a log or rock on top so the next person doesn't step in it.

➤ Carry along a plastic baggie to pack out used toilet paper for disposal later. Always bury or burn your toilet paper if you do not plan to pack it out.

➤ Blend the site into natural surroundings by rescattering leaves or pine needles.

➤ When urinating, you do not need to dig a hole; surface disposal leads to quicker decomposition in most environments.

Additional tips for special circumstances include:

➤ A couple or small group should try to spread the impact by not sharing a common toilet site.

➤ A group of five or more will be hard pressed to find enough available places to spread out their wastes. Groups should dig a twelve-inch-deep pit for common use, with each person "flushing" by sprinkling dirt over the feces with a handy shovel. The pit should be completely buried and re-blended with the surroundings upon leaving the site.

➤ When the ground is covered with snow, be sure to dig through the snow and create a cat hole several inches beneath the topsoil. Otherwise, you may leave behind an unpleasant surprise when the snow melts.

➤ If the ground is frozen, you will have to carry out your waste to be disposed of later. Use a zipper-locked bag as your "toilet" and then double bag it.

Using a cat hole isn't my favorite part of a hiking trip, but it really isn't that big a deal—especially when compared to holding out for porcelain splendor during a week-long trek. Your backcountry bathroom may even boast an awesome view.

BREAKING CAMP

When it comes to breaking camp, when and how to do it differ according to individual preference, as with any other aspect of backpacking. Some folks love to wake up at dawn and get out with the rising of the sun. Others prefer to take their time, slowly sipping their coffee as the sun spreads its warmth over the landscape.

Whether you take down your tent before you eat breakfast or afterwards is really a matter of preference. What matters the most, though, is to leave your campsite looking as if it had never been used. Or, if it is an established site, with as little additional damage as possible.

For some people, beating the early bird to the worm is just another form of masochism. But for even the slackest of packers, there almost always comes a day when there is a need to break camp in record time. Fortunately, there are a number of ways to hasten your retreat:

➤ Use a watch alarm to wake up early. This is the most obvious way to get an early start and break camp quickly. If you can hit the trail at sunrise, you've already gained an hour or two on your day.

➤ Sleep under the stars. If weather permits, you can gain minutes in the morning by not having to take down your tent.

➤ Pre-pack. The night before you need to break camp early, pack up any gear you will not need to use in the morning.

➤ Be water ready. At night, go ahead and filter or boil any water you might need the following morning to cook and fill water bottles.

➤ Share tasks. While one person is preparing the morning meal, the other can be taking down the tent. While one is cleaning up, the other can be breaking camp.

➤ Don't dawdle. If you need to get out of camp in a hurry, don't waste time lingering over the morning cup of coffee. Make it a game or competition and see how quickly each task can be accomplished.

➤ Go cold. If the weather permits, try not cooking at all. Rather than fixing a warm bowl of oatmeal, munch on a Power Bar or some granola or gorp, and sip from your water bottle rather than a hot cup of cocoa before hitting the trail.

Keeping a Journal

It's horrifying when you need to jog your memory, and upon opening your journal, you discover nothing but, "Hiked 17.2 miles today to Half Moon camp. Ate mac and cheese, then crashed." Surely something worth noting happened in that 17.2 miles.

One of my favorite journal entries details the two frigid nights we spent in a rickety barn with 13 Boy Scouts when we were delayed before climbing the upcoming balds. The event seemed so newsworthy that the journal entry read like a series of newspaper articles complete with headlines and a banner—The Not Yet Over the Humps News.

You do not have to be a writer or even extremely creative to add some interest to your journal, and facts such as how far you hiked and what you ate can be helpful later. The following should help:

➤ Details make the difference. In addition to mileage, add things you saw, sounds you heard, what you felt, smelled, and tasted. Illustrations add interest to your entries as well.

➤ Don't worry about spelling, punctuation, and grammar. Let it flow. No one has to read this so there is no need to feel self-conscious.

➤ Don't feel it's necessary to highlight only the high points of a trip. If you're feelings are negative, say so. A journal reflects your experiences as they are not as you hope they will be.

➤ Try to write something every day. The more time that passes between journal entries, the more vague the details become.

➤ Use a "journal" that fits your needs. From a spiral-bound and lined notebook to loose sheets of watercolor or charcoal paper, use what works for you. If your journal is mostly drawings, then plain sheets of paper may work best. Fill-in-the-blank journals are a possibility for those who need prompting.

➤ Pens are more legible but always carry a pencil as well since it will never run out of ink.

➤ Always date your entries as well as the outside of your journals so you can keep track of not just where you hiked but when.

➤ Simplify your bear bag. Attach a plastic hook to the end of your bear-bag rope so the bag clips on and off, and you avoid fumbling in the dark with the knots.

When taking down your tent in the rain, you may be able to do most of the work beneath the fly, keeping the tent a bit drier.

The Backcountry Kitchen

Backpackers are noted for their tremendous appetites. Anyone who has done any long-distance hiking or met long-distance hikers has a tale to tell about how much a backpacker can eat.

From gallons of ice cream to all-you-can-eat (AYCE) buffets, hikers consume copious amounts of food whenever they hit a town near the trail. While hiking the Appalachian Trail, Phil Hall was so impressed with Shoney's AYCE breakfast bar in Virginia that he hitched a ride back there when he reached New Hampshire.

Long-distance hikers often leave a town dreaming about what epicurean delights the next town might have to offer. Because you really do want to keep your pack light, you must often hike with a less than satisfying amount of food in tow. The challenge is getting the best bang out of what you carry

NUTRITION

Nutrition on the trail is a Catch-22. While it is easy enough to carry sufficient food to account for calories burned during a day or weekend hike, it is difficult and often impossible to do so for extended trips.

The more food you carry, the heavier your pack. The heavier your pack, the more calories you burn. The more calories you burn, the more you need. It's a vicious cycle for long-distance hikers as well as those who are already on the thin side. While you're sure to lose weight on an extended hike, there is no need to sacrifice your health.

Since you'll be burning close to five thousand calories per eight-hour hiking day on a backpacking trip, it is important that the food you carry has high nutritional value and a high carbohydrate count. The complex carbohydrates should make up about 50 percent of the backpacker's daily caloric intake. Fortunately, this is an easy requirement to fill. Bread, pastas, cookies, dried fruit, candy, and honey are all high in carbohydrates.

Twenty percent of your day's calories should consist of fats, which the body converts into stored energy. You need a higher percentage of fats in the winter, and you can get your fats from margarine, cheese, peanut butter, nuts, and salami. High-altitude hikers and climbers need to increase their carbo intake and lower their fat consumption during climbs because the body will confiscate oxygen to process fats into stored up lipoproteins. Most climbers can't spare the oxygen for this process, and they have more energy on a high carbohydrate diet.

Protein is also important to the backpacker, but if you eat too much, it will be converted to glycogen and stored as fat. You can get your proteins from peanut butter, oat and wheat cereals with powdered milk, sausage, cheese, beef jerky, or other dried or fresh meats. A better solution is to get your protein from plants—raw or cooked beans, soybeans, nuts, and olives—that also supply important vitamins, minerals, carbohydrates and fiber.

Whether or not you should take vitamins on an extended trip is debatable. During our six-month trek, we took vitamins when we remembered (which wasn't often) and both of us caught a severe cold. Two years later I began taking vitamins religiously (when carrying my daughter, Griffin) and I have suffered only one brief cold in two years. Whether or not it is the vitamins or the lack of exposure, I couldn't tell you. Once again, it is a matter of preference, but I recommend taking some sort of vitamin supplement on an extended trip, particularly vitamins C and B. It is hard to maintain a balanced diet under such strenuous conditions, so a multivitamin is your best bet during a long-distance hike.

Food sources high in calcium are particularly important to long-distance hikers. Powdered milk, milk products such as cheese, and sardines in oil are good sources of calcium. Dried fruit, though not particularly high in calcium content, can add greatly to the total calcium and vitamin A intake when eaten on a regular basis.

Experts recommend that you vary your backpacking diet as much as possible. While it may not bother you to eat cold cereal for breakfast, gorp for lunch, and macaroni and cheese for dinner every day, your body may soon tire of it. I learned the hard way with macaroni and cheese. We ate so much of it that by the end of our trip I literally had to gag the stuff down and often couldn't finish my serving. The most important aspect of a varied diet is the guarantee that you will be getting all the nutrients your body needs to function efficiently.

I know of backpackers who subsist on the same thing for every meal, seven days a week. I also know of backpackers who thought they were in peak condition until they had to undergo open-heart surgery. Your body can only do so much on its own. It depends on you to do what's right for it. As The Fonz said, "You live in your body most of your life."

THINGS TO CONSIDER WHEN SHOPPING FOR FOOD

In addition to nutrition, there are several other things to consider when shopping for backpacking trips: the weight of the food, ease of preparation, taste and cost are of varying importance to different people.

Remember that your pack can only hold so much. While you may want steak every night, the weight alone precludes your carrying it. The lighter the food the better and, fortunately for backpackers, there are a lot of options on the market.

Ease of preparation also is important. After a long day of hiking, it is unlikely that you will want to spend hours preparing your meal. Read package labeling before purchasing a food product. How long will it take to prepare the meal? How long do you want to wait? On days when we reached our destination early, we didn't mind waiting 20 minutes for our lentils and rice to simmer. Other days, we could hardly wait for the macaroni to finish cooking and often ate it a bit more al dente than we usually liked. Buying food with various preparation times (but with a majority on the short side)

will give you some options when you stumble into camp for the night.

Taste is something else to think about when purchasing food. If you can't stomach peanut butter at home, you sure as heck won't like it in the outdoors, especially if you're forced to eat it. Macaroni and cheese was not the only thing I got sick of while backpacking. During our six-month trip, it seemed we always ate our sardines on cold, rainy days. It wasn't long before I associated being miserable with those smelly little fish.

Although I can eat both macaroni and sardines again, they are no longer a staple when it comes to backpacking meals. If you are unsure whether a certain backpacking food will be unsavory to you, try it before you hike. When you have end-of-the-day hunger pangs, you don't want to find yourself facing an unpalatable meal. A lot of your time hiking will be spent anticipating your next meal.

Backpacking food (as with anything) can cost as much or as little as you like. From the expensive, extra-lightweight, specially packaged foods to the inexpensive, homemade alternative, the backpacker has many choices. You know how much you have to spend. Once again, the key is diversity. Don't buy a week's worth of blueberry pancakes and lasagna; round it out with eggs and toaster pastries, macaroni and cheese, pasta salad, and lentils.

TYPES OF FOODS

Dehydrated and Freeze-dried Foods

Until someone invents something amazingly lightweight, filling, tasty, inexpensive, and convenient, hikers will have to make do with what's available. Thanks, no doubt, to the ever-increasing number of women in the workforce, supermarkets are filled with easy-to-fix, just-add-water dinners. A couple of years ago, we would have recommended that hikers stick to the low-cost supermarket brand dinners made by Kraft, Lipton, and others, but specialty dehydrated foods designed for backpackers have come a long way. Though still expensive, they add variety to the macaroni-and-cheeses and Ramen noodle dinners many hikers subsist on.

We decided to test a few different brands of meals and were pleasantly surprised by what came out of our cook pot. For breakfast, we tried an omelet with potatoes and sautéed onions. The two-serving egg dish was not a bad buy. A bit of a pain to clean up, it definitely adds variety to the staples of oatmeal and toaster pastries. Pancake mixes are also available in foil pouches.

For lunch, you have your choice of many dehydrated main courses as well as the standards—soups and sandwiches. You might want to cook your lunch, as opposed to eating a cold meal, for variety. Think about lunch at home or work—you might alternate soups, sandwiches, salads, and occasionally main courses. You have the same choices when backpacking—except for salads, which are generally impractical.

For supper, we tried a dinner described as "grains, brown rice, turkey, vegetables, and wild rice in a tangy sour cream sauce." The no-cook entree was actually quite palatable (though it wasn't actually no-cook—

Examples of pre-packaged freeze dried food.

when you hike, even boiling water is cooking). The dinner says it serves two although a hungry hiker, especially a hungry male hiker, would probably have to eat the entire dinner just to get halfway full. We had freeze-dried ice cream for dessert—the thought of it intrigued us. The two-serving portion of Neapolitan ice cream was good but expensive—and it would be just one serving for a hungry hiker. We recommend sticking to cobblers, pies, and more filling desserts.

Among the companies that supply backpackers with dehydrated and freeze-dried foods are Adventure Foods, AlpineAire, Harvest Foodworks, Mountain House, Natural High, Nature's Pantry, Richmoor, Trail Wise, and Wee Pack. Taste Adventure offers meals boxed in tiny "milk" cartons. These vegetarian, dehydrated meals prepare quickly and are inexpensive. We tried both the black bean chili and lentil soup, which were tasty and provided large portions for two people.

Although we still do not recommend relying solely on these specially dehydrated and freeze-dried backpacking foods, we do believe they are a wonderful way to add variety to your diet. Keep in mind, though, that main dishes tend to cost two to three times as much as ordinary store-bought macaroni, pasta salads, and rice dishes.

Supermarket Fare

Add the ever-growing market of backpacking foods to the supermarket fare listed below and contemporary backpackers are already farther down the trail than their compatriots of a decade earlier.

Grocery stores offer a wide variety of fare to choose from. You're limited only by what the store has in stock. If you search for meal ideas at oriental and health food stores as well, you open yourself up to even more variety. On our long-distance hike, we chose to purchase food along the way rather than send any ahead. This meant there were times when we ate macaroni and cheese three times in one week and other times when we had a different meal to choose from every night.

Self-dehydrated Foods

Many hikers depend on food they dehydrate themselves. Dehydrators can be purchased through most outdoor stores. All manner of food can be dehydrated—fruit, meat, and vegetables.

Although it takes time and effort, dehydrating your own food can be an inexpensive alternative. My mother swears by her dehydrated tuna, and Bill and Laurie Foot by their beef. Cindy Ross and Todd Gladfelter, who have hiked more than twelve thousand miles between them, dry most of the food they use for their trips.

Dehydrators cost between $50 and $100, and are to be used before you hike since they are both too heavy and bulky (not to mention electric) to carry with you.

Fresh Food

Fresh foods are available to hikers although you can't rely solely on fresh foods for your backpacking diet. Those hiking short distances have more freedom in the different types of foods they can carry because they have more room in their packs to carry the heavier, bulkier foods. If you're going for an overnighter, you can carry steaks, hamburgers, fish, or chicken to cook over your grill. Although long-distance hikers have the option to carry fresh meat, vegetables, or fruit, they have to eat this motherlode their first night back on the trail after a shopping stop or they risk rotten and decaying food. The weight is also a problem; the sooner you eat the heavier food, the more immediate the relief to your back.

We usually stick to hot dogs (turkey or chicken) on longer hikes because they are the only meat that won't drip blood all over our packs. Hot dogs roasted over a fire with some cheese make a delicious meal alternative and you don't have to worry about ketchup, mustard etc. We also occasionally carry apples, oranges, pears, carrots, and other fruits and vegetables that are not easily bruised.

With a little planning, weekenders can still enjoy fresh foods. For example, if you intend to have hamburgers your second night out, freeze the meat before you go. By the end of the second day, it should be thawed. Make sure you keep it in a zipper-lock bag or you could end up with a messy backpack. One of the greatest advantages of short hikes is that your diet is limited only by the amount of time you want to spend cooking.

Living Off the Land

Unless you know your edible wild plants backwards and forwards, I would suggest sticking to store-bought and homemade foods when backpacking. Many edible plants can be easily confused with poisonous plants.

While attending a lecture on mushrooms, we were dismayed to find that a mushroom we had feasted on in Maine was potentially fatal. This mushroom has the color and taste of lobster and is parasitic, growing off both a safe and a very dangerous mushroom. Obviously, we were lucky and we've decided we'll never take a chance like that again.

There are some obvious edibles though. Blueberries grow profusely in the wild and are great in pancakes, on cereal, and in oatmeal. Blackberries, gooseberries, currants, raspberries, and wild strawberries can also be found trailside. Mulberries, unless fully ripe, can be dangerous. Another safe wild plant is the ramp or wild leek. It's strong onion odor distinguishes it; use as you would an onion.

MEAL SUGGESTIONS

Breakfasts

Breakfasts are easier to choose than lunches since there are so many breakfast products on the market. Most are "vitamin-fortified"—generally a gimmick to make mothers feel that they are providing a healthy breakfast for their child even when the product is stuffed full of sugar. Of course, the extra carbohydrates are an added boon for hikers!

Suggested Breakfasts:

Cold cereal with powdered milk
Granola with powdered milk

Gorp with powdered milk

Oatmeal (flavored and plain varieties)

Cream of Wheat

Toaster pastries (such as Pop Tarts)

Eggs (eggs will keep for several days)

Canned bacon

Bacon bars

Bread with peanut butter

Bagels with cream cheese (cheese also keeps for several days)

Snickers or other candy bars

Granola bars

Breakfast bars (such as Nutrigrain Breakfast Bars)
    Pancakes (bring the dry mix, and add powdered
    milk and water)

Instant hash browns

Instant grits

English muffins

Raisin bread

Lunches

Lunches are always a problem for us, both at home
and on the trail. Unless it is really cold, we never feel
like taking the time to cook a lunch; but on the trail,
there are only so many things you can do to improvise
a cold lunch. We recommend that you do what suits
you best. Some people hike better after a big, hot
meal, but most do best with a simple repast. The temperatures during your hike may also determine your
midday meal. When it is cold, we often choose to keep
moving, eating snack foods while we hike, rather than
stopping to prepare a meal.

Suggested Lunches:

Sardines

Cheese

Nuts

Pemmican (complex protein bars)

Cookies

Graham crackers (perhaps spread with peanut butter)
    Other crackers (also perhaps spread with peanut

butter or cheese; a number of pre-spread cookies can be purchased)

Cheese sandwiches (pita is a great hiking bread—stuff it with salami and cheese for a calorie-packed sandwich)

Peanut butter and jelly sandwiches

English muffins and peanut butter

Crackers and tuna

Beef jerky

Pepperoni

Sausage (hard types like salami, summer sausage, etc.)

Corned beef or Spam

Vienna sausages

Apples, oranges, and other fresh fruit

Dried fruit (including rolls and bars; raisins are a good choice)

Lipton Pasta or Noodles and Sauce

Dried soups

Hard-boiled eggs

Granola bars

Candy bars

Snack foods (Little Debbie brand is especially popular)

Gorp (a mixture of dried fruit, nuts, M&Ms, sunflower seeds, etc.)

Fruit cake

Suppers

Supper should be your most time-consuming meal of the day. It is time to relax, settle down for the night, and enjoy the great outdoors. You no longer have to worry about whether or not you'll reach your goal for the day. Your camp is set. Dinner is your only concern. Despite the fact that many backpackers eat macaroni and cheese night after night, there are many alternatives when choosing dinner on the trail.

Suggested Suppers:

Macaroni and cheese (a real favorite; meat or dried soup is often added)

Chef Boyardee spaghetti

Lipton brand noodle dinners

Ramen noodles

Pasta salads
Instant potatoes and potato dishes (mashed, au gratin,
    etc.)
Instant rice dishes (instant gravies and cheese sauces
    can be added)
Lentils
Pilafs (made with lentils, wheat, or rice)
Couscous (a Middle Eastern wheat dish similar to grits)
Stove Top or other stuffings
Instant soup
Tuna and other canned meats (used with any dinners)
Pepperoni, dried beef, and sausages
Sardines and fish steaks (hot dogs also show up
    occasionally)
Specialty dehydrated meals

Beverages
As I mentioned in the chapter on water, drinking is a very
important part of hiking. Becoming dehydrated will seriously impair your body's ability to perform normal func-
tions. The best thing to drink is water, but when the water
tastes like iodine you'll probably want to disguise its taste
with a powdered drink mix such as Kool-Aid. Because we
prefer the flavor, we have developed the practice of constantly carrying a full liter of a Kool-Aid-type drink mix
and a spare liter (or two if the weather is hot) of water.

The next best thing to water is an electrolyte solution such as Gatorade or Gookinaid ERG. These help
replace the electrolytes, as well as the water, that you
lose when you perspire, respire, etc. Some physiologists
debate this claim and believe that electrolyte solutions
do more harm than good.

Very few of us are willing to give up our morning
cup of coffee when we hit the trail. If you do drink coffee or cocoa (unless decaffeinated), keep in mind that
they are diuretics and you will need to drink more water
to compensate.

Suggested Beverages:

Water
Powdered fruit drinks (such as Kool-Aid—unsweetened
    or with your preferred sweetener added)

339

Powdered iced tea (often mixed with fruit drinks)
Powdered fruit teas
Jell-O mix (used as a tasty, hot drink that also supplies
extra calories)
Instant coffee
Non-dairy creamer (for tea or coffee)
Powdered spiced cider
Powdered eggnog
Gatorade (powdered)
Gookinaid E.R.G.
Hot tea
Cocoa/Hot chocolate

Desserts

Desserts are a nice way to finish your evening meal.
They supply you with a few extra calories and help fill
that last empty spot in your belly. They also make dinner special. Although pudding is a favorite, there are a
number of easy-to-make desserts on the market.

Suggested Desserts:

Instant puddings
Instant cheesecakes
Cookies
Instant mousse
Jell-O or other flavored gelatins
Powdered milk (mostly used to add to other foods)
Snack cakes
Easy-bake cakes
Specialty dehydrated desserts

Spices and Condiments

Not everyone uses spices and no one carries all of
those indicated below, but those who bring spices tend
to use a variety. For their weight, spices and condiments can add a lot to a meal.

A good way to carry spices is to put them in film
containers. This keeps them both dry and compact.
Shaker tops for film containers are available through
most outdoors stores for about two dollars for two lids.

Suggested Spices:

Garlic
Salt
Pepper
Italian seasoning
Seasoned butter
Tabasco
Red pepper
Curry powder
Chili powder
Oregano
Cumin
Onion powder
Squeeze margarine (this lasts approximately one week in
    hot weather and almost indefinitely in cold weather)

Trail Snacks
I've never been a snacker, but I find it important when
hiking. Because you don't want to stuff yourself at
meals—for comfort's sake as well as the fact that a too-
full stomach can make you drowsy—it is a good idea to
snack on high energy food during breaks and while hiking. One of the most popular trail snacks is Gorp, a
mixture of nuts, dried fruit, and M&Ms. Actually, Gorp
can consist of anything you like, but the following is a
list of some popular ingredients. Mix and match your
favorites: peanuts, almonds, pecans, walnuts, filberts,
cashews (if you can afford them), M&Ms (plain, almond,
or peanut), Reese's Pieces, shredded coconut, chopped
dates, raisins, banana chips, dried pineapple, figs,
prunes, sunflower seeds, and cereals like Cheerios.

    Other trail snacks include: hard candy, Skittles
candy, semisweet chocolate, mixed nuts, and fruit bars
and rolls. There are many packaged snack bars on the
market these days. Use your imagination. As long as it
is within easy reach and will keep in the outdoors for
more than a day, it will make a good snack. Remember
too that snacks can round out dinners and often make
up your entire lunch.

PACKING YOUR FOOD

Packaging is only a problem if you are unable to repackage the food yourself. Don't buy rigid, heavy-weight containers if they must go straight into your pack. Unless you have room for food at the top of your pack where it won't get smashed, make sure the packaging is sturdy enough to survive the weight you intend to subject it to.

Proper packing is essential. Hikers joke that the "yellow-and-blue-makes-green" Gladlock brand plastic bags are one of the great backpacking inventions of our time. This might be a little exaggerated, but not much. In the interest of space, weight, and waterproofing, you will want to repackage your food into plastic bags or some other waterproof container. Other options include reusable, plastic, squeezable food tubes. A clip at the bottom is used to squeeze the food upward toward the spout. I have only seen these used for peanut butter and jelly, but because both peanut butter and jelly now come in plastic containers, it is just as easy to use them in their containers. Also, it isn't a simple process to transfer these sticky foods from one container to another.

Rigid plastic egg cartons are also available for less than three dollars from most outdoor stores. They come in both the dozen and half-dozen size and are a wonderful way to carry eggs if you eat a lot of them while hiking. These containers will hold small and medium-size eggs only.

To pack food for backpacking, sort your boxes and other packages into meals. Open the boxes and pour the contents into plastic bags of appropriate sizes. You do not need to do this with meals that come in foil or other waterproof pouches. On short trips, you can cut down on weight and space by adding the powdered milk, salt, pepper, etc., to the bag at home and leaving the condiments behind. If you need the directions, cut out the portion of the box with instructions and put it in the bag with the meal.

Some food products do better in plastic bags with twist ties. If you are carrying powdered milk, for example, it is best to double bag it and shut it with a twist tie because the grains of milk tend to get caught in a "zipper" and keep it from closing properly.

Food for a Week or More

If you are hiking for more than a week, will you be able to buy food along the way? Would it be better to send something ahead to a post office? The majority of long-distance hikers suggest using both methods. Buying some food ahead of time and some as you hike allows you to be adaptable along the trail and leaves some leeway as to where and when you stop. It also allows for much less preparation before the hike and is easier on the support crew at home.

The option to purchase food along the way eliminates the need to time your arrival in town to coincide with the hours of a post office. (It's nice not to have to depend on the U.S. Postal Service for food.) It also allows you to satisfy any cravings you may have!

CLEANING UP AFTER MEALS

Cleaning pots, dishes, and utensils is an absolute necessity. Many hikers have found out the hard way that giving cleaning the short shrift can result in severe gastrointestinal problems not dissimilar to giardiasis. Cleaning should be done away from the campsite or shelter, as well as far from the water source.

There are several reasons to clean your pots as soon as you have finished eating, not the least among them being the growth of bacteria. Dirty pots also beg for the appearance of pests such as raccoons, skunks, mice, and even bears (and dried-on macaroni and cheese can be harder to clean up than superglue). The best solution is to carry a little biodegradable soap and a pot scrubber.

Bill and Laurie Foot offer these suggestions: "Use two pots for hot meals. You should never need to cook food in your large pot. It is for heating water and rinsing dishes only. Add your hot water to the entree in the smaller pot, and after you've eaten, add more water and some soap to the smaller pot to use as a washpan. The remainder of the hot water in the large pot becomes your rinse water."

The following are some tips to make KP a bit easier:

➤ Fill your biggest pot with water, heat it, and wash away. Warm, soapy water on a chilly night makes dish duty a bit more bearable.

➤ If you are with a crew, try using a collapsible bucket. Fill it with clean rinse water for the final dip. The bucket will also be useful for hauling large amounts of water.

➤ If you lose your scrubbing sponge, substitute your hiking partner's toothbrush. OK—not! Try using ashes or sand instead. They work great as an abrasive. Toss them in your pot and use your hand or a cloth to scrub them against the metal.

➤ If you absolutely cannot abide the idea of doing dishes, confess your abhorrence but make sure you make up for it by taking on another chore instead.

➤ Short trip? Leave the soap behind. Trips of a week or longer will require soap to remove the grease buildup in your pots. Make sure the soap is biodegradable, though.

➤ Once again, never wash dishes within two hundred feet of your water source, biodegradable soap or not.

➤ Protect your stove by packing it inside your pots.

➤ Use a lid when boiling your water. Boiling time will be much faster and you will conserve fuel.

Camping Green

"It began to be noticed that the greater the exodus, the smaller the per capita ration of peace, solitude, wildlife, and scenery, and the longer the migration to reach them."

-Aldo Leopold

As Aldo Leopold wrote years ago, it is getting harder and harder to find solitude. Even wilderness areas seem to overflow with humanity at times. Backpacking is a way to get away from the mass of people and be alone (or at least among the noble few who will respect your wish for solitude). But, are we as backpackers destroying the last vestiges of wilderness in our selfish quest for peace and communion with nature?

Like Kermit the Frog says, it's not easy being green. Backpacking is not really the greenest form of recreation. Although we revel in the environment, do we trade price, nutrition and convenience for environmental quality? Are the products we buy and use dangerous to the health of people and animals? Do they cause damage to the environment during manufacture, use, or disposal? Do they consume a disproportionate amount of energy and other resources during manufacture, use, or disposal? Do they cause unnecessary waste due to either excessive packaging or a short useful life? Do they involve the unnecessary use of or cruelty to animals? And, finally, do they use materials derived from threatened species or environments?

These are all questions John Elkington, Julia Hailes, and Joel Makower say should be asked when deciding whether or not a product is "green." In their book *The Green Consumer* they agree that it is difficult to find a perfectly green product. But when purchasing equipment, you may want to take some of these factors into account. Fortunately, backpacking gear already has one major factor in its favor—minimal packaging! Most backpacking gear comes as is: sleeping bags and tents packed in stuff sacks; packs purchased off the rack; stoves in environmentally sound cardboard cartons.

In the book *Shopping for a Better World*, by the Council on Economic Priorities, manufacturers are rated on how green they are. Criteria used to determine the rating include: how environmentally clean the company is, if animals are tested, and if the company is associated with South Africa or nuclear weapons. The book focuses on manufacturers of food, personal care products, and other items typically found in a grocery store. To find out about the manufacturers of boots, backpacks, tents, and other backpacking equipment, contact the company and question them about your concerns.

These days a number of companies are striving to be green. Some outdoor businesses are involved in the Outdoor Industry Conservation Alliance, working together to address ecological and environmental issues and providing grants to grassroots conservation organizations. Other businesses are helping to purchase and preserve land, working with organizations such as the Nature Conservancy. Chevrolet, Coleman, ACG (Nike), AT&T, Canon, Duofold, Kodak, Merrell, Mountainsmith, Nalgene, Nature Valley Granola Bars, Nike Hiking, REI, Spenco, Trek, Wild Country USA, and Yakima are corporate sponsors of the new American Discovery Trail.

RECYCLED GEAR
One of the biggest changes that took place in the 1990s was the manufacture of backpacking equipment using recycled products. For example, Patagonia's recycled Synchilla fleece jackets are made from recycled plastic soft drink bottles. They contain 80 percent recycled polyester (including post consumer plastic) and 20 percent virgin fibers.

Other products using recycled materials include Nike boots, which use reground rubber in the soles, and Reebok's lightweight Telos hiking books, which include pigment-free leather and recycled plastic soft drink bottles in the uppers. The Telos also have outsoles manufactured in large part (75 percent) from recycled car tires.

In addition to the use of recycled materials in the products themselves, some manufacturers are using recycled materials in their packaging or they are decreasing the packaging.

MINIMUM IMPACT CAMPING
In addition to watching what we purchase, we should also consciously seek to make as small an impact on the environment as possible when hiking. In recent years, "minimum impact camping" has become the catchphrase for responsible outdoors behavior.

Groups such as the Boy Scouts, who once espoused techniques like trenching your tent to prevent water from running under it, have adopted low-impact techniques. Minimum impact camping is a philosophy once summed up by the National Park Service as "Take nothing but pictures, leave nothing but footprints." The following are measures you can take to eliminate any trace of your presence along the trail.

Pack It Out

Every piece of trash you create, even organic trash, should be packed out . There is nothing more annoying than heading back into the woods and following a trail of candy bar wrappers and cigarette butts. And though orange peels, apple cores, and egg shells may strike you as natural trash, easily biodegradable, they can take a long time to rot and become one with the earth. In the meantime, animals dig up the trash, scattering it for everyone to see. The worst case is going to relieve yourself only to discover a trail of paper proving you weren't the first to have this idea at this spot. Soggy, used toilet paper is probably one of the uglier reminders of human presence.

Whether you smoke, munch on candy bars, or snack on fruit while hiking, keep a sack handy to store your waste. Pack it in, pack it out, and you're already one giant step toward preserving the environment you've supposedly escaped to.

Carry Out Trash Left by Others

A friend of mine who maintains a section of trail in Virginia once disgustedly told me of the miles of string he had to pick up when that section of trail was being measured; the measurer who neglected to clean up after himself should have known better. The trails abound with trash. For some reason, people who wouldn't dare throw trash on the ground at home do so freely in the outdoors. You can make the outdoors an even better place by stopping occasionally to pick up other people's trash. You don't have to be ridiculous and carry out nasty toilet paper or rotting organic material, but you can take a minute to cover it with leaves, moss, dirt, and twigs. If you pick up trash, you'll find you'll feel a lot better about yourself. If your trip is a long one and there aren't many stops available to drop off trash, it is perhaps understandable (but not excusable) that you carry no more than your own trash. Unfortunately, the enviro-conscious do not outnumber the users and abusers of America's trails, and we have to make up for the ignorance and sloth of others by picking up after them.

Use a Stove

It is now illegal in many forests to build campfires—and for good reason. If not cared for properly, they can start forest fires. They are also damaging to the environment. Scars from fire rings last a long time. Blackened earth and rocks are messy and far from aesthetically pleasing to the eye. Using a cook stove puts less wear and tear on the environment.

If you must build a fire, do not burn or leave trash in the fire pit. Burning trash often releases toxic gases into the air. And once you start to burn something, you'll have the tendency to leave it in the pit whether it is fully burned or not. Do not put tinfoil-lined packages in fire pits because they will not entirely burn up. The easiest thing to do is to avoid this problem altogether by packing out all your trash.

If you do decide to build a fire, do so only in designated fire pits. As I said earlier, fire pits deeply scar the earth. If there is a pit already available, use it, and use only downed wood in it. Breaking branches from trees or chopping dead or live trees for wood should not even be considered a possibility. Killing plant life for atmosphere is inexcusable. Obviously, if a life or death situation is involved, all rules change.

Camp in Designated Sites

Similarly, when camping on a backpacking trip, make sure you camp in designated areas only. These spaces are chosen because they are more resistant to constant use. If you feel it is too dangerous (in griz country, for example) to camp in a designated area or if one is not available, camp well off the trail. Trails already receive a lot of impact and camping away from the trail will cut down on its wear and tear.

When you leave a campsite, take a long, hard look at it. It should look better than when you found it. If you camp off the trail, it should look as if you had never been there. It can be done. We've even gone so far as to rescatter leaves and fluff up grass so that you could not tell where our tent had been pitched. It only takes a few minutes, and the peace of mind you gain will more than compensate your efforts.

Limit Group Size

Any time you have ten or more people camping in one spot, you're going to have a major impact on the environment. You've got ten people using the surrounding area as a toilet, ten people beating down the ground to set up tents, ten people wandering around the kitchen area. The environmental impact of such a group on a campsite is shocking. Obviously, not all large groups are detrimental to the outdoors, but enough are that they make a bad impression on those who are environmentally conscious. If you become involved with a group that is interested in backpacking trips, make sure that you divide yourselves into groups of ten or fewer before you set out.

Stay on the Designated Trail

The switchbacks are there for a reason; they slow down the erosion of trail on steep climbs. Sure, it may seem easier to scramble up the hillside the ten yards or so to the next section of trail, but if too many people do that, rain will start using the newly exposed earth as a watercourse—washing away both trail and mountain in its wake. Stay on the designated trail. You may curse the person who blazed it and those who attempt to keep it passable for you, but remember that just about any trail you hike was built and is maintained by volunteers.

Don't Use Soap In or Near Streams

As discussed earlier, there are a number of reasons to avoid the use of soap in or near a stream. Unless you are using a biodegradable soap, you could poison the water for any animal that drinks from it, including yourself. Even biodegradable soap should be used well away from streams and rivers, ponds and lakes.

Streams are often water sources when backpacking. Even if you do have biodegradable soap, do you really want to drink water that has soap in it? If you need to wash your body, your hair, or your dishes, use stream water, but carry it well away from the stream before using it.

One method for washing your hair is to get it wet while at the water source. Then, fill a pot or waterbag with water, walk about two hundred feet away from the water source, and wash and rinse your hair there. If you have a waterbag with a shower attachment, you can hang the bag from an appropriate tree and wash and rinse your hair out with ease.

The same goes for washing clothes and dishes. Carry the water away from the water source. You can wash both dishes and clothes in your largest cooking pot.

Solid Waste Management

In other words, how to dispose of your excrement. Kathleen Meyer has written a book, which she calls "an environmentally sound approach to a lost art." To learn about the fine details of relieving yourself in the woods, Meyer provides plenty of advice in *How to Shit in the Woods*, which is available from Ten Speed Press.

Disposing of your feces when backpacking is absolutely necessary. Always, always, always (I can't say it too many times) dig a hole. More importantly, make sure you're at least two hundred feet from the nearest water source. If you're hiking in a canyon through which water runs, climb up. If it's winter and snowing and you can't dig through the frozen snow and ice (if you can, make sure you dig into the earth as well), pack it out. Yes, it sounds horrifying but if it's cold enough, it can be done. Just line a hole in the snow with a plastic bag, do your thing, and then tie-twist or zip it shut and pack it out. Otherwise, when the snow melts, your feces will end up on the surface of the ground, making an unwelcome sight (not to mention odor) for any springtime hikers. There's more to being green than just packing out your trash. Disposing properly of your solid waste will keep the wilderness much more appealing.

Trail Maintenance

One of the biggest ways you can give back to the trail and the hiking community is by becoming involved in trail maintenance. The vast majority of trails in this country are maintained by volunteers.

Maintaining a section of existing trail or helping out regularly with the blazing of new trails is a good way to pay back the outdoors for the good times you have received from it. Trails are beginning to crisscross the entire country, and there is sure to be a new or old trail somewhere near you. Contact your local trail clubs to see what you can do to help out. A list of trail-related clubs and organizations appears in the back of this book.

The late Henry Lanham would often speak of the users and the givers—those who used the trails selfishly, with no thought of offering even a day's work to help what had given them so much pleasure, and those who paid back many times over all the joy the trails had given them, spending not only days but weeks and years working on the trails. Henry was a giver. Active in the Natural Bridge Appalachian Trail Club for years, Henry died in 1991 while cutting a new trail in Idaho.

WHAT ELSE CAN YOU DO?

There are a number of little things you can do to decrease your environmental impact:

➤ Reuse your zipper-lock bags. Not only can they be reused during a trip but once home, you can wash and dry them to use on your next trip. Don't reuse bags that carried raw meat or human and animal waste.

➤ Buy hiking equipment (tents, backpacks, etc.) in environmentally eye-pleasing colors such as forest green, gray, light blue, tan, and brown.

➤ Purchase environmentally-sound toiletries by manufacturers such as Aubrey Organics, St. Ives, and Tom's of Maine. Catalogs from The Body Shop, The Compassionate Consumer, Ecco Bella, Seventh Generation, and others offer environmentally safe products. The Green Consumer supplies lists of both catalogs and manufacturers. There is also a 304-page guide on how to buy in the best interest of the environment—*The Consumer's Guide to Effective Environmental Choices: Practical Advice from the Union of Concerned Scientists* by Michael Brower and Warren Leon.

➤ Always change into a pair of lightweight, soft shoes when you make camp to lessen your effect on the site.

This chapter is not a list of rules; it is a way of living that is becoming increasingly important to adopt. If these techniques are not used by everyone (and currently they're not), the trail will lose its natural beauty.

Nature is resilient but its ability to fight back is limited. It takes a long time for a campsite to recover from a single overnight stay by an inconsiderate group of hikers.

But a little bit of help goes a long way toward improving the world we're escaping to. If everyone pitches in—even just a little bit—we'll be able to enjoy our backcountry experiences even more.

Remember, Earth, despite her condition, will be here forever. It is the human race that needs saving. If we can't preserve our environment, we can't preserve ourselves.

Gear Repair and Maintenance

Even if you're just going out for an overnight hike, it is wise to carry along a few small items to help you out in a pinch. Most problems can be taken care of with these miniature repair kits. Here is a suggested list of some of the items you can include in a basic repair kit:

➤ Duct tape, perhaps wound several times around your Nalgene.

➤ Swiss Army knife or small Leatherman.

➤ Sewing kit, including assorted thread, a few buttons, and several sizes of needles and safety pins.

➤ Dental floss.

- ➤ Alcohol swabs for cleaning.
- ➤ A few rubber bands.
- ➤ Small patch of self-adhesive nylon tape.
- ➤ Small lighter.
- ➤ Extra backpack pins and rings.
- ➤ Stove repair kit, including operating instructions, jet-cleaning tool, spare jet and O-rings, and any other spare pieces your model might need.

PACK REPAIR

Pack pins and rings are the most frequent cause of problems. You'll be surprised at the number of rings you'll see littering frequently packed trails. Frank's three-week-old pack lost a ring in the Shenandoahs. Rings, small circles of overlapping wire, are used to keep the pins in place on external frame packs. All

Though you can create your own repair kit, Gear Aid provides an already assembled kit you can purchase at outdoor retail stores.

those rings on the trail represent pins that are about to work their way loose from hikers' packs, causing pack bags to sag or hip belts and shoulder straps to spring loose from the frame. Carrying a couple of extra pins and rings could save you much discomfort on a hike. Pack repair is mostly done by prevention. Check seams and buckles before you hit the trail because they are easier to replace at home than on the trail.

TENT REPAIR

We always carry a tent repair kit. Boy does it come in handy—and not just for our tent. I've used it to repair my sleeping bag stuff sack and Frank's (and Craig Jolly's) rain pants.

Tent repair kits usually include tent fabric tape (adhesive-backed, waterproof ripstop nylon of two types), a small amount of duct tape, a needle and thread, a short length of cord, an aluminum splint for tent poles, and no-see-um netting. A good kit, manufactured by Outdoor Research, costs five dollars and weighs only 2.5 ounces.

If you're going to be hiking more than two or three months, you'll want to send some seam sealer ahead of you. Extensive use is hard on a tent, and you'll need to reseal the seams every two to three months, depending on how much you use your tent. Because broken zippers are among the most common breakage problems on the trail, some ingenious fellow has come up with the Zipper Rescue Kit. In two sizes, basic and deluxe, the kit includes materials you need for repair at home and in the field. These can be purchased from ZRK Enterprises, PO Box 1213, McCall, ID 83638, (208) 634-4851.

STOVE REPAIR

"Carry a stove repair kit or learn how to build fires," is long-distance hiker Phil Hall's advice. Stoves will break or have problems when you least expect or desire it. If the manufacturer of your stove offers a kit, it is wise to purchase one. Repair kits weigh approximately two ounces, and packing that weight is well worth the peace of mind. We use ours, and everyone else we know uses theirs.

Not all stove manufacturers offer repair kits for their stoves; some stoves are not designed for field repair. Depending on the stove, follow the manufacturer's instructions. If possible, stoves should be cleaned at home, where cleaning is much easier. Maintenance suggestions include oiling the pressure-pump plungers before hitting the trail and replacing the O-rings each year. Following these two maintenance suggestions and keeping your stove clean will help prevent many of the problems you could have on the trail.

CLOTHING REPAIR

You can purchase a miniature sewing kit, complete with a number of different colored threads, needle, thimble, scissors, needle threader, snaps, and buttons, at almost any drug, discount, grocery, or outfitter store. If you're trying to save room, you can throw an extra needle and applicable thread into your tent-repair kit instead.

I carry an entire sewing kit (approximately two by three inches) that weighs about an ounce; and I have used it innumerable times. Dental floss is high strength sewing material if an emergency should strike. For hikes of a week or less, a sewing kit is probably unnecessary.

PAD REPAIR

There are a few simple things you can do to make sure your pad stays as healthy as possible:

➤ In camp, make sure you keep your pad away from fires, stoves, and abrasive surfaces.
➤ Minimize your pad's exposure to ultraviolet rays and DEET-based insect repellents.
➤ Unroll your self-inflating pad and open its valve as soon as you get to camp. This will give your pad the maximum amount of time to inflate before you hit the sack. Also, limit your capping off of the inflation to just a couple of puffs of air. Because your breath contains water vapor, even the sturdiest foam pad will eventually break down.

➤ Back at home, give your pad a quick sponge bath after each camping trip. Make sure you give it plenty of time to dry.

Store your self-inflating pad unrolled and with the valve open so that you don't trap moisture inside and cause your pad to mildew. Even foam pads should be stored flat; Storing any pad rolled up will weaken the foam.

If you can't find a repair kit, make your own. Store in a zipper-lock bag: one tube of contact cement, two small swatches of coated nylon, and a couple of alcohol wipes for cleaning.

To fix a punctured pad, try the following:

1. Boil a quart of water in a flat-bottomed pot.
2. Wipe the pad clean and cleanse the area around the puncture with cool water and then allow the pad to dry.
3. Open the valve. You can ruin the pad if you forget this step.
4. Squeeze a liberal amount of contact cement into the exposed foam, work it into the material, then spread a thinner amount around the hole. Do this just as the water is boiling so the cement doesn't dry out.
5. With the water now boiling, peel the backing from the patch and smooth it over the puncture.
6. Place the hot pot over the patch and leave it there for at least thirty minutes. The heat-sealed bond should hold permanently.

BOOT MAINTENANCE

Boot leather needs periodic waterproofing; hikes of two weeks or more, particularly in wet seasons, will wear the waterproofing off your boots.

If you intend to be out for more than two weeks, you will need to either carry along Sno-Seal (or whatever you use to waterproof your boots—Silicone Water Guard, Biwell Waterproofing, Aquaseal) or send it up the trail ahead of you. Waterproofers for boots cost from three to eight dollars.

WATER PURIFIER MAINTENANCE

Should your filter become clogged anyway, and at some point it probably will, a repair kit with these items should be of help. As the Boy Scouts say, be prepared.

➤ A scrubber sponge or toothbrush to clean the filter element. Scrub the element once, rinse and then scrub again. Check your manufacturer's suggestions first, though. Some filters aren't meant to be scrubbed.

➤ Spare O-rings to replace the ones that might break or crack and cause leaks. The manufacturer should be able to supply these.

➤ A lubricant. O-rings can dry out and ruin the seal on a filter. A tube of lubricant (also available from the manufacturer) can alleviate this problem. No lubricant? Use cooking oil or spit. No petroleum-based products, please. I think we all know how many problems they can cause.

➤ A bandanna and a rubberband. As mentioned above, a bandanna used as a pre-filter can significantly increase the life of your filter. Secure it with the rubber band to free your hands for pumping or whatever.

➤ And always, always, always carry along that emergency pack of iodine pills. Make sure you have a recently-purchased bottle of iodine pills in your repair kit.

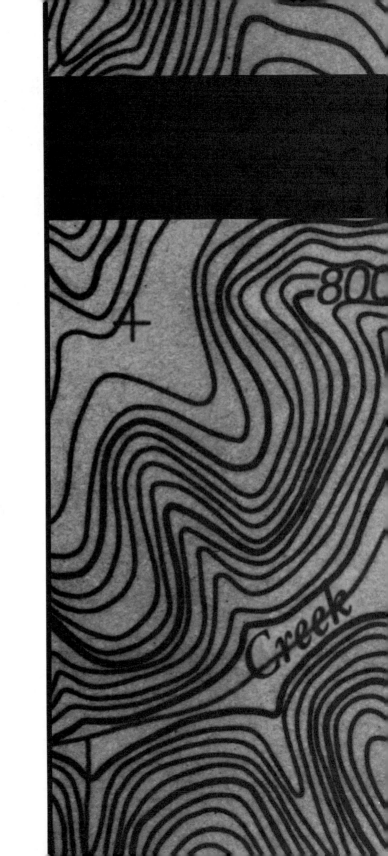

Appendices

PART FOUR

Glossary

Aiming Off (verb):   The technique of purposefully erring to one side when following a compass bearing. Mistakes naturally occur when walking along a compass bearing as you navigate around trees, boulders or even clumps of impenetrable underbrush. Always try to go around obstacles to one side. Then when you arrive at a baseline, you will know which direction to look for your intended destination. If you go to the right around all obstacles, the destination should be to the left when you get to the baseline.

Base Camp Trip (noun):   This trip involves hiking into an area, setting up camp, and then hiking out from camp on short day hikes. This allows you to leave your heavy gear in one place for several days and enjoy a number of opportunities in the surrounding area whether it be fishing, climbing and/or hiking.

Baseline (noun):   A line of reference crossing your path of travel used to make following a compass bearing closer to foolproof. When following a compass bearing, many factors conspire against you following an exact course. These include natural objects, such as trees and boulders, you must go around, and other technical factors like properly setting the compass to account for declination. A baseline is used to set the odds in your favor. Baselines include roads, powerlines, railroad tracks, and rivers.

If you are heading to a bridge over a river, set the compass bearing for the bridge. If you are off by several degrees, you will arrive at your baseline of the river, knowing that you need to look for the bridge. To make this even easier, try aiming off.

Bearing (noun):   The direction of one point from another point. In working with a map and compass, the first point is always true north (or magnetic north if your compass has not been adjusted for declination). When you take a bearing, you measure the degree of the angle between the point you are determining the bearing for and true north.

Bench Mark (noun):   A metal disk set into the ground for use as an exact reference point by surveyors. Bench marks are indicated on a topographic map with an **X** and the letters BM with an elevation next to it.

Blaze (noun):   A paint mark on a tree or rock marking the route of a trail. Originally trails were "blazed" by hacking a mark in the tree bark with an axe to mark the route. Today, most trails use a combination of signs and paint blazes.

Blue Blaze (noun):   The color often used to paint blazes on the side trails off main trails such as the Appalachian Trail.

Blue Blaze (verb): To take trails other than the official trail you are hiking because they offer a shorter or easier alternative to your route.

Cairn (noun): A manmade pile of rocks used to mark the route of a trail through a treeless area. In California, these are sometimes referred to as "ducks."

Check Point (noun): A landmark, that can be easily identified on the ground to let you know when to leave a handrail and begin a new course. For example, when following a stream, you will want to note a tributary crossing your path, near or at the point when you need to follow a new bearing away from that stream. Having a check point will allow you to follow a handrail without constantly checking your position on the map.

Conductive Heat Loss (noun): Although this is usually a relatively minor way to lose heat, it can be dangerous in certain circumstances. Conductive heat loss occurs when the body loses heat to the air, water or fabric that is in contact with the body at a lower temperature. Falling into cold water, for example, you lose all your body heat to the water, a potentially fatal situation.

Convective Heat Loss (noun): This most common form of heat loss occurs when air and water come into contact, or near-contact, with your body and carry heat away with them. Materials such as pile, down, wool, PolarGuard and Hollofil, and Thinsulate work as a barrier against convective loss, retaining most of your body's heat.

Elevation (noun): The height of a mountain or other landmark given in the number of feet above sea level. The elevation is indicated on both significant landmarks and along the index lines on topographic maps. Planimetric maps (such as road maps) rarely indicate the elevation.

Evaporative Heat Loss (noun): When you sweat, you lose heat through the evaporation of the liquid. This is great in warm weather because it cools the body; but when it is cold and once you stop moving, your clothes remain wet and so do you. This can lead to hypothermia. Fortunately for backpackers, materials such as polypropylene have been designed to wick away the moisture or sweat. These materials work by removing the moisture from the skin before it evaporates.

Flip-Flop (verb):   To hike continuously, time-wise but not necessarily in the same direction. For example, one might flip-flop on the Appalachian Trail by hiking north to Harpers Ferry, WV, and then hiking south to Harpers Ferry from Mount Katahdin in Maine.

Handrail (noun):   A long stream, road, or other feature that runs parallel to your course of travel. Once you begin to follow a stream, bank for example, you can hold on to that "handrail" without constantly checking your compass bearing and position on the map. You will need to first find a check point on the map that will indicate when to turn away from the handrail.

Loop Trip (noun):   A trip in which you start and finish at the same trailhead with very little retracing of steps.

Out-and-back Trip (noun):   A trip in which you hike to a destination then retrace your steps back to the trailhead.

Power Hiker (noun):   Someone who hikes twenty miles or more daily while on an extended backpacking trip.

Purist or White Blazer (noun):   A backpacker who hikes the official route of a trail no matter the circumstances.

Radiant Heat Loss (noun):   Another minor method of heat loss is when heat radiates out from your body into your clothes. Unless the fabric you are wearing reflects the heat back to you, the heat is lost to the air. Vapor barriers reflect the heat back to your body.

Slackpack (verb):   To hike without your pack on by either leaving it at a hostel, hotel or friend's home or by having someone shuttle it up the trail for you; also to take one's time when hiking by hiking slower than the average hiker.

Shuttle Trip (noun): This is a point-to-point trip that requires that you either leave a vehicle at both ends of the hike or pre-arrange a shuttle to pick you up at the end of the hike or to drop you off at the beginning.

Trail Angels (noun): People who befriend hikers and do special things for them out of the goodness of their hearts rather than for profit or gain.

Trail Magic (noun): The special things that happen and the generosity that hikers experience while on a backpacking trip.

Trail Name (noun): A chosen or given nickname a hiker may adopt while backpacking.

White Blaze (noun): The white blaze is the signature marker of the Appalachian Trail.

White Blaze (verb): To follow the trail's official route.

Yellow Blaze (verb): To hitchhike or skip sections of trail rather than to hike it.

Yogi (verb): Called after Yogi the Bear because of his habit of making off with people's picnic baskets in the cartoon. Backpackers "yogi" when they entice a non-hiker out of something they need or want without actually asking for it.

Yo-Yo (noun): A round-trip hike of a long-distance trail.

Equipment Checklists

EQUIPMENT FOR A DAY HIKE

(This list assumes you are already wearing comfortable clothes and good walking shoes.)

Day pack or fanny pack
One-liter (minimum) Nalgene-style bottle
Rain gear
Food for the day
Lighter or waterproof matches
First aid (bandages, moleskin)
Toilet paper, trowel
Map and/or guidebook*

Camera and film*
Binoculars*
Gloves and knit cap•
Extra shirt•
Bandanna*

EQUIPMENT FOR AN OVERNIGHT HIKE
Light- or medium-weight hiking boots
Internal or external frame pack
Sleeping bag
Sleeping pad
Tent/tarp and groundcloth
Stove and fuel
Cooking pot and eating utensils
Knife (pocket)
Water purifiers (or plan to boil your water)
More than adequate food for length of hike
Spices*
One-liter (minimum) Nalgene-style bottle
Drinking cup
Rain gear including pack cover
Gaiters*
One pair of shorts
One pair of loose fitting, long pants*
One to two short-sleeve shirts
One long-sleeve shirt or sweater
Knit cap
Balaclava•
Down- or synthetic-fill parka•
Two pairs liner socks
Two pairs socks
One or more bandannas
Long johns•
Underwear (two pair)*
Toilet paper, trowel
Biodegradable soap and washcloth
Deodorant*
Toothbrush and toothpaste
Shaving kit*
Nylon cord (at least ten feet)

Maps, guidebooks
Compass
Flashlight with new batteries
Watch or clock*
Sunglasses*
First Aid kit (including moleskin)
Space blanket
Swimsuit and towel*
Extra shoes*
Repair equipment (for pack, tent, and stove)*
Camera and film*
Radio with headphones*
Insect repellent
Sunscreen/lotion
Hiking stick*

ADDITIONAL EQUIPMENT NEEDED FOR LONGER HIKES

Repair equipment for pack, tent, stove, and clothes
Trash bag (a small one for your own trash)
Long-sleeve shirt or sweater
Long johns
Film mailers*
Reading material*
Journal*
Crampons and ice ax

*   *Optional*
•   *Seasonal*

Gear Manufacturers

Arc'Teryx Equipment, Inc.
170 Harbour Ave.
North Vancuver, BC, Canada V7J 2E6
(800) 985-6681
Web: www.arcteryx.com
internal frame packs

Artiach/Appalachian Mountain Supply
P.O. Box 8526
Atlanta, GA 31106
(800) 569-4110
Web: www.amsgear.com
sleeping pads

Asolo
1 Sportssystem Plaza
Bordentown, NJ 08505
(800) 892-2668
Web: www.asolo.com
boots

Bibler Tents
2084 East 3900 South
Salt Lake City, UT 84124
(800) 241-8690
Web: www.biblertents.com
single-wall tents and sleeping bags

Camp Trails
1326 Willow Rd.
Sturtevant, WI 53177
(800) 572-8822
Web: www.jwa.com
packs, tents, and sleeping bags

Camping Gaz
3600 N Hydraulic
Wichita, KS 67219
(800) 835-3278
stoves

Cascade Designs
4000 1st Ave. S
Seattle, WA 98134
(800) 531-9531
Web: www.cascadedesigns.com
sleeping bags and pads

Dana Design
19215 Vashon Highway SW
Vashon, WA 98070
(888) 357-3262
Web: www.danadesign.com
packs and tents

Danner Shoe Manufacturing
P.O. Box 30148
Portland, OR 97294
(800) 345-0430
Web: www.danner.com
boots

Diamond Brand
P.O. Box 249
Naples, NC 28760
(800) 258-9811
packs and tents

Eastern Mountain Sports (EMS)
1 Vose Farm Rd.
Peterborough, NH 03458
(888) 463-6367
Web: www.emsonline.com
retail stores offering a full line of outdoor
    gear

Eureka!
1326 Willow Rd.
Sturtevant, WI 53177
(800) 572-8822
Web: www.jwa.com
packs and tents

Feathered Friends
119 Yale Ave. N
Seattle, WA 98109
(206) 328-0887
Web: www.featheredfriends.com
sleeping bags

Ferrino USA
P.O. Box 4383
Charlottesville, VA 22905
(888) 219-8641
Web: www.ferrino.it
packs, tents and sleeping bags

General Ecology
151 Sheree Blvd.
Exton, PA 19341
(800) 441-8166
Web: www.general-ecology.com
water filters

Granite Gear
P.O. Box 278
Two Harbors, MN 55616
(218) 834-6157
Web: www.granitegear.com
packs

Gregory Mountain Products
100 Calle Cortez
Temecula, CA 92590
(800) 477-3420
Web: www.gregorymountainproduct.com
packs

Hi-Tec Sports USA
4801 Stoddard Rd.
Modesto, CA 95356
(800) 521-1698
Web: www.hi-tec.com
boots

Integral Designs
5516 3rd St. SE
Calgary, AB, Canada T2H 1J9
(403) 640-1445
Web: www.integraldesigns.com
single-wall tents and sleeping bags

Jack Wolfskin
166-A Fesler St.
El Cajon, CA 92020
(888) 378-9653
Web: www.wolfskin.de
packs

JanSport
P.O. Box 1817
Appleton, WI 54913
(800) 552-6776
Web: www.jansport.com
packs

Kelty
6235 G Lookout Rd.
Boulder, CO 80301
(800) 423-2320
Web: www.kelty.com
packs, tents, and sleeping bags

Lafuma America
6662 Gunpark Dr., Suite 101
Boulder, CO 80301
(800) 514-4807
Web: www.lafuma.fr
packs and sleeping bags

LaSportiva USA
3280 Pearl St.
Boulder, CO 80301
(303) 443-8710
Web: www.sportiva.com
boots

Limmer Boot
HC 68, Box 248C
Center Conway, NH 03813
(603) 694-2668
boots

L.L. Bean
Casco St.
Freeport, ME 04033
(800) 809-7057
Web: www.llbean.com
mail order and retail outlets for a full line
of outdoor gear

Lowa Boots
P.O. Box 407
Old Greenwich, CT 06870
(203) 353-0116
boots

Lowe Alpine Systems
P.O. Box 1449
Broomfield, CO 80038
(303) 465-0522
Web: www.lowealpine.com
packs

Marmot Mountain
2321 Circadian Way
Santa Rosa, CA 95407
(707) 544-4590
Web: www.marmot.com
packs, tents, and sleeping bags

Merrell Footwear
9341 Courtland Dr. NE
Rockford, MI 49351
(888) 637-7001
Web: www.merrellboot.com
boots

Montrail
1003 6th Ave. S
Seattle, WA 98134
(206) 621-9303
Web: www.montrail.com
boots

Moonstone Mountain Equipment
833 Indiana St.
San Francisco, CA 94107
(800) 390-3312
Web: www.moonstone.com
sleeping bags

Moss Tents
P.O. Box 81227
Seattle, WA 98108
(800) 859-5322
Web: www.mosstents.com
tents

Mountain Hardwear
950 Gilman St.
Berkeley, CA 94710
(800) 579-9093
Web: www.mountainhardwear.com
tents and sleeping bags

Mountain Safety Research (MSR)
P.O. Box 24547
Seattle, WA 98124
(800) 877-9677
Web: www.msrcorp.com
stoves

Mountainsmith
18301 Colfax Ave.
Golden, CO 80401
(800) 426-4075
packs

Optimus
2151 Las Palmas Dr., Suite G
Carlsbad, CA 92009
(800) 543-9124
Web: www.optimus.se
stoves

Osprey Packs
P.O. Box 539, 504 Central Ave.
Dolores, CO 81323
(970) 882-2221
Web: www.ospreypacks.com
packs

Outbound Products
8585 Fraser St.
Vancouver, BC, Canada V5X 3Y1
(604) 321-5464
packs, tents, sleeping bags, and stoves

Outdoor Research
2203 1st Ave. S
Seattle, WA 98134
(888) 467-4327
Web: www.orgear.com
sleeping bags

Peak 1
P.O. Box 2931
Wichita, KS 67201
(800) 835-3278
Web: www.coleman.com
a full line of outdoor gear

Primus
2151 Las Palmas Dr., Unit G
Carlsbad, CA 92009
(800) 543-9124
Web: www.primus.se
stoves

PUR
9300 N 75th Ave.
Minneapolis, MN 55428
(800) 787-5463
Web: www.Purwater.com
water filters

Quest
3333 Yale Way
Fremont, CA 94538
(800) 613-1225
packs, tents, and sleeping bags

Raichle Molitar USA
Geneva Rd.
Brewster, NY 10509
(800) 431-2204
Web: www.raichle.com
boots

Recreational Equipment Inc. (REI)
1700 45th St. E
Sumner, WA 98390
(800) 426-4840
Web: www.rei.com
mail order and retailer with a full line of
outdoor gear

Salomon North America
400 E. Main St.
Georgetown, MA 01833
(877) 272-5666
Web: www.salomonsports.com
boots

Sierra Designs
1255 Powell St.
Emeryville, CA 94608
(800) 635-0461
Web: www.ecotravel.com/sierradesigns/
tents and sleeping bags

Slumberjack
P.O. Box 7048-A
St. Louis, MO 63177
(800) 233-6283
Web: www.slumberjack.com
tents, sleeping bags, and pads

Stephensons-Warmlit
22 Hook Rd.
Gilford, NH 03246
(603) 293-7016
tents, sleeping bags, and pads

SweetWater
4000 1st Ave. S
Seattle, WA 98134
(800) 531-9531
Web: www.cascadedesigns.com
water filters

Technica
19 Technology Dr.
West Lebanon, NH 03784
(603) 298-8032
Web: www.technicausa.com
boots

The North Face
407 Merrill Ave.
Carbondale, CO 81623
(800) 447-2333
full line of outdoor gear

Timberland
200 Domain Dr.
Stratham, NH 03885
(800) 445-5545
Web: www.timberland.com
boots

Tough Traveler
1012 State St.
Schenectady, NY 12307
(800) 468-6844
Web: www.toughtraveler.com
kid carriers, packs, and sleeping bags for
  children

Vasque
314 Main St.
Red Wing, MN 55066
(800) 224-4453
Web: www.vasque.com
boots

Walrus, Inc.
8330 Military Rd. S
Seattle, WA 98180
(800) 550-8368
Web: www.walrusgear.com
tents and sleeping bags

Wiggy's
P.O. Box 2124
Grand Junction, CO 81502
(800) 748-1827
Web: www.wiggys.com
sleeping bags

ZZ Manufacturing
1520A Industrial Park St.
Covina, CA 91722
(800) 594-9046
Web: www.gorp.com/zzstove
stoves

Hiking Organizations

National Trail Organizations:

American Discovery Trail Society
P.O. Box 20155
Washington, DC 20041-2155
(800) 851-3442
Web: www.discoverytrail.org/

American Hiking Society
1422 Fenwick Lane
Silver Spring, MD 20910
(301) 565-6704
Web: www.americanhiking.org/index.html

Appalachian Long Distance Hikers
Association
10 Benning St., Box 224
West Lebanon, NH 03784
Web: www.aldha.org

American Long Distance Hikers
Association-West
P.O. Box 651
Vancouver, WA 98666
Web: www.gorp.com/nonprof/aldhaw/

Appalachian Trail Conference
P.O. Box 807
Harpers Ferry, WV 25425
(304) 535-6331
Email: info@atconf.org
Web: www.appalachiantrail.org

Continental Divide Trail Alliance
P.O. Box 628
Pine, CO 80470-0628
(303) 838-3760
Email: cdnst@aol.com
Web: www.cdtrail.org

Continental Divide Trail Society
3704 N Charles St., #601
Baltimore, MD 21218
(410) 235-9610
Email: cdtsociety@aol.com
Web: www.gorp.com/cdts

Ice Age Park & Trail Foundation
207 E Buffalo St., Suite 515
Milwaukee, WI 53202
(414) 278-8518
Email: IAT@execpc.com
Web: www.iceagetrail.org

North Country Trail Association
49 Monroe Center NW, Suite 200B
Grand Rapids, MI 49503
(800) 454-NCTA
Email: NCTAssoc@aol.com
Web: www.northcountrytrail.org

Pacific Crest Trail Association
5325 Elkhorn Blvd., PMB #256
Sacramento, CA 95842
(800) 817-2243
Email: info@pcta.org
Web: www.pcta.org

Rails-to-Trails Conservancy
1100 17th St. NW, 10th floor
Washington, DC 20036
(202) 331-9696
Web: www.railtrails.org

State Trail Organizations:

Alabama
Appalachian Trail Club of Alabama
P.O. Box 381842
Birmingham, AL 35238-1842
Web: sport.al.com/sport/atca

Vulcan Trail Association
P.O. Box 19116
Birmingham, AL 35219-9166
(205) 982-4022
Email: Vulcan_trail@mindspring.com

Alaska
Fairbanks Area Hiking Club
P.O. Box 80954
Fairbanks, AK 99708
(907) 479-9736
Email: fahc@mosquitonet.com
Web: www.fairbankshiking.org

Arizona

Arizona Trail Association
P.O. Box 36736
Phoenix, AZ 85067-6736
(602) 252-4794
Email: ata@aztrail.org
Web: www.primenet.com/~aztrail

Glendale Hiking Club
P.O. Box 10997
Glendale, AZ 85318-0997
(602) 815-9026

Huachuca Hiking Club
P.O. Box 3555
Sierra Vista, AZ 85636-3555
(520) 459-8959

Arkansas

TAKAHIK River Valley Hikers
217 Canterbury Circle
Russellville, AR 72802
(501) 968-5005
Web: www.cswnet.com/~dlhale/River
  ValleyHikers.htm

Ozark Highlands Trail Association
411 Patricia
Fayetteville, AR 72703
(501) 442-2799
Email: TimErnst@compuserve.com
Web: Wilderness.ArkansasUSA.com/
  OHTA.html

California

Bay Area Ridge Trail Council
26 O'Farrell St., Suite 400
San Francisco, CA 94108
(415) 391-9300
Web: www.ridgetrail.org

Bay Area Trails Preservation Council
330 W. Blithedale Ave.
Mill Valley, CA 94941

Berkeley Hiking Club
P.O. Box 147
Berkeley, CA 94701

Coastwalk
1389 Cooper Rd.
Sebastopol, CA 95472
(707) 829-6689
Email: coastwalk@sonic.net
Web: www.sonic.net/coastwalk

Historic Trails Council
3570 Williams Pond Lane
Loomis, CA 95650
(916) 652-9056

La Canada Flint Ridge Trail Council
P.O. Box 852
La Canada Flint Ridge, CA 91012
(818) 790-2679

Orinda Hiking Club
P.O. Box 934
Orinda, CA 94563-2700
(510) 254-3689

Red Bluff Trails United
14600 Chico Ct.
Red Bluff, CA 96080
(530) 529-1134

Trail Center
3921 E. Bayshore Rd.
Palo Alto, CA 94303
(650) 725-1159
Email: trailexe@aol.com
Web: www.trailcenter.org

Colorado
Big City Mountaineers, Inc
210 Beaver Brook Canyon Rd., #200
Evergreen, CO 80439
(800) 644-2122
Web: www.bigcitymt.org

Colorado Fourteeners Initiative
710 10th St., #220
Golden, CO 80401
(303) 278-7525
Email: Cfi@coloradofourteeners.org
Web: www.coloradofourteeners.org

Colorado Mountain Club
710 10th St., #200
Golden, CO 80401
(303) 279-3080
Web: www.cmc.org/cmc

Connecticut
Connecticut Forest & Park Association
16 Meriden Rd.
Rockfall, CT 06481
(860) 346-2372
Email: conn.forest.assoc@snet.net
Web: www.ctwoodlands.org/

Delaware
Wilmington Trail Club
4934 S Raintree Ct.
Wilmington, DE 19808
(302) 656-1155
Web: www.wilmingtontrailclub.org

District of Columbia
Capital Hiking Club
6519 Bannockburn Dr.
Bethesda, MD 20817

Center Hiking Club
1412 Montague St. NW
Washington, DC 20011
(202) 829-7749

Florida
Florida Trail Association
P.O. Box 13708
Gainesville, FL 32604-1708
(800) 343-1882
Email: Fta@florida-trail.org
Web: www.florida-trail.org

Georgia
Benton Mackaye Trail Assn.
P.O. Box 53271
Atlanta, GA 30355-1271

Georgia Appalachian Trail Club
941 Clifton Rd. NE
Atlanta, GA 30307
(404) 634-6495
Email: InfoEd@georgia-atclub.org
Web: www.georgia-atclub.org

Georgia Pinhoti Trail Association
P.O. Box 1362
Tucker, GA 30085
(770) 414-0211
Email: pedoneap@aol.com

Idaho
Boulder-White Clouds Council
P.O. Box 6313
Ketchum, ID 83340
(208) 726-1065
Email: bwcc@micron.net
Web: www.idahorivers.org/bwcc.htm

Illinois
Illinois Hiking Society
1142 Winkleman Rd.
Harrisburg, IL 62946

Indiana
Hoosiers Hikers Council
P.O. Box 1327
Martinsville, IN 46151

Indianapolis Hiking Club
35 N County Rd. #900E
Indianapolis, IN 46234

Iowa
Iowa Trails Council
P.O. Box 131
Center Point, IA 52213-0131

Kansas
Kansas Trails Council Inc
510 Utah
Lawrence, KS 66046-4846

Louisiana
Louisiana Hiking Club
18360 Fortier Lane
Prairieville, LA 70769
(225) 677-8954
Email: ALFHiker@aol.com
Web: hometown.aol.com/lahkgclub/
    club/index.htm

Maine
Maine Appalachian Trail Club
P.O. Box 283
Augusta, ME 04330
Web: www.matc.org/

Maryland
C & O Canal Association
P.O. Box 366
Glen Echo, MD 20812

Friendly Trails Wandering Club
5457 Enberend Terrace
Columbia, MD 21045

Mountain Club of Maryland
4106 Eierman Ave.
Baltimore, MD 21206
Web: www.netcom.com/~sburket/
    mcm.html

Massachusetts
Appalachian Mountain Club
5 Joy St.
Boston, MA 02108
(617) 523-0655
Email: Information@amcinfo.org
Web: www.outdoors.org

Chatham Trails Association
P.O. Box 74
Bethel, MA 04217

Michigan
Michigan Trailfinders Club
2680 Rockhill N.E.
Grand Rapids, MI 49525-1292

Minnesota
Kekekabic Trail Club
309 Cedar Ave. S.
Minneapolis, MN 55454-1030
(800) 818-4453
Email: Info@kek.org
Web: www.kek.org

Superior Hiking Trail Association
P.O. Box 4
731 7th Ave.
Two Harbors, MN 55616
(218) 834-2700
Email: suphike@mr.net
Web: www.shta.org

Missouri
Ozark Greenways Inc.
P.O. Box 50733
Springfield, MO 65805

Montana
Red Lodge Hiking Club
Rt. 2, Box 3465
Red Lodge, MT 59068

Nebraska
Nebraska Trails Council
P.O. Box 3383
Omaha, NE 68103-0383

New Jersey
Outdoor Club of South Jersey
P.O. Box 433
Sewell, NJ 08080-0433
(609) 268-7492
Web: www.voicenet.com/-ubert4/ocsj

New Mexico
Moreno Valley Trekkers
P.O. Box 1234
Angel Fire, NM 87710

New Mexico Rails-to-Trails Association
P.O. Box 44
Cloudcroft, NM 88317
(505) 682-3040
Nmrails@zianet.com
Web: www.cloudcroft.net/rails.htm

New York
Adirondack Mountain Club
814 Goggins Rd.
Lake George, NY 12845-4117
(518) 523-3480
Email: adkinfo@adk.org
Web: www.adk.org

Foothills Trail Club
1331 Brookfield Dr.
N. Tonawanda, NY 14120

Genesee Valley Hiking Club
259 Rye Rd.
Rochester, NY 14626

NY-NJ Trail Conference
232 Madison Ave., Rm. 802
New York, NY 10016-2901
(212) 685-9699
Email: nynjtc@aol.com
Web: www.nynjtc.org

Southampton Trails Preservation Society
P.O. Box 1171
Bridgehampton, NY 11932-1236

Thendara Mountain Club
13 Nassau Ave.
Plainview, NY

Valley Stream Hiking Club
67 East Fairview Ave.
Valley Stream, NY 11580

North Carolina
Carolina Mountain Club
P.O. Box 68
Asheville, NC 28802
cmcinfo@carolinamtnclub.com
Web: www.carolinamtnclub.com/

Nantahala Hiking Club
31 Carl Slagle Rd.
Franklin, NC 28734
Web: www.smnet2.net/users/nhc/

Piedmont Appalachian Trail Hikers
P.O. Box 4423
Greensboro, NC 27404
Web: www.path-at.org

Ohio
Buckeye Trail Association
P.O. Box 254
Worthington, OH 43085
(740) 585-2603
Email: Info@buckeyetrail.org
Web: www.buckeyetrail.org

Cleveland Hiking Club
P.O. Box 347097
Cleveland, OH 44134-7097

Cuyahoga Valley Trails Council
810 Cedar Grove Circle
Sagamore Hills, OH 44067

Oregon
Friends of Wildwoods and Trails Inc
P.O. Box 472
Lincoln City, OR 97367

Pennsylvania
Blue Mountain Eagle Climbing Club
P.O. Box 14982
Reading, PA 19612

Keystone Trails Association
P.O. Box 251
Cogan Station, PA 17728
(717) 322-0293
Email: Keyhike@mail.sunlink.net
Web: www.kta-hike.org

Susquehanna Appalachian Trail Club
P.O. Box 61001
Harrisburg, PA 17106-1001
Web: www.libertynet.org/susqatc

Tennessee
Cumberland Trail Conference
Route 1, Box 219A
Pikeville, TN 37367
(423) 533-2620
Email: cumberlandtrail@rocketmail.com
Web: users.multipro.com/cumber
  landtrail

Smoky Mountains Hiking Club
P.O. Box 1454
Knoxville, TN 37901
(615) 922-3920
Email: SMHClub@aol.com

Tennessee Trails Association
RR 1, Box 219A
Pikeville, TN 37367-9743
(423) 533-2620

Texas
Lone Star Hiking Trail Club
2119 Green Knoll Dr.
Houston, TX 77067-2703
(281) 837-8114
Email: trailguide@lshtclub.com
Web: www.lshtclub.com

West Texas Trail Walkers Inc.
5103 Plantation Colony Dr.
Sugar Land, TX 77478

Vermont
Green Mountain Club, Inc
4711 Waterbury-Stowe Rd.
Waterbury Ct., VT 05677
(802) 244-7037
Email: gmc@sover.net
Web: www.greenmountainclub.org

Virginia
Natural Bridge Appalachian Trail Club
P.O. Box 3012
Lynchburg, VA 24503
Web: www.inmind.com/nbatc

Potomac Appalachian Trail Club
118 Park St. S.E.
Vienna, VA 22180
(703) 242-0693
Fax: (703) 242-0968
Web: www.patc.net

Rivanna Trails Foundation
P.O. Box 1786
Charlottesville, VA 22902
(804) 295-5104
Email: john@papercraft.com
Web: www.monticello.avenue.va.us/
   rivanna

Roanoke Appalachian Trail Club
P.O. Box 12282
Roanoke, VA 24024

Tidewater Appalachian Trail Club
P.O. Box 8246
Norfolk, VA 23503
Web: www.geocities.com/Yosemite/9125

Washington
Cascadians
P.O. Box 2201
Yakima, WA 98907-2201

Cascade Mountain Backpackers
P.O. Box 1024
Stevenson, WA 98648-1024

Chinook Trail Association
P.O. Box 997
Vancouver, WA 98666-0997
Email: Cta@chinooktrail.org
Web: www.chinooktrail.org

Mountaineers
300 3rd Ave. W.
Seattle, WA 98119-4100
(206) 284-6310
Email: BrookeD@Mountaineers.org
Web: www.mountaineers.org

Pacific Northwest Trail Assn.
P.O. Box 1817
Mount Vernon, WA 98273
Web: www.pnt.org

Washington Trails Association
1305 Fourth Ave., #512
Seattle, WA 98101-2401
Web: www.wta.org

West Virginia
WV Scenic Trails Association
P.O. Box 4042
Charleston, WV 25364
Email: wvsta@hotmail.com
Web: www.wvonline.com/wvsta

West Virginia Trails Coalition
P.O. Box 487
Nitro, WV 25143
(304) 755-4878
Email: Wvtc@wvtrails.org
Web: www.wvtrails.org

WV Rails-to-Trails Council
P.O. Box 8889
S. Charleston, WV 25303-0889

Wisconsin
Waupaca County Ice Age Trail Club
811 Harding St.
Waupaca, WI 54981

Wisconsin Go Hiking Club
6860 S. 111th St.
Franklin, WI 53132-1426
Web: www.homestead.com/wisconsingo
   hiking

Internet Resources

The Internet offers a dizzying array of ever-changing websites devoted to the outdoors. The following short list is devoted to the few key sites that can be counted on for providing quality information and a good source of links to the other related sites on the web. The author's own website is at:
members.aol.com/franklogue/

Backpacker Magazine (**www.bpbasecamp.com**)
The magazine has a very nicely done website with good hiking information from the Weekend Wilderness section. Their site includes an online encyclopedia for backpackers.

The Backpacker (www.thebackpacker.com)
This general purpose site on backpacking contains good information. It is not affiliated with the magazine.

Great Outdoor Recreation Pages (www.gorp.com)
A mammoth site with planning information on tons of destinations and lots more good information.

Highpoints (www.americasroof.com/)
This site has info on the high points in every state in America.

Hikenet (members.aol.com/hikenet/intro.html)
This entertaining site has stories and photos of backpacking experiences and links to other similar stories and photos on other web pages.

L.L. Bean's ParkSearch (www.llbean.com/parksearch/)
The mail-order giant has a unique search engine any hiker should look into before heading into the backcountry.

The National Outdoor Leadership School (www.nols.edu/)
NOLS has long been a leader in low impact technique through classes. Their book *Soft Paths* and now a website.

National Park Service (www.nps.gov/)
The NPS has a well-designed site giving basic information on all of the units of the National Park Service. Some of those units have further enhanced their sites into worthwhile destinations in their own right.

Index

medical emergencies, 277–279
How to Shit in the Woods (Meyer), 172
the human factor, 213
hunting season, 213–214
hybrid-loading backpacks, 136
hydration, 248–249
hydration bladder/feeder tube, 140
hyponatremia, 278
hypothermia
    alcohol and, 43
    treatment of, 17, 270–271
    vapor barrier system to avoid, 95

Ice Age National Scenic Trail, 9
ice ax
    described, 18
    self-arrest technique using, 204–205
incisions, 284
infants, 26–29
insect repellents, 309
insects, 303–308
insurance, 61–62
internal frame backpacks, 132–136,
    139–140
International Appalachian Trail, 10
isobutane, 116

journals, 326
Journey on the Crest (Ross), 49

Kamikaze bears, 288–289, 292
kerosene, 116
knots, 181–185

latrines, 323–324
legs
    first-aid treatment for, 273–275
    fractures, 276–277
    strains/sprains, 275–276
    stretching exercise for, 238–239
lighting equipment
    flashlights, 41, 165–166
    headlamps, 166–167
    lanterns, 163–165

lightning, 279–280
lithium batteries, 179–180
long-distance hikes
    blue-blazing, 53
    flip-flopping on, 52
    impact of, 62
    information on, 52
    preparations for
        managing supplies, 57–62
        mapping route, 50–51
        money issues, 54–55
        shelter, 55–56
    pros and cons of, 13–14, 47–50
    section hiking on, 52–53
    trail registers/trail names, 56–57
losing your way, 235–236
lunches, 337–338
Lyme disease, 308–309

mail drops, 60–61
maps
    care of, 224–225
    colors on USGS, 218–219
    using a compass and, 233–234
    contour lines on, 220–222
    legend on, 222–224
    measuring distance on, 235
    orienting, 230–232
    symbols on USGS, 219–220
    types of, 218
massage
    benefits of, 241
    techniques used for, 243–248
    tips for, 242 |
    when not to, 241
meals, *See also* food
    beverages, 339–340
    breakfasts, 336–337
    cleaning up, 343–344
    desserts, 340
    lunches, 337–338
    spices/condiments for, 340–341
    suppers, 338–339
    trail snacks, 341

treatments for purifying, 256–259
   while desert hiking, 210–211
"webhead," 19
whistles, 176
white gas, 117
Wilderness Medical Associates, 264
Windchill Chart, 274
women
   backpack features for, 141
   personal hygiene, 172–173
   rain gear for, 92–93
   sleeping bags for, 108
wood/solid fuel, 117
wounds, 282–284

zip-locked bags, 44